T0305379

Exploring Transgenerational Entrepreneurship

THE SUCCESSFUL TRANSGENERATIONAL ENTREPRENEURSHIP PRACTICES SERIES (STEP)

Series editor: Pramodita Sharma, *University of Vermont and Babson College, USA*

The success of passing a family business from one generation to another depends not only on instilling business ideas and leadership in future generations, but also on engendering the entrepreneurial spirit in those business leaders to come; this is the practice of transgenerational leadership. Successful Transgenerational Entrepreneurship Practices, more commonly known as the STEP Project, was put in place to help facilitate family enterprising. An innovative research initiative that spans the globe, it offers insight, partnership and solutions for current and future family leaders. As part of the STEP Project, academic experts in entrepreneurship and business collaborate with prosperous multigenerational family businesses to explore and identify those practices that will help family businesses grow and prosper. The project focuses on three key tenets: venturing (launching new businesses), renewal (revitalizing existing businesses), and innovation (introducing new products and processes). By creating a stream of powerful practices and cases that empower families to build their entrepreneurial legacies, the members of the STEP Project are rapidly moving their discoveries from research into practice.

Current STEP Affiliates and Collaborators

Europe
- Alba Graduate School of Business, Athens, Greece
- Dublin City University, Dublin, Ireland
- ESADE Business School, Barcelona, Spain
- Jönköping International Business School, Jönköping, Sweden
  - Collaborating with University of the Western Cape, South Africa
- Lancaster University Management School, Lancaster, England
- RANEPA of the President of Russia, Institute of Business Studies, Moscow, Russia
- Università Bocconi, Milan, Italy
  - Collaborating with Università degli Studi di Bergamo, Bergamo, Italy
- Università della Svizzera Italiana, Lugano, Switzerland
- Universität St. Gallen, St. Gallen, Switzerland
- Universität Witten-Herdecke, Witten, Germany
- Universiteit Antwerpen, Antwerp, Belgium
- University of Edinburgh, Edinburgh, Scotland
  - Collaborating with Makerere University Business School, Uganda & University of Strathclyde, Glasgow, Scotland
- Windesheim University, Zwolle, Netherlands

Latin America
- Fundação Dom Cabral, Belo Horizonte, Brazil
- IESA Instituto de Estudios Superiores de Administración, Caracas, Venezuela
- Universidad Interamericana de Puerto Rico (UIPR), San Germán, Puerto Rico
- Pontificia Universidad Católica Madre y Maestra, Santiago De Los Caballeros, Dominican Republic
- Tecnológico de Monterrey, Mexico City, Mexico
- Universidad Adolfo Ibáñez, Santiago, Chile
- Universidad de Los Andes, Bogotá, Colombia
- Universidad San Francisco de Quito, Quito, Ecuador
- Universidad de San Andrés, Buenos Aires, Argentina

Asia Pacific
- Bangkok University, Bangkok, Thailand
- Bond University, Gold Coast, Australia
- China Europe International Business School, Shanghai, P.R. China
- Chinese University of Hong Kong, Hong Kong
- Indian School of Business, Hyderabad, India
- National Sun Yat-Sen University, Kaohsiung, Taiwan
- Singapore Management University, Singapore
- Universiti Tun Abdul Razak, Kuala Lumpur, Malaysia
- Waseda University, Tokyo, Japan
- Zhejiang University, Hangzhou, P.R. China

North America
- Babson College, Massachusetts, USA
  - Collaborating with Syracuse University, New York, USA
- Baylor University, Texas, USA
- Dalhousie University, Nova Scotia, Canada
  - Collaborating with Virginia Polytechnic and State University, Virginia, USA
- HEC-McGill, Quebec, Canada
- Northwestern University, Illinois, USA
- Oregon State University, Oregon, USA
- Stetson University, Florida, USA
- University of Vermont, Vermont, USA
  - Collaborating with Universidad ICESI, Colombia
- Utah State University, Utah, USA
  - Collaborating with Seattle University, Washington, USA
- Worcester Polytechnic Institute, Massachusetts, USA
  - Collaborating with Hangzhou Dianzi University, China & Northeastern University, Massachusetts, USA

Exploring Transgenerational Entrepreneurship

The Role of Resources and Capabilities

Edited by

Pramodita Sharma
University of Vermont and Babson College, USA

Philipp Sieger
University of St. Gallen, Switzerland

Robert S. Nason
Syracuse University, USA

Ana Cristina González L.
Universidad ICESI, Colombia

Kavil Ramachandran
Indian School of Business, India

THE SUCCESSFUL TRANSGENERATIONAL ENTREPRENEURSHIP PRACTICES SERIES

Edward Elgar
Cheltenham, UK • Northampton, MA, USA

Published by
Edward Elgar Publishing Limited
The Lypiatts
15 Lansdown Road
Cheltenham
Glos GL50 2JA
UK

Edward Elgar Publishing, Inc.
William Pratt House
9 Dewey Court
Northampton
Massachusetts 01060
USA

A catalogue record for this book
is available from the British Library

Library of Congress Control Number: 2013943222

This book is available electronically in the ElgarOnline.com Business Subject Collection, E-ISBN 978 1 78100 362 6

ISBN 978 1 78100 361 9

Typeset by Servis Filmsetting Ltd, Stockport, Cheshire
Printed and bound in Great Britain by T.J. International Ltd, Padstow

Contents

Contributors

Kevin Au, The Chinese University of Hong Kong

Nunzia Auletta, IESA-Venezuela

Waswa Balunywa, Makarere University Business School, Uganda

Jeremy C.Y. Cheng, The Chinese University of Hong Kong

Mircea-Gabriel Chirita, HEC Montreal, Canada

Luis Cisneros, HEC Montreal, Canada

Eric Clinton, Dublin City University, Ireland

Bérangère Deschamps, Grenoble University, CERAG, France

Rocki-Lee DeWitt, University of Vermont, USA

Alberto Gimeno, ESADE, Spain

Gustavo González C., Universidad de los Andes, Colombia

Ana Cristina González L., Universidad ICESI, Colombia

Florence H.C. Ho, The Chinese University of Hong Kong

Patricia Monteferrante, IESA-Venezuela

Shakilah Nagujja, Makarere University Business School, Uganda

Robert S. Nason, Syracuse University, USA

Diana Nandagire Ntamu, Makarere University Business School, Uganda

Luz Elena Orozco C., Universidad de los Andes, Colombia

Maria José Parada, ESADE, Spain

Kavil Ramachandran, Indian School of Business, India

Aramis Rodriguez, IESA-Venezuela

Peter Rosa, University of Edinburgh, UK

Pramodita Sharma, University of Vermont and Babson College, USA

Philipp Sieger, University of St. Gallen, Switzerland

Figures

Tables

1. Introduction: exploring transgenerational entrepreneurship: the role of intangible resources

Robert S. Nason, Ana Cristina González L. and Pramodita Sharma

> *There is a close relation between the various kinds of resources with which a firm works and the development of the ideas, experience, and knowledge of its managers and entrepreneurs . . . they facilitate the introduction of new combinations of resources – innovation – within the firm.*
> (Penrose, 1959: 85)

INTRODUCTION

Families are engines of economic activity around the world. In many cases their economic impact lasts for centuries and generations. This phenomenon is referred to as transgenerational entrepreneurship (TE) and is defined as the processes, resources and capabilities used by an enterprising family to create financial and socio-emotional value across generations (cf., Habbershon et al., 2010). TE shifts the level of analysis to the family. It examines how the longevity of family enterprises extends beyond the life cycle of any individual operating entity (Zellweger et al., 2013).

As Penrose highlights in her seminal work, *Theory of the Growth of the Firm* (1959), the nature of the firm's resources impacts its ability to innovate as new value creation comes from the novel combination of different types of resources. The aim of this book is to understand how successful enterprising families in different contexts build and exploit resources and capabilities to create entrepreneurial ventures across generations. We focus on a specific theme within TE – the role of intangible resources and capabilities. Our interest is to understand how intangible resources are built and how they impact family based entrepreneurship.

To accomplish this objective, a life history reconstruction of 26 business families in 12 countries is used to explore TE across several hundred years of economic activity of enterprising families. Whereas previous books in this series have explored the concept of TE in the unique institutional contexts of Europe (Nordqvist and Zellweger, 2010), Latin America (Nordqvist et al., 2011) and the Asia Pacific (Au et al., 2011), this volume takes a global perspective of TE. The context of the studies extends to firms in Africa, Asia, Europe, Latin and North America. While some controlling families of these enterprises follow the nuclear family structure, others are from extended families. We leverage an unparalleled collection of rich qualitative data on leading global families.

Families are able to initiate and sustain value creation over time by utilizing unique resources, including tangible ones like financial and physical capital as well as intangibles like social and human capital (Sharma, 2008). While tangible assets are quite readily quantifiable, intangibles are more elusive since they do not show up on any firm financial statements or organizational charts. However, both tangible and intangible resources are important to value creation. When resources are combined in novel ways, they generate value for individual actors and the economy as a whole (Penrose, 1959; Schumpeter, 1934). Families have resource combination advantages because of their unique ability to influence, generate and acquire valuable resources (Habbershon et al., 2003). In the knowledge-driven economy, intangible resources are of primary importance (Grant, 1996) and increasingly the basis for new value creation. Intangible family resources are the primary concern of this book. We examine how families utilize unique intangible resources to create economic and social value over time.

It is clear from recent literature that intangible resources represent a very different type of resource for contemporary firms and one which can be combined with other resources in ways that were previously unimaginable (Molloy et al., 2011). However, we still do not know much about this rather broad class of intangible resources and the impact they have on family based entrepreneurship. This book seeks to bring clarity to this question in two primary ways. First, we provide a structure to examine intangible resources by differentiating between internal and external intangible resources. Second, we link internal and external intangible resources to distinct outcomes within the framework of TE.

Internal intangible resources reside within the boundaries of family firms and are often deeply embedded in their routines. These include important resources such as strongly held values, virtues and tacit knowledge that can only be learned through experience over time. Internal resources generate a base of inimitable resources which bond the organization together. On the other hand, external resources bridge the organization with its external environment. External resources include relationships with individuals and organizations outside of a firm's boundaries and reputation which extend to the public at large. These resources connect a firm to its institutional environment and allow it to adapt and change over time.

Internal and external resources are both critical to TE. Chapters in this book shed significant light on how this is so. Internal intangible resources facilitate the creation and continued renewal of products and services that an enterprise offers to its customers. Strong family values positively impact not only firm performance, but also the broader non-financial outcomes that satisfy other important firm stakeholders (for example, Chapters 2 and 3). Deep tacit knowledge and learning across generations is critical to develop superior products to the competition (Chapters 4 and 5). Bonds between family members are critical to navigate the tricky waters of intergenerational succession (Chapters 5, 6, 7).

External intangible resources facilitate the identification of opportunities that can create new streams of value and fuel growth in different environmental contexts as illustrated by Chapters 7, 8 and 9 that collectively study African, Latin American and European family firms. External resources also protect the firm from changes in environmental conditions over time as evidenced by the cases in Chapter 8. However, identifying opportunities and protecting the organization are not the only factors needed to ensure value creation across generations. Rather, family firms need to provide excellence in the products they do produce in order to be sustainable over time.

This introductory chapter provides an overview and introduction to the relationship between intangible resources and TE. The chapters of this book provide an in-depth exploration of specific intangible resources and their entrepreneurial outcomes. Each chapter starts with a short case vignette that serves as a practical illustration of the types of issues transgenerational family enterprises face. The chapter then elaborates on the theoretical perspectives that shed light on the issues being dealt with in the illustration. The concluding chapter then ties these findings back together and sets a course forward to explore what is yet to be discovered.

We begin this introductory chapter by reviewing the concept of TE and why it is important. We then discuss the role of resources generally, and intangible resources specifically, in TE. We close with direct evidence from each chapter that sheds light onto unknown domains in the link between intangible resources and TE.

TRANSGENERATIONAL ENTREPRENEURSHIP

TE explores how families create social and economic value over time. This represents a distinctive domain within the management literature.

First, the level of analysis is the family. Much like literature on serial or portfolio entrepreneurs, the level of analysis is shifted away from the firm and towards a level which may incorporate several firms over time. This opens up a whole range of economic and social value creation which may be completely missed if focused exclusively on the firm level (Sieger, et al., 2011). Second, TE examines a distinct type of firm performance. Rather than shareholder value or profitability at a point in time, TE focuses on creating a broad set of economic and social value, repeatedly and for generations not yet born. This emphasis on long-term social and economic value creation is of great importance (Lumpkin and Brigham, 2011; Zellweger, 2007).

In order to understand the process of TE, the Successful Transgenerational Entrepreneurship Practices (STEP) research framework provides two central constructs. The first is an entrepreneurial mindset which is motivated and seeking to create new value (Lumpkin and Dess, 1996). This entrepreneurial orientation is a necessary component and one which has been addressed in its relationship to TE elsewhere (Zellweger et al., 2012). However, while an entrepreneurial mindset is a necessary requirement for TE it is not a sufficient one. In order to achieve new value creation, there has to be action. In the STEP framework, that is where resources play a critical role. We draw on the Schumpeterian and Penrosian perspective that sees entrepreneurship and new value as the result of the novel combination of resources. However, the weight of resource importance is quickly changing in today's economy. Land, labor and capital are no longer the dominant factors of production. These traditional factors are being supplanted by information and knowledge. As a result, the role of intangible resources is increasingly important, but unfortunately remains not very well understood. In the next section, we review the role of resources in management literature, its link to TE and some pending questions regarding intangible resources.

THE ROLE OF FIRM RESOURCES

The view of the firm as a collection of resources stretches back to Edith Penrose's (1959) groundbreaking work on firm growth. Penrose reacted against the dominant economic conceptions of the firm in her development of the *Theory of the Growth of the Firm* (1959). Such approaches had treated firms largely as uniform actors in the larger economic system, fulfilling the supply and demand equation. However, Penrose recognized significant differences between firms which could not be attributed to their environment. As a result, she focused her attention on the idiosyncratic factors within firm boundaries that lead to growth (Penrose, 1959).

To address the research question of what causes and governs firm growth, she viewed the firm not only as an administrative organization which coordinates activities (Barnard, 1938), but went further to conceptualize the firm as a collection of productive resources. The purpose of this organization is to 'organize the use of its "own" resources together with other resources acquired from outside the firm for the production and sale of goods and services at a profit' (Penrose, 1959: 28).

Penrose's work has had a significant impact on fueling the growth of the field of strategic management (Nair et al., 2008; Kor and Mahoney, 2004). Wernerfelt (1984) built on Penrose, coined the term 'resource-based view' (RBV) and suggested it as an alternative perspective to examining firm products. Barney (1991) defined critical characteristics of resources as valuable, rare, inimitable and non-substitutable and specifically linked these types of resources to competitive advantage. This has led to a proliferation of research examining internal sources of competitive advantage specifically using RBV as a dominant theoretical frame.

Within this stream of resource-based research, the importance of a particular set of resources – broadly referred to as intangible resources – has been highlighted (Molloy et al., 2011). In seminal articles arguing for the importance of heterogeneous resource stocks across firms, authors have routinely pointed to the importance of such intangible resources as reputation (Dierickx and Cool, 1989), complex social relationships (Barney, 1991), trust between management and employees (Amit and Schoemaker, 1993), tacit knowledge (Nelson and Winter, 1982), and organizational culture (Barney, 1986). Indeed, an entire branch of resource-based theory has emerged that views the intangible resource of knowledge as the most critical of all resources (Grant, 1996; Spender, 1996).

Several characteristics distinguish intangible from tangible resources. For example, intangibles are generic non-tradable resources that do not deteriorate with use (Gedajlovic and Carney, 2010). Multiple actors can simultaneously use intangibles. Being immaterial they are not readily accessible or transferable from one individual to the next (Molloy et al., 2011). These characteristics make intangible resources rather elusive to capture since they do not readily appear on firm balance sheets, accounting processes or organizational charts.

THE FAMILY INFLUENCE ON FIRM RESOURCES

The family has been shown to be an especially relevant context in which to discuss firm resources (Habbershon and Williams, 1999; Habbershon et al., 2003). The family represents an idiosyncratic context which allows for the creation of imperfectly imitable resources (Barney, 1991). The inimitable set of unique family-influenced resources is referred to as 'familiness' (Habbershon and Williams, 1999). Resource inimitability is critical because these characteristics represent 'isolating mechanisms' (Rumelt, 1984) which allow the controlling firm alone to appropriate the value from their corresponding rent streams (Amit and Schoemaker, 1993) and prevent both ex-ante and ex-post limits to competition (Peteraf, 1993). These conditions provide critical components of the foundation for sustained competitive advantage (Barney, 1991).

Intangible resources, while increasingly recognized as the most important type of resources (Molloy et al., 2010), are also very difficult to imitate. We suggest that this inimitability is a source of advantage for family enterprises as the continuity of the controlling family across generations enables a context wherein the transfer of such elusive resources is more of a possibility than it is in organizations with a shorter continuity of values of personnel. To review previous literature on intangible family resources, we find Barney's (1991) mechanisms for resource inimitability on three dimensions – unique historical conditions, causal ambiguity and social complexity – to be helpful.

Unique Historical Conditions

Family firms are often recognized for the unique way in which they are influenced by their history. Issues of legacy (Sharma and Manikutty, 2005), long-term orientation (Zellweger, 2007) and intentions to pass on the business play an influential role in how a family firm is managed (Zellweger et al., 2012). Such non-financial considerations have been referred to as the socio-emotional wealth of a family firm, which fundamentally alters the decision-making process of firms and their subsequent performance outcomes (Gomez-Mejia et al., 2011). As a result, family firms represent a fertile context for intangible resources that are historically dependent. This may be the result of 'time compression diseconomies' (Dierickx and Cool, 1989). In their classic article, Dierickx and Cool (1989: 1507) illustrate this concept through a conversation between a British Lord and his American visitor:

> 'How come you got such a gorgeous lawn?' 'Well, the quality of the soil is, I dare say, of the utmost importance.' 'No problem.' 'Furthermore, one does need the finest quality seed and fertilizers.' 'Big deal.' 'Of course, daily watering and weekly [mowing] are jolly important.' 'No sweat, jest leave it to me!' 'That's it.' 'No kidding?!' 'Oh, absolutely. There is nothing to it, old boy; just keep it up for five centuries.'

In a manner similar to a beautiful lawn cultivated over generations, the unique experience of family members in the firm builds deep levels of tacit knowledge over time (Chirico and Salvato, 2008). In addition, the competitors cannot easily replicate or acquire the legacy and reputation of a successful family firm because such intangible assets may have been idiosyncratically developed over hundreds of years. The intangible legacies transmitted across generations constitute a driving force behind family business vision and goals (Chrisman et al., 2005: 568). In addition, family firms may be more likely to positively or negatively develop path dependencies (Barney, 1991; Nelson and Winter, 1982) across very long periods of time. For instance, family firms become less capable of undergoing strategic change or divesting underperforming assets (Sharma and Manikutty, 2005), which concurs with Barney's (1991) argument that firms are intrinsically social and historical entities and their aversion to change is closely related to their stage of development.

Causal Ambiguity

Causal ambiguity refers to the inability of firms to recognize the source of their sustained competitive advantage. Intangible resources are likely to be causally ambiguous precisely because of the difficulty in capturing and measuring such resources (Molloy et al., 2011). If you cannot measure a resource, how can it be clearly linked to competitive advantage?

This is particularly pronounced in the family firm context. Family firms represent a complex systemic interaction between individuals, family and firm (Habbershon et al., 2003) which leads to a near inability to trace the precise source of outcomes, let alone begin to replicate it. Further, family firms are recognized as often managing through intuitive means, which implies a lack of ability to articulate or even clearly identify the source of successes. Sirmon and Hitt (2003) suggest that resource inventory, resource creation and resource leveraging are three challenges that family businesses face, especially if these family-influenced resources are the source of their competitive advantage.

Social Complexity

Social complexity refers to firm resources which are part of a complex social phenomenon (Barney, 1991). Since such resources arise out of social interaction, they are unlikely to be solely tangible or material resources. The family firm represents a particularly complex social phenomenon. Family firms represent a unique overlap in terms of family and business actors (Tagiuri and Davis, 1992). This fact alone creates an especially complex network of individuals. Such conditions lead to overlap in family and firm identity (Zellweger et al., 2013), a complex systemic interaction (Habbershon et al., 2003) and a deeply embedded network of relationships (Pearson et al., 2008). Indeed, some scholars have argued that the internal social capital bonds represent one of the most critical resources of the family firm (Pearson et al., 2008). However, the social complexity of family firm resources has also led to mixed results regarding the impact of family on firm performance (van Essen et al., 2010).

For these reasons, it seems clear that families influence firm resources in ways which incorporate unique historical conditions, causal ambiguity and social complexity. Family firms are a fertile context for the development of intangible resources. It is likely for this reason that family firm resource portfolios have been characterized as an idiosyncratic bundle (Habbershon and Williams, 1999) of generic non-tradable assets (Gedajlovic and Carney, 2010) and structural, cognitive and relational social capital (Pearson et al., 2008). As indicated by these references, research explorations have begun in earnest to understand the elusive intangible elements of family firm resources, taking their well-deserved place in the intellectual foundations of the family business field (Chrisman et al., 2010).

THE NEXT FRONTIER FOR INTANGIBLE FAMILY RESOURCES

While some early conceptualization has appeared in the literature, there is limited empirical evidence to indicate the dimensions of intangible resources or the processes involved in their formation, growth and transfer across generations. Meta-analytic reviews of related literature suggest a tendency in the literature to treat intangible resources as an umbrella concept to describe a homogeneous group (Crook et al., 2008). However, a deeper investigation into the specific differences and impact of types of intangible resources is necessary. To accomplish this objective, we believe precision is needed regarding the types of intangible resources. In this book, we find it helpful to delineate intangible resources based on where they reside – either within a family as are the values discussed in Chapter 2, or in the family enterprise in the form of knowledge, learning, decision-making, professionalization and bonding social networks (Chapters 3–7), or in the external environment outside the organizational boundaries such as reputation or bridging social capital, discussed in Chapters 7–9.

Starting with Penrose (1959), the resource-based tradition has been focused on almost exclusively analyzing resources within the firm. Indeed, Barney's (1991) article described the RBV as providing a framework to analyze the internal strengths and weaknesses of a firm. While such a perspective was warranted and perhaps even necessary as a reaction against economic and structure-conduct-performance models, which saw firms as either homogeneous or simply a reflection of their environment (Schmalensee, 1985), it is important to now take the environment into account when assessing a firm's intangible resources. Amit and Shoemaker (1983) may provide insights into how this can effectively be done. Within this book, we consider the role that intangible resources play in assisting families to navigate a broad array of external environmental conditions. For instance, in Chapter 8, Rodriguez et al. explicitly address the relationship between intangible resources (social capital and resilience) and the family firm's ability to manage a hostile environment. From a different perspective, Chapter 7 explores the circumstances under which intangible resources (bridging social capital) built over the years by the leader of the family and the business puts the business at risk when he thinks about leaving to get involved in local politics.

Moreover, resources that are critical to a firm's survival and growth often do not exist within the boundaries of the firm. As a result, firms must access or develop resources outside of the firm's boundaries to help them achieve their goals. This is especially true in the knowledge economy where the most valuable factors of production, such as knowledge or social relationships, cannot be exclusively possessed and exploited by any individual actor (Nahapiet and Ghoshal, 1998). This book investigates a broad range of specific intangible resources, including social capital (Chapters 7 and 8) and reputation (Chapter 9), that exist primarily outside organizational boundaries.

The inability of firms to exclusively control intangible and especially external resources links to the fact that merely possessing resources does not ensure competitive advantage or value creation. As Sirmon and Hitt (2003) suggest, resources need to be actively managed in order to exploit their latent value. This is done through structuring, bundling and leveraging resource stocks (Sirmon et al., 2007). Family firms may have some advantages in resource management (Sirmon and Hitt, 2003) and bundling may be especially important to innovation in family firms (Carnes and Ireland, forthcoming).

In Penrosian terms, the only way new streams of value become relevant to TE is through the novel combinations of resources. This means envisioning, marshalling and configuring resources in unexpected ways. The malleability of intangible resources dramatically increases the potential number of unique configurations that can be constructed from a family's resource base. Chapters in this book explore such configurations by delving into the process of intangible family resource management. While a firm's current intangible resources may be the result of time compression diseconomies and visible as an exceptionally rich 'garden' as in Dierickx and Cool's (1989) example shared above, more needs to be known about how resource stocks and flows are managed across time in order to end up with a particular bundle of idiosyncratic resources (Sharma, 2008). Deeper insights into the transfer of intangible resources across salient family firm transitions within the same family (Chapters 6 and 7) and to a non-founding family (Chapter 5) are revealed. Using the distinction between internal and external resources, we are able to isolate unique intangible resource development processes.

SUMMARIES

While our chapters demonstrate a unified theme in their focus on intangible assets, they show great variety in the types of intangible assets which family firms possess. Table 1.1 presents an overview of the topical and contextual focus of each chapter. Following the 'inside-out' logic of discussion, the book starts with intangible values that reside deep within the controlling family (Chapter 2), progressing to those that are clearly deeply embedded in the firm (Chapters 3–6), to social capital resources that straddle the organizational boundaries (Chapter 7 and 8) and, finally, to resources such as reputation that clearly exist outside of the boundaries of the firm (Chapter 9). The concluding chapter (Chapter 10) wraps up with a synthesis of insights from research in this book and some future-oriented reflections. Below we provide a brief overview of the research contributions of Chapters 2–9.

Table 1.1 Internal vs external intangible resources

Chapter #	Authors	Resource	Internal/external	# of family firms	Countries
2	Orozco & González	Values/virtues	Familial/internal	8	Colombia
3	Gimeno & Parada	Decision-making/ professionalization	Internal	2	Spain
4	Cheng, Ho & Au	Learning/knowledge building	Internal	1	China
5	DeWitt & González	Tacit knowledge	Internal	1	United States
6	Cisneros, Chirita & Deschamps	Tacit knowledge/social capital	Internal	6	Canada
7	Balunywa, Rosa, Ntamu & Nagujja	Social capital	Internal/external	1	Uganda
8	Rodriguez, Auletta & Monteferrante	Social capital	External	6	Venezuela, Sweden, Costa Rica, El Salvador, Germany
9	Clinton, Nason & Sieger	Reputation	External	1	Ireland

Internal Intangible Family Resources

'Family firms and entrepreneurial families as breeding grounds for virtues' by Orozco and González

Using evidence from eight Colombian entrepreneurial family firms, the authors illustrate the distinctiveness of family values and actionable virtues based on these values. This research signals that family firms are natural settings to seed and breed values and that these values impact desirable goals pursued by both the family and the business. For this purpose, they illustrate the way in which different sets of values – understood as positive moral actions – become capabilities when they turn into virtues that drive performance.

Interestingly, Orozco and González identify specific sets of values associated with particular business goals and explain the rationale behind each relationship in the context of family businesses. For instance, they relate diversification to temperance and prudence; business growth to wisdom; and courage, perseverance and economic sustainability to commitment. Nevertheless, they point out how the emphasis on specific values may change over time, even if the influence of the founder on firm values is strong from the beginning, a topic worth studying in future research.

'Professionalization of the family business: decision-making domains' by Gimeno and Parada

Based on a longitudinal study of a pharmaceutical company with more than 175 years of history in Spain, this chapter explores the multidimensional professionalization processes a family business undertakes in decision-making. The authors' main argument is twofold. First, they signal that professionalization is a process, not a one-time, stand-alone simple decision. Second, they suggest that establishing practices to become professional in the decision-making domain and to acquire capabilities necessary to make decisions are contingent on the development of family businesses.

In order to do this, they describe the way decisions were made in the different stages this pharmaceutical company faced and the mechanisms introduced to the business at each stage. By dividing the decision-making domain into three sub-dimensions, namely administrative, operational and strategic, Gimeno and Parada illustrate how different generations of family members can take the responsibility of formalizing governance structures, building mechanisms to gather necessary information from internal and external sources, and develop decision-making capabilities. It is observed that founders and more experienced leaders tend to rely more on intuitive decisions, whereas the later generation and less experienced leaders make decisions based more on analytic tools. Nevertheless, the need to balance between intuitive and analytical decision-making is permanent, as family enterprises professionalize over time. The latter is their most significant contribution.

'Transgenerational entrepreneurship and entrepreneurial learning: a case study of Associated Engineers Ltd in Hong Kong' by Cheng, Ho and Au
Based on the history of Associated Engineers Ltd, a Chinese family business from Hong Kong founded in 1961, this chapter portrays the stages in a family business life cycle in which entrepreneurial learning is developed as a key intangible resource. The activities and interactions that foster this type of learning across generations include a combination of education, family meetings, work experience inside and outside the enterprise as well as founding experience with siblings and non-family members. Each activity and interaction is aimed to facilitate the acquisition of knowledge and skills to find new business opportunities.

Regardless of the path chosen by a particular family business across time, the authors conclude that entrepreneurial learning prepares current and subsequent generations to face uncertainty and pursue business ventures. This indicates that entrepreneurial learning influences the relationship between family specific resources and the capacity of a firm to create value across time. Furthermore, they suggest and elaborate the argument that entrepreneurial learning moderates two key relationships: first, the relationship between entrepreneurial orientation and firm performance; and second, the relationship between familiness and firm performance.

'Successful family business ownership transitions: leveraging tacit knowledge' by DeWitt and González
This chapter focuses on a family business that fails to effect a fifth-generational transition and goes through two non-family ownership transitions before becoming an owner-controlled private family firm after 144 years in business. DeWitt and González develop the argument that even though strategic changes – ownership and leadership ones – can become a major threat to any type of business, tacit knowledge within a family business can be leveraged to achieve business longevity. Through the analysis of different stages, the authors focus on the role of tacit knowledge – stocks and influxes – not only in family members but in employees and outsiders, in protecting the business from major disruptions and in pursuing new business opportunities when it is properly managed.

'The role of social capital in succession from controlling owners to sibling teams' by Cisneros, Chirita and Deschamps
Although succession is a topic that has been widely studied in family businesses, the authors' main contribution to the literature stems from their approach to the role of social capital, tacit knowledge and reputation in succession from controlling owners to sibling partners. This chapter explores the contingencies and processes that help to build leadership teams of siblings in each step of a succession process. Tacit knowledge, they suggest, is a precursor of collective successions, and reputation and networks are intangibles that trigger the need to develop a team with complementary capabilities to run the family business. The authors focus on the processes involved in the transfer of social capital – particularly tacit knowledge – in earlier stages of the succession process, and reputation as a trigger in later stages to decide on collective teams. Both resources contribute not only to successful transitions, but also to the formation of sibling teams that bring complementary capabilities to family business leadership.

Balancing the Internal and External Intangible Family Resources

'Opportunities and dilemmas of social capital: insights from Uganda' by Balunywa, Rosa, Ntamu and Nagujja
This chapter explores the role of social capital in the very interesting and unexplored continent of Africa. Balunywa and colleagues explain the cultural, political and social dimensions that influence a family business and for the first time in family business research they illustrate the threats of having too much social capital. Through a set of propositions, they first examine the role of extended families – a cultural and social specific feature in sub-Saharan Africa – in business continuity. They propose that extended families bring more support, knowledge and networks, but at the same time, as the family grows, its members tend to drain the resources available.

Second, they compare the opposite influences of bonding social capital in family business outcomes. On the one hand, if a family business develops in a highly cohesive society, social capital benefits both the family and the business. On the other hand, this effect is counterbalanced by the social costs of maintaining strong community relationships.

Lastly, the duality of bridging social capital is exposed. On the one hand, it brings advantages to the family business in the form of new business opportunities. But, at the same time, a bridge brings disadvantages if that intangible resource is centralized solely in the patriarch. This chapter opens up a broad set of research possibilities around the different dimensions that can affect the relationship between intangible resources and family business outcomes, particularly the dangers present when the leader pursues different interests and gradually leaves the business fragile without key intangible resources.

External Intangible Family Resources

'Bridging for resilience: the role of family business social capital in coping with hostile environments' by Rodriguez, Auletta and Monteferrante

This chapter uses bridging social capital and resilience capacity as intangible and unique resources to explore the ways in which family businesses in five countries around the world face uncertain environments. The authors provide a set of propositions to present the different circumstances – location and sector – in which flows of capital, between family businesses and their tiers, contribute to family business resilience to handle external shifts and disruptions. Such capital flows include knowledge, information, financial capital, advice, supplier flexibility and access to distribution channels, among others. The main contribution to family business theory and practice resides in the study's implication that if family businesses invest in their external social capital, that is, participate in guilds, increase their business contacts, exchange information and knowledge among peers, it fosters their resilience capacity across generations.

'Reputation for what? Different types of reputation and their effect on portfolio entrepreneurship activities' by Clinton, Nason and Sieger

This study explores the relationship between reputation as a unique family resource and a business family's entrepreneurial portfolio activity. The chapter argues that while a strong positive reputation has a significant impact on the opportunities for family enterprises, reputation is not a homogeneous construct. Therefore, the main contribution of this study lies in its introduction of three sub-dimensions of reputation – long-term orientation, trusted business partners and entrepreneurial spirit – as intangible resources that can contribute to different entrepreneurial portfolio activities, according to the dimension addressed.

Through an analysis of the Irish Smith family, the authors illustrate how different positive perceptions from outsiders contribute to a business family's entrepreneurial opportunities. By focusing on an 80-year-old family business, the study contributes to TE by suggesting that entrepreneurial portfolio activity can be fostered by different types of intangible resources, in this case, reputation in its different sub-dimensions.

CONCLUSION

This book has been in the making since August 2011 when we submitted a proposal to Edward Elgar Publishing for the 'Global Successful Transgenerational Entrepreneurship Practices Series', with the first volume focusing on understanding the role of resources and capabilities in the development of transgenerational entrepreneurship (TE). Prior to this proposal, three of us – Nason, Sieger and Sharma (w. Zellweger) – had compiled findings from 38 authors in 18 countries, indicating the crucial role of resources in TE around the world (Sieger et al., 2011). Each chapter in this book is a response to an open call for submissions sent to STEP scholars in early 2012. These submissions went through several rounds of review and revisions aimed at sharpening the focus of the opening vignettes and theory presented in the chapters.

The body of novel research in this book sheds light on the relatively unexplored arena of intangible resources in TE. In going through the chapters, the critical role of intangible resources to family firms' ability to generate and sustain new streams of revenue across time becomes evident. Furthermore, the longitudinal studies upon which each chapter is based bring to life the dimensions and processes that underlie intangibles such as values, virtues, decision-making, professionalization, tacit knowledge, learning, social capital and reputation. In this endeavor we hope to have opened up many new promising avenues for future research to explore. Enjoy!

REFERENCES

Amit, R. and P.J. Schoemaker (1993), 'Strategic assets and organizational rent', *Strategic Management Journal*, **14** (1), 33–46.

Au, K., J. Craig and K. Ramachandran (2011), *Family Enterprise in the Asia Pacific: Exploring Transgenerational Entrepreneurship in Family Firms*, Cheltenham, UK and Northampton, MA, USA: Edward Elgar.

Barnard, C.I. (1938), *The Functions of the Executive*, Cambridge, MA: Harvard University Press.

Barney, J.B. (1986), 'Organizational culture: can it be a source of sustained competitive advantage?' *Academy of Management Review*, 656–65.

Barney, J. (1991), 'Firm resources and sustained competitive advantage', *Journal of Management*, **17** (1), 99–120.

Carnes, C.M. and R.D. Ireland (2014), 'Familiness and innovation: resource bundling as the missing link', *Entrepreneurship Theory and Practice*, in press.

Chirico, F. and C. Salvato (2008), 'Knowledge integration and dynamic organizational adaptation in family firms', *Family Business Review*, **21** (2), 169–81.

Chrisman, J.J., J.H. Chua and P. Sharma (2005), 'Trends and directions in the development of a strategic management theory of the family firm', *Entrepreneurship Theory and Practice*, **29** (5), 555–76.

Chrisman, J.J., F.W. Kellermanns, K.C. Chan and K. Liano (2010), 'Intellectual foundations of current research in family business: an identification and review of 25 influential articles', *Family Business Review*, **23** (1), 9–26.

Crook, T.R., D.J. Ketchen, J.G. Combs and S.Y. Todd (2008), 'Strategic resources and performance: a meta-analysis', *Strategic Management Journal*, **29** (11), 1141–54.

Dierickx, I. and K. Cool (1989), 'Asset stock accumulation and sustainability of competitive advantage', *Management Science*, **35** (12), 1504–11.

Gedajlovic, E. and M. Carney (2010), 'Markets, hierarchies, and families: toward a transaction cost theory of the family firm', *Entrepreneurship Theory and Practice*, **34** (6), 1145–72.

Gomez-Mejia, L.R., C. Cruz, P. Berrone and J. De Castro (2011), 'The bind that ties: socioemotional wealth preservation in family firms', *The Academy of Management Annals*, **5** (1), 653–707.

Grant, R.M. (1996), 'Toward a knowledge-based theory of the firm', *Strategic Management Journal*, **17**, 109–122.

Habbershon, T.G. and M.L. Williams (1999), 'A resource-based framework for assessing the strategic advantages of family firms', *Family Business Review*, **12** (1), 1–25.

Habbershon, T.G., M. Nordqvist and T. Zellweger (2010), 'Transgenerational entrepreneurship', in M. Nordqvist and T. Zellweger (eds), *Transgenerational Entrepreneurship: Exploring Growth and Performance in Family Firms across Generations*, Cheltenham, UK and Northampton, MA, USA: Edward Elgar, pp. 1–38.

Habbershon, T.G., M. Williams and I.C. MacMillan (2003), 'A unified systems perspective of family firm performance', *Journal of Business Venturing*, **18** (4), 451–65.

Kor, Y.Y. and J.T. Mahoney (2004), 'Edith Penrose's (1959) contributions to the resource-based view of strategic management', *Journal of Management Studies*, **41** (1), 183–91.

Lumpkin, G.T. and K.H. Brigham (2011), 'Long-term orientation and intertemporal choice in family firms', *Entrepreneurship Theory and Practice*, **35** (6), 1149–69.

Lumpkin, G.T. and G.G. Dess (1996), 'Clarifying the entrepreneurial orientation construct and linking it to performance', *Academy of Management Review*, **21** (1), 135–72.

Molloy, J.C., C. Chadwick, R.E. Ployhart and S.J. Golden (2011), 'Making intangibles "tangible" in tests of resource-based theory: a multidisciplinary construct validation approach', *Journal of Management*, **37** (5), 1496–518.

Nahapiet, J. and S. Ghoshal (1998), 'Social capital, intellectual capital, and the organizational advantage', *Academy of Management Review*, **23** (2), 242–66.

Nair, A., J. Trendowski and W. Judge (2008), 'The theory of the growth of the firm, by Edith T. Penrose. Oxford: Blackwell, 1959', *Academy of Management Review*, **33** (4), 1026–8.

Nelson, R.R. and S.G. Winter (1982), *An Evolutionary Theory of Economic Change*, Cambridge, MA: Belknap Press of Harvard University Press.

Nordqvist, M. and T. Zellweger (2010), *Transgenerational Entrepreneurship:*

Exploring Growth and Performance in Family Firms across Generations, Cheltenham, UK and Northampton, MA, USA: Edward Elgar.

Nordqvist, M., G. Marzano, E.R. Brenes, G. Jiménez and M. Fonseca-Paredes (2011), *Understanding Entrepreneurial Family Businesses in Uncertain Environments: Opportunities and Resources in Latin America*, Cheltenham, UK and Northampton, MA, USA: Edward Elgar.

Pearson, A.W., J.C. Carr and J.C. Shaw (2008), 'Toward a theory of familiness: a social capital perspective', *Entrepreneurship Theory and Practice*, **32** (6), 949–69.

Penrose, E.T. (1959), *The Theory of the Growth of the Firm*, New York: John Wiley.

Peteraf, M.A. (1993), 'The cornerstones of competitive advantage: a resource-based view', *Strategic Management Journal*, **14** (3), 179–91.

Rumelt, R.P. (1984), 'Toward a strategic theory of the firm', in R. Lamb (ed.), *Competitive Strategic Management*, Englewood Cliffs, NJ: Prentice Hall, pp. 556–70.

Schmalensee, R. (1985), 'Do markets differ much?', *The American Economic Review*, **75** (3), 341–51.

Schumpeter, J. (1934), *Capitalism, Socialism, and Democracy*, New York: Harper & Row.

Sharma, P. (2008), 'Commentary: familiness: capital stocks and flows between family and business', *Entrepreneurship Theory and Practice*, **32** (6), 971–7.

Sharma, P. and S. Manikutty (2005), 'Strategic divestments in family firms: role of family structure and community culture', *Entrepreneurship Theory and Practice*, **29** (3), 293–311.

Sieger, P., R. Nason, P. Sharma and T. Zellweger (2011), *The Global STEP Booklet: Evidence-based, Practical Insights for Enterprising Families*, Wellesley, MA: Babson College.

Sieger, P., T. Zellweger, R.S. Nason and E. Clinton (2011), 'Portfolio entrepreneurship in family firms: a resource-based perspective', *Strategic Entrepreneurship Journal*, **5** (4), 327–51.

Sirmon, D.G. and M.A. Hitt (2003), 'Managing resources: linking unique resources, management, and wealth creation in family firms', *Entrepreneurship Theory and Practice*, **27** (4), 339–58.

Sirmon, D.G., M.A. Hitt and R.D. Ireland (2007), 'Managing firm resources in dynamic environments to create value: looking inside the black box', *Academy of Management Review*, **32** (1), 273–92.

Spender, J.-C. (1996), 'Making knowledge the basis of a dynamic theory of the firm', *Strategic Management Journal*, **17**, 45–62.

Tagiuri, R. and J.A. Davis (1992), 'On the goals of successful family companies', *Family Business Review*, **5** (1), 43–62.

Van Essen, M., M. Carney, E. Gedajlovic, P.P.M.A.R. Heugens and J. van Oosterhout (2010), 'Do US publicly-listed family firms differ? Does it matter? A meta-analysis', paper presented at the 10th Annual Family Businesses Research Conference (IFERA 2010), Lancaster, UK.

Wernerfelt, B. (1984), 'A resource-based view of the firm', *Strategic Management Journal*, **5** (2), 171–80.

Zellweger, T. (2007), 'Time horizon, costs of equity capital, and generic investment strategies of firms', *Family Business Review*, **20** (1), 1–15.

Zellweger, T.M., F.W. Kellermanns, J.J. Chrisman and J.H. Chua (2012), 'Family control and family firm valuation by family CEOs: the importance of intentions for transgenerational control', *Organization Science*, **23** (3), 851–68.

Zellweger, T.M., R.S. Nason, M. Nordqvist and C.G. Brush (2013), 'Why do family firms strive for nonfinancial goals? An organizational identity perspective', *Entrepreneurship Theory and Practice*, **37** (2), 229–48.

2. Family firms and entrepreneurial families as breeding grounds for virtues

Luz Elena Orozco C. and Gustavo González C.

CAN A SCHOOL REFLECT A FAMILY'S VALUES?

Bucaramanga, Colombia's fifth largest city, is renowned for its first-rate private schools. Colegio Nueva Castilla (CNC) is ranked 12th among the country's 200 leading public and private high schools – the result of 40 years of hard work by Tomás, the principal, and Alicia, his wife and CNC's student counselor.

Tomás's teaching vocation complements his business acumen. As an undergraduate majoring in psychology, he and a professor offered weekend courses to young managers, enabling Tomás to save enough money by the time he graduated to make a down payment on a small private school he renamed. At first Tomás was the school's principal, manager and teacher, making ends meet by living in the building's cellar. To attract students, he offered a local radio station a fee for each student enrolled as a result of the station's publicity – a daring move.

Enrolment at CNC soon increased. Tomás paid off his debts and married his childhood sweetheart. A practicing psychologist, Alicia joined the school as a teacher while serving as student-parent counselor.

At the same time, Tomás was keen on business – investing in convenience stores, running a small cargo business and looking into real estate ventures. He purchased a sizable property on the outskirts of the city and used it to leverage loans to expand other businesses. Meanwhile, the school's enrolment continued to grow, and facilities and student services improved. Tomás and Alicia also raised four children.

By the time the children were in high school, Bucaramanga's schools had gained academic recognition and much of the city's affluent population was moving to the suburbs. Land values in the area virtually doubled, as did Tomás's investment. It was also time to consider moving the school and designing entirely different facilities from those available at its downtown location. Tomás and Alicia took the bold step of selling their businesses and focusing on the future of CNC by building state-of-the-art classrooms and sports facilities. The goal was to achieve national league standing.

Thirty years elapsed and CNC was up and running at its new location. Junior (the couple's eldest son) had earned a degree in management, and worked as chief financial officer of a leading non-profit organization based in Bogotá, the capital city. He offered to work for CNC and help his parents attain their ambitious academic goal – to make it one of Colombia's top ten private schools. Junior, now the school's manager, knew that achieving such a goal would require financial leveraging. He hired a management consultant to guide his parents through a strategy exercise that included several options – including bringing in a majority CNC shareholder. Such discussions led to reflection centering on the school as representing the family's core values: respect, honesty, loyalty, faithfulness, responsibility and a sense of humor.

Junior approached the local banks with a CNC expansion plan based on revenue from a new wave of enrolment growth. The next step was obtaining international accreditation. Tomás had long thought of applying for the University of Cambridge International Certificate. This meant recruiting bilingual teachers, making use of new technology learning methods and launching a preschool program. Happily, all of the siblings were suited to the new demands: Natalia, who had followed her mother's example and held a degree in psychology, designed and established the preschool offering; and Oscar, the second son, took on the introduction of new learning technologies. Junior continued as general manager and the school recruited a new principal.

CNC growth entailed entering a number of business ventures. Students had to be bussed to and from the school, which meant setting up a firm to operate a fleet of vehicles and hiring drivers; a bakery catering to local hotels and other customers was set up to make more efficient use of CNC cafeteria staff and equipment. The sports complex, the city's first to feature night lighting and artificial turf, was rented out-of-hours to local teams. Junior guided his brother, sisters and assorted in-laws in running the new business firms, and found time to launch new cargo, mining and real estate ventures with other partners. A family holding company was established to oversee CNC operations and share in Junior's new ventures.

These developments triggered a host of questions concerned with managing the new holding company – the potential risk from new ventures and operating an expanded CNC. Was Junior making too many time commitments? Should the business portfolio continue to expand or should the family focus on fewer projects? If Junior stepped down, would Oscar be capable of running CNC? What values did the school represent for all members of the family? What values should guide the family strategy going forward? What was to happen once Tomás and Alicia retired from active service and CNC lost their guiding strength, values and virtues, especially in such a value-virtue dependent organization as a school?

Once again, the family agreed to take on an external management consultant. S/he would have to understand the role played by the school as a bonding factor for the family, let alone Junior's entrepreneurial initiatives and the risk that the holding company might at some point overextend its business commitments. What steps would you advise the family to take in light of the above-mentioned queries?

INTRODUCTION

The importance of values in family firms has been recognized since the inception of family business studies. Describing values as a 'vast source of strength and energy in business', Dumas and Blodgett (1999: 214) argue that 'a healthy owning family with strong values . . . may be the greatest resource a business can have'. Tapies and Ward (2008) argue that the values of the owning family drive the key decisions regarding: strategy, structure, competitive advantage, culture, employee recruitment, governance, succession, owners' cohesion, commitment and constitution or protocol. Distelberg and Blow (2010) find that families with coherent values enjoy a healthy family business system and Barker et al. (2004) use values as a resource to identify organizational culture. In a recent survey of the most frequent dependent variables and outcomes researched for family firms (FF) in the past decade, the authors found, in descending order of importance: family involvement in business, family values, family business characteristics, attitude towards family business/family members and succession processes (Yu et al., 2012: 43). From this perspective, values can be viewed as either independent or dependent variables, independent because they are linked to different FF outcomes and dependent to the extent that they are specifically looked for by FFs as an objective in their existence. In short, the role of values in FFs has been studied from several perspectives. However, a theoretical foundation to link family values with firm outcomes has yet to be developed – a task we undertake in this chapter.

As values represent an intangible, difficult-to-imitate asset that may provide competitive advantage for a FF, they may be treated as resources. This has prompted us to seek insights from the resource-based view of the firm in order to understand the relationship between family values and firm-level outcomes. Scholars working from this perspective differentiate between resources and capabilities. While resources are viewed as stocks that can be built up or drawn upon over time, capabilities indicate the flow of stocks that put the resources into productive use (for example, Dierickx and Cool, 1989; Eisenhardt and Martin, 2000). Inspired by this subtle yet critical distinction, we differentiate between values and virtues. We view values as belonging to the mental and emotional spheres of an individual or a family. Virtues on the other hand, are lived values. That is, the visible behavioral outcomes when values are embodied and acted upon.

This theoretical distinction enables us to understand the role of values and virtues in FFs in several ways. First, by treating values as a resource we are able to analyze why and how values influence financial and non-financial firm outcomes. Second, and relatedly, examining action-oriented virtues provides insight into the idiosyncratic capability development process within FFs. This process combines actions and reactions between members of the family and the firm, creating a breeding ground for the development of 'core' family virtues and their impact on firm-level outcomes. Third, our framework provides future research with a tool for examining values and virtues between family and non-family firms. For instance, scholars like Tapies and Ward (2008) have argued that the dominant values in non-family firms are technically and economically biased with a focus on efficiency and profitability, whereas FFs are guided by socio-emotional values such as reputation, stewardship, and so on. We observe that FFs continuously experience the tension between values and action-oriented virtues. The framework and methodological approach developed in this chapter illustrates one way to capture family virtues, a topic given little attention in FF literature, and furthermore understand their impact on firm-level outcomes.

Our opening case exemplifies the tensions between values and virtues within a family. Driven by the family values of prudence and self-regulation, the founders focused their efforts on building the school, while remaining open to broader entrepreneurial opportunities, indicating a combination of human and economically focused values guiding behaviors. Building on this foundation, both sets of values are visible in the next generation, with Junior being more driven by economic values while his siblings continue to run the school with family values. The dilemma now is how to settle the tension between the two sets of values in action-oriented virtues.

To shed light on such dilemmas, we examine the lived values in eight Colombian FFs in several industries. Sixty-six interviews with family and non-family members were conducted from 2007 through to 2011 following the STEP (Successful Transgenerational Entrepreneurship Practices) methodology for exploring transgenerational entrepreneurship. Coding was undertaken to understand the values and virtues as resources and capabilities respectively, as well as firm-level outcomes. We find that action-oriented virtues emerging from interactions of members in the FF system have an impact on the outcomes. The longitudinal nature of the cases allows us to elaborate on changes in virtues over time and generations of family leadership. In terms of methodology, we are intrigued by the power of using speech to identify and understand the virtues (lived values) of individuals and their relationship to FFs' performance.

The next section clarifies the relationship between values, virtues and character strengths. This is followed by an examination of these concepts using tenets of the resource-based view of the firm. Salient virtues identified from the Colombian cases are then discussed, relating them to distinct outcomes in the family and business domain. This analysis leads us to a discussion of transfer and evolution of selected virtues across generations. The chapter concludes with a reflection on the theoretical and practical implications of our research.

VALUES AND VIRTUE ETHICS IN THE LITERATURE

Values when considered as principles and standards of moral conduct are ideals or desired behavior, and so are not always practiced. Virtues, on the other hand, are lived values, that is, human qualities. Virtues are preferred dispositions towards good behavior, open to any person who sets his/her mind, will and heart to master them. In other words, virtues are manifestations and dispositions of willpower (Baumeister and Tierney, 2011). A virtuous person not only acts according to these dispositions but also makes the best effort to exhibit good behavior when acting.

For the purpose of this chapter we insist on considering 'values' to be judgments of the worth of positive moral actions, which are intellectually and emotionally agreed to, and so belong to the realm of ideals. When a value is more than just agreed to, when it is lived, enacted, embodied, practiced and habituated we are then in the realm of a 'virtue'. A virtue is not only an embodied disposition towards that positive moral behavior desired – due to its worth – but that behavior acted.

Moral values and virtues come into play when discussing ethics. This subtle distinction between values (ideals) and virtues (embodied action) arose recently in business ethics. This branch of ethics can be thought of as a name given to a special scholarship, a corporate movement or a social expectation. Business ethics when referring to an academic field consider different theoretical approaches.[1] The approach we will endorse is Aristotelian, which claims that ethical behavior draws on the character traits of the person, called virtues. It is from the latter tradition that virtue ethics draws its inspiration (De George, 2005).

Ethics usually refers to complying with rules, norms and the law. Another venerable tradition is that of ethics as a branch of philosophy that endorses virtue: action that is praiseworthy, that is good, that provides the good life. Since moral goodness is a complex issue, positive psychology approaches a person's good character as a totality of positive traits, each of which exists to a degree. To convey the multidimensionality of character, Peterson and Park (2006) call its components *character strengths*. They arrived at this group of character strengths by identifying core virtues recognized across world cultures throughout history and taking into consideration the different ways these are manifest.

The core virtues they refer to are courage, temperance, humanity, wisdom/knowledge, justice and transcendence. Nevertheless, with mounting research – scholarship has increased in the past 12 years since the movement started (Donaldson and Ko, 2010) – a proven number of positive traits have been associated with each virtue. These traits constitute character strengths of the individual that have guided research in verifying their adequacy to describe the virtue they intend to express (Peterson and Seligman, 2004).

The pillars underpinning this endeavor are positive subjective *experiences*; positive *traits* that include talents, interests, creativity, meaning, purpose, growth and enthusiasm; and positive *institutions* like positive schools, businesses, families, communities and societies. This is 'the study and application of positively oriented human resource strengths and psychological capacities that can be measured, developed and effectively managed for performance improvement in today's workplace' (Luthans, 2002: 16). It can be helpful in actionable research on FFs and even improve relations among members of the owner/managing family.

There are some promising findings such as character strengths like *hope, zest, curiosity* and *love* that are associated with life satisfaction across a range of occupation types, from unskilled laborer to chief executive officer (CEO). For example, *hope,* a character strength associated with the virtue of transcendence, is a salient feature of Colombian culture: 'Researchers have claimed the importance of hope in sustaining the efforts of workers and organizations in an environment increasingly threatened by mergers, downsizing, bankruptcies, new technologies, an uncertain global economy and terrorism. Hope is a strength that allows people to overcome uncertainty and to stay the course' (Peterson and Park, 2006: 1151).

The character strengths associated with the virtue of wisdom/knowledge are creativity, curiosity, open-mindedness, love of learning, perspective;

those linked to courage are bravery, persistence, integrity and vitality. Likewise, the virtue of humanity is related to the character strengths of love, kindness and social intelligence; justice is associated with citizenship, fairness and leadership; temperance with forgiveness and mercy, humility/modesty, prudence, self-regulation; and transcendence with appreciation of beauty and excellence, gratitude, hope, humor and spirituality (Peterson and Seligman, 2004: 29).

The growing literature has documented the empirical development of constructs and the relationships between character strengths and performance, especially at work, but all this has been studied mostly at the individual level. Less has occurred at the group level, and still less in the family and FF domains. Nevertheless, the scientific approach on which this scholarship is based would allow in time for understanding the role of the entrepreneur family in shaping those character strengths (to which virtues are related, as we claim throughout our chapter) that constitute capabilities in order to increase FF performance.

Thus, although any person willing to acquire virtues can do so, their incorporation into the particular FF setting via family members who embody them constitutes a dimension of 'familiness' and may become a position barrier, as we describe further.

Habbershon and Williams (1999) refer both to *organizational* and *process* capital resources. Competencies and culture are elements of the former while knowledge, disposition and leadership are elements of the latter. Thus, virtues, the main concept introduced in this chapter, can assume the quality of both organizational and process capital resources.

In subsequent work, Habbershon et al. (2003) offer a unified systems perspective of FF performance: the family social system, they argue, consists of three subsystem components: (1) the controlling family unit; (2) the business entity; and (3) the individual family member – representing the interests, skills and life stage of the participating family owners/managers. Virtues exist in the individual family member subsystem. Moreover, it is through FF leaders that virtues interact systemically with the other two components.

We intend to demonstrate in the following sections how these character strengths –that conform virtues – are reflected in the words and actions (practices) that family members and non-family members of FFs describe in the interviews of our eight STEP cases.

VALUES AND VIRTUES CONSIDERED FROM THE RESOURCE-BASED VIEW (RBV)

'Familiness', the unique bundle of resources created by the interaction of individual family members, family and business (Habbershon and Williams, 1999), plays a crucial role in raising transgenerational potential. According to Habbershon et al. (2003), transgenerational potential increases the wealth of FFs in the long-term.

The values of individuals – appraisals of desired positive moral behavior – can assume the quality of firm resources; and virtues – lived values – of capabilities, to the extent they allow for an increasing capacity to deploy positive moral action that influences performance. In the RBV, capabilities refer to a firm's capacity to deploy resources, usually in combination, using organizational processes to affect a desired end (Amit and Schoemaker, 1993).

Individuals acquire virtues by exercising positive moral actions; in time, a positive moral habit takes hold. However, a virtue can erode as well. Virtues are not always explicitly stated; they are immanent to decisions, practices and attitudes within the business organization and the family organization. For subsequent generations, having experienced the leader's example at home and at work provides lasting lessons. Virtue ethics is consistent positive action (in thoughts, words and deeds); a virtuous leader/manager will be so at home, in the office and on the street.

Adams and colleagues in Habbershon and Williams (1999) highlight that FFs are less likely to have a formal code of ethics and that FFs emphasize personal and family values over corporate values, meaning that role models prevail in such firms. For leaders of non-FFs, managing by values requires establishing values as goals to guide behavior and decisions; values become something of which they need to be mindful and willing to invest effort and time to cultivate.

Children assimilate the family's lifestyle over time without being aware of this process or of the virtues that underpin it. Later on, if they happen to participate in the FF, in all probability they will fit well into the founder's business style, without awareness of the virtues at play. In contrast, for non-FF managers the provisional character of their jobs precludes the acting out of moral guidance and practices that thrive only with time.

Values in FFs, on the one hand, manifest the founder's values as well as those of the family. They are worthy and rare organizational resources, imperfectly imitable and with no strategically equivalent substitutes, which become a source of competitive advantage (Barney, 1991). Virtues, on the other hand, are not marketable; hiring a virtuous individual does not automatically make the organization's other members virtuous; these are rare capabilities. Virtues of family members involved in the FF (by ownership/managing) are imperfectly imitable since they require the founding member's wish to transmit their values and virtues to newer members (legacy), and the parallel deference of the latter to learn from the former for the organization's survival and success. A direct result of these facts is that FFs reap competitive advantages.

Willingness, time, practice and habituation embody a value and convert it into a virtue. In addition, time allows for the molding of character through virtue; acting out a virtue produces feedback that enhances that same capacity for further virtuous action. For instance, being fair is a consequence of first answering questions like *Why* be fair? *How* to be fair? *Where* to be fair? Knowledge, deliberation and acting with immutable character are prerequisites to behaving with fairness, as a fair person is expected to act (Aristotle, 1984: NE: 1105b1).

The growth of virtues within a family business contributes to the family's idiosyncrasy that reflects the complexity of a particular FF, which is not imitable by another organization (Habbershon et al., 2003; Habbershon and Williams, 1999).

This being the case, should values be regarded as resources and virtues as capabilities in light of the resource-based view of the firm? Which virtues are lived in the FF? Moreover, what kind of consequences may be associated with these virtues? The opening case, for instance, shows clearly that while Tomás practices temperance through prudence, Junior values his father's prudence but may risk the FF by developing less prudence in his entrepreneurial initiatives. Hopefully the following analysis based on Colombian cases will help clarify the ethical discourse where 'values' usually refer to the realm of norms that inspire action, while 'virtues' belong to the realm of action or the capacity to practice values.

VIRTUES IN COLOMBIAN FF CASES

Our interviews with STEP families have pointed to virtues, all of them mentioned above at least through some character strength. This section considers in detail character strengths related to *courage* and *temperance* (Peterson and Seligman, 2004: 29) in order to illustrate how these traits exist in FFs, and summarizes findings for other virtues at the end of the section. Table 2.1 describes the analyzed Colombian cases.

The 66 interviews were conducted, recorded and transcribed by researchers as part of the STEP project from 2007–2011. The authors further coded these interviews for the specific purpose of this chapter. Sentences and complete paragraphs were coded using definitions given by Peterson and

Table 2.1 Summary of Colombian STEP cases

Family	Economic sector	Size	Interviews
Abisaad	Oil drilling	Medium	6
Suarez	Financial services	Medium	5
Lozano	Egg production and distribution	Small	5
Lopez	Food industry	Large	17
Caballero	Cargo, logistics	Large	11
Reinoso	Newspaper	Small	6
Muñoz	Entertainment, insurance and car dealers	Medium	8
Rincón	Education	Small	8

Notes:

Small firms house 1–50 employees, medium 50–500 and large 500+ employees.
Families' last names were changed to guarantee confidentiality.

Seligman (2004) as starting points and interpreting statements despite their not referring to the character strength explicitly. Analysis considered the frequency of codes in the complete set of interviews for each family. For the Colombian cases studied, some family members (especially leaders) develop virtues at different degrees of intensity, even though most of these virtues are common to all. Figure 2.1 shows the average importance of each virtue according to the response of each FF member interviewed.

COURAGE

The virtue of courage is 'the exercise of the will to accomplish goals in the face of opposition, external or internal' (Peterson and Seligman, 2004: 29). It is the main virtue in six of these families and the second largest in the Reinoso and Suarez cases. The character strengths associated with courage are:

Bravery (valor): 'not shrinking from threat, challenge, difficulty, or pain; speaking up for what is right even if there is opposition; acting on convictions even if unpopular' (Peterson and Seligman, 2004: 29). The Muñoz family exhibited bravery when negotiating their father's ransom, in spite of his declared wish for them not to do so in the event of his kidnapping. Once freed and after paying a considerable ransom, he took the reins of the business against the advice of friends and relatives who proposed his fleeing the country.

Persistence (perseverance, industriousness): 'finishing what one starts, persisting in a course of action in spite of obstacles; taking pleasure in

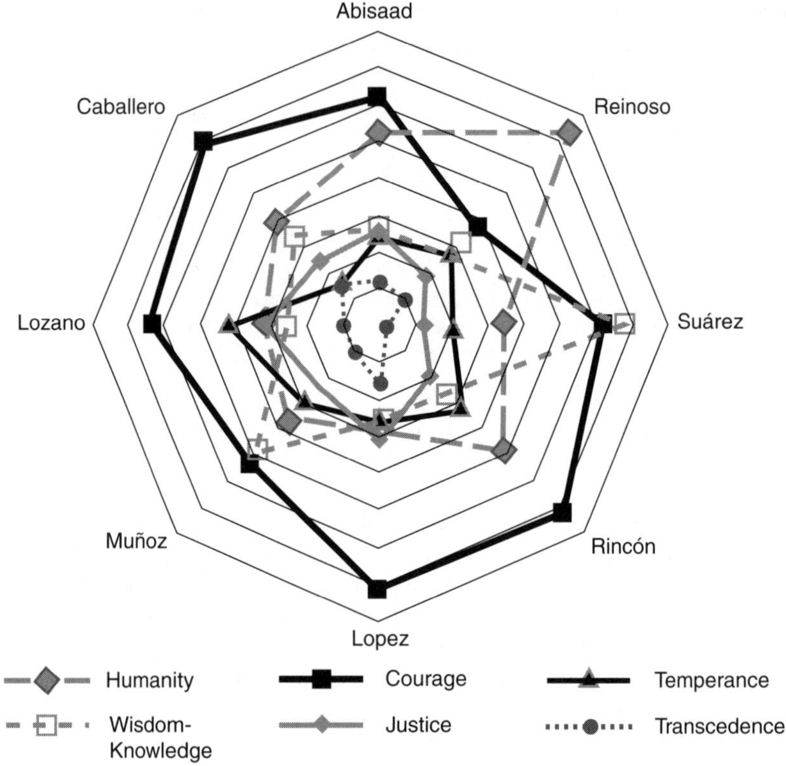

Note: The distance from the center represents the percentage of the speech that referenced a specific virtue in the whole set of interviews for a specific family.

Figure 2.1 Importance of virtues for family firms

completing tasks' (Peterson and Seligman, 2004: 29). Persevering belongs to the essence of any entrepreneur. Any family entrepreneur might retreat in the face of some well-known risk – after all, the family's future wealth is at stake – but s/he does not cower at hurdles that entail just plain hard work. All of our cases demonstrated persistence, but we highlight two specific elements here: first, materially deprived family settings moved the Lopez and Caballero brothers to work while still teenagers, their persistence over time resulting in their current businesses. A second element is the view of perseverance reflected in what José Agustín Caballero stated concerning his own entrepreneurship: 'The best investment for research is hardship and not always succeeding [. . .] such failure will surely lead to discovering new things.'

Vitality (zest, enthusiasm, vigor, energy): 'approaching life with excitement and energy; not doing things halfway or half-heartedly; living life as an adventure; feeling alive and activated' (Peterson and Seligman, 2004: 29). It is what Alejandra observed and lived in the cargo company when accompanying her father in the family's four-wheeler along risky roads in order to evaluate their fitness for larger cargos; it left in her a lasting feeling of adventure and admiration that made her want to follow in his footsteps. Or the case of Carlos Antonio, second-generation member CEO of all the Lopez FFs, who with his characteristic vigor proposed that the three largest palm oil producers in the country soften their harsh competitive approach in order to merge and build what is today a successful multinational that serves many Latin American markets.

Integrity (authenticity, honesty): 'speaking the truth but more broadly presenting oneself in a genuine way and acting in a sincere way; being without pretense; taking responsibility for one's actions and feelings' (Peterson and Seligman, 2004: 29). In Colombian culture, where paying corporate taxes that are due is not a generalized practice, FFs are the exception. Somehow, sustainability and legacy relate to truthfulness and honoring contracts. Integrity includes not only strict adherence to legal requirements, but also honoring one's word. Referring to his father and mother, the Rincón family's young leader explains: 'Both are absolutely straight and open; here you will never see in our books an entry for my mother's personal expenses or anything like that.' These were characteristics in all our cases.

TEMPERANCE

Peterson and Seligman (2004: 30) define the virtue of temperance as 'all those strengths that protect against excess'. The character strengths associated with temperance are:

Forgiveness and mercy: 'forgiving those who have done wrong; accepting the shortcomings of others; giving people a second chance; not being vengeful' (Peterson and Seligman, 2004: 30). What more could be asked of the Muñoz family than for them to forgive their kidnappers? During our interviews, family members uttered not a single bitter phrase regarding this event.

Humility/modesty: 'letting one's accomplishments speak for themselves; not seeking the spotlight; not regarding oneself as more special than others' (Peterson and Seligman, 2004: 30). Members of FFs see themselves as similar to others; Rose Abisaad highlights modesty by saying:

> I believe that the key to greatness is humility. We were brought up this way; my father did not even paint our farm's roof in order not to bring attention. My father was low profile; his social sensitivity did not allow him to own a luxury car in order not to provoke envy in others. Our ancestors migrated in boats and were not blue bloods. I believe our only right in life is to be humble, which does not rule out striving for great projects. We might have shoes today, but we might not have them tomorrow. However, we do have to be committed to using our intelligence and working capacity at its most. That is what our kids have to learn.[2]

Prudence: 'being careful about one's choices; not taking undue risk; not saying or doing things that might later be regretted' (Peterson and Seligman, 2004: 30). Some of the Lopez's FFs deal with large palm oil plantations and many times its CEOs could not visit such operations personally due to terrorist threats. 'Managing by video' was the most appropriate means, supported by very reliable and loyal employees who worked in production. This character strength together with the above-mentioned *bravery* accompanied efforts to meet the needs of poor peasants who worked in the plantations. Schools, housing and health services were provided at company expense. In a way, the gratitude of the population served as a barrier to the terrorists' plans; informants would warn beforehand of an intended kidnapping.

Self-regulation (self-control): 'regulating what one feels and does; being disciplined; controlling one's appetites and emotions' (Peterson and Seligman, 2004: 30); in other words, building strong willpower. For the eight cases, second and third generations recognized the austerity of the founders. They knew no luxuries, either in their lifestyles or in their businesses. Modesty and humility is another common factor among family entrepreneurs.

Given the high scores that the virtues of wisdom and humanity also reported in the Colombian FFs (see Figure 2.1), Figure 2.2 highlights some factors that highlight their importance.

We now turn to exploring, based on our cases, the outcomes that such capabilities produce.

OUTCOMES FROM VIRTUES IN FAMILY FIRMS FOR COLOMBIAN CASES

In this section, we offer a detailed analysis in order to argue that for FFs values and virtues become important resources and capabilities, respectively, which enhance transgenerational potential. For this analysis we codified the interviews according to what Gomez-Mejía et al. (2011) iden-

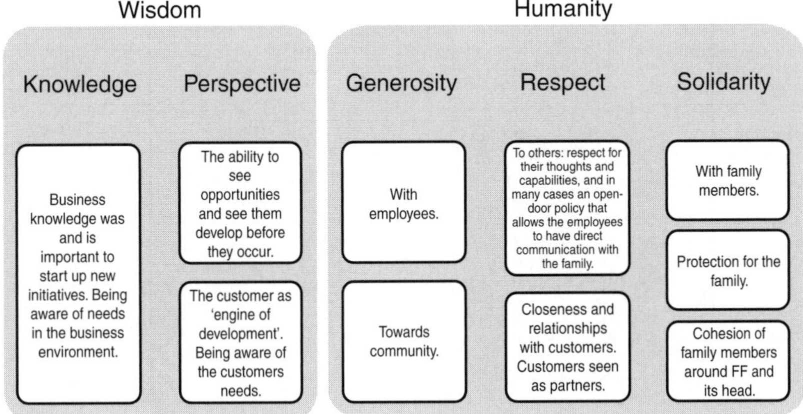

Figure 2.2 Relevant factors for other virtues and character strengths

tify as choices. Likewise, we include other choices that emerged from our cases, some of which complement the proposed model for socio-emotional wealth. The analysis is based on the frequency of sequences between the two sets of codes: choice codes and the codes of character strengths used above. For this analysis, the interviews of all the cases were considered as a whole. Consequently, there is no distinction among frequencies of outcomes in each FF studied. The figures in Table 2.2 show the Z value in such a way that the higher the Z value, the less likely such a sequence between the two specific codes is attributable to chance.

Our findings show that some relationships between choices and virtues occur more often than the average frequency of each relationship. The most frequent relationships in Table 2.2 (Z value at 99 percent of confidence), whose explanation follows, are: sustainability with commitment (2.8), growth with perseverance (3.6) and perspective (3.4), diversification with prudence (3.7), governance with hope (3.6) and family welfare with family love (3.6).

Economic sustainability refers to the firm's capacity to exist and generate profit over time; it is a must for the endurance of FFs and accounts for the business viability and the economic support of the family.

From the difficult conditions that founders usually endure, emerges the motivation for improving their standard of living in spite of former austere practices. However, there is more than knowledge and hope of it; there is commitment (a character strength illustrating the virtue of courage) that leads entrepreneurs both to reach their goals and move on to new ones.

Under these circumstances, FF *growth* arises in a natural way, with

Table 2.2 *Relationship between virtues and outcomes*

Strategic choices	Humanity			Courage					Temperance		Wisdom		Transcendence
	Generosity	Social intelligence	Family love	Perseverance	Vitality/passion	Integrity honesty	Industriousness	Commitment	Prudence	Self-regulation	Open-mindedness	Perspective	Hope
Sustainability								**2.8**				-1.8	
Growth				**3.6**								**3.4**	
Diversification					**2.2**				**3.7**				
Mastery competence										1.9			
Reputation						**2.3**							
Socio-emotional endowment							1.8	**2.0**					
Governance													**3.6**
Family welfare			**3.6**					**2.5**					
Others' welfare	**2.4**	1.7				**2.0**							
Loyalty others											**2.5**		

Notes:

Values represent the Z value at 90% of confidence for the sequence of codes; bold values are above 95% of confidence.
The virtue of justice was omitted given the low levels of significance of its relationships with the strategic choices.
Negative values represent the opposite sequence of the two codes in the text.

perseverance (virtue: courage) and perspective (virtue: wisdom) as important elements. Growth refers to the increase of a firm's wealth and size. For the Colombian cases, after reaching a level of profit, FFs invest their surplus earnings in the firm or in other FF initiatives. FF sustainability is an engine for FF growth; even more, for sustainable growth (Collins, 2011), which occurs as an outcome of built-in perspectives rather than in terms of growth as an objective per se.

Corporate diversification is one of the strategic choices for FFs (Gomez-Mejía et al., 2011) that reflects the FF's decision to invest in other businesses. Our results show diversification as related to prudence (virtue: temperance) and vitality/passion (virtue: courage). Vitality/passion is what moves the family members towards both working for the FF and forging new initiatives; after all, they are entrepreneurs. FF leaders give free rein to their impulses, harnessed by their self-knowledge, and so develop their initiatives with prudence in a dynamic explained by Sieger and colleagues (2011).

Governance represents the family interest in having a formal and hierarchical organization to manage their relationship with the firm. Governance is less pressing when families have few members. However, when the number of members increases, there arises the need for an organizational structure that allows for the FF's survival.

For the Colombian cases, governance is unusually related to hope (virtue: transcendence). Our interpretation of this result is that desire and hope for the survival of their businesses manifest in families building hierarchical structures for the FFs.

Family welfare relates to socio-emotional wealth (Gomez-Mejía et al., 2011). In some families, more than others, there are permanent reasons and actions preserving family cohesion (love of family as a character strength of humanity as a virtue). Some family members (Abisaad, Suarez, Muñoz, Lozano) often develop activities for maintaining family bonds outside the business. In other cases, family togetherness persists despite it not being possible for all members to meet, given their large numbers and global residences. Family welfare also includes the fact that family members involved in management or boards are committed to the business as a mechanism to provide economic support for families. The Lopez FF's CEO is also committed to providing dividends to the surviving widow of a founder.

Table 2.2 shows other important findings. For instance, for some FFs, *reputation, the prestige or esteem that FFs have among their partners*, is based on offering quality products or services and demonstrating *integrity*. Originally, FFs were usually small businesses arising from some specialized knowledge previously acquired by the founders in a related activity. For some, this experience and their relationships as employees support their future relationships as entrepreneurs. Recognizing this, subsequent generations cultivate reputation so that quality and relationships continue to play a leading role in the FF's economic sustainability.

Honesty and transparency (character strength of the virtue of courage) are salient characteristics of the relationships sustained by founders. 'One's word is honored' would seem to be the slogan in all of the companies, whose founders did not hesitate in making onerous decisions to comply with verbal agreements. Integrity becomes manifest in FFs whose activities relate to the performance of commodities in large markets. The Lopez's policy of trading with previously set restraints and avoiding speculation is a case in point. Likewise, reputation is a worthy asset due to the emotional component of family relationships; current generations feel admiration for previous generations and are morally committed to preserving such a legacy.

Our findings also show what Gomez-Mejía et al. called socio-emotional endowment (2011: 656). Many families are fond of their businesses; for some members, family and the FF have fuzzy boundaries because they were brought up in both settings. This emotional attachment to the firm becomes not only an engine for *industriousness* and *commitment* to the FF but also a key decisional factor in some critical situations; for instance, when the Reinoso family had to decide whether to sell its newspaper, which was emblematic of the city's culture. Likewise, the Abisaad and Muñoz families do not think about their businesses without recalling the pioneering units of the past, despite their low profitability at present.

Table 2.2 also shows that the interest of FFs in *welfare* is not restricted to their families; in all the observed cases, family members are motivated to provide more than conventional living conditions for employees and communities, what we have called *others' welfare*. Three arguments support *others' welfare*: first, FF leaders feel responsible for the continuance of jobs for employees, explaining the very low turnover in these FFs. When deciding whether to close a business unit, a key decision factor is the number of employees and families who depend on that business unit. Second, some family members consider that they owe the existence of their business to their employees. Third, generosity is a shared practice among family members towards non-family members, which in some cases reaches wider environments; for instance, the López family's abovementioned social programs for communities that welcome their business units, and the Reinoso family's projects promoting the cultural development of their city. This welfare towards their staff and community is often reciprocal in terms of *loyalty* and esteem towards the family and the FF: another found outcome of the virtues of FFs.

VIRTUES THAT FOSTER A DYNAMIC THROUGH GENERATIONS

Our analysis of the eight Colombian cases indicates that virtues are enacted over generations. However, factors such as the FF's experiences, family size and technological changes influence the transmission and development of virtues across generations and the means to transmit them.

Sustainability and family welfare motivate commitment (character strength of courage) and family love (character strength of humanity) respectively in hard-working family entrepreneurs. For the first generation, the 'right to a job', thereby employing even in-laws, involves new family members in the firm and develops the family's cohesion. First-generation members see their effort as a means to improve their extended family's welfare. In contrast, members of following generations concentrate on their own families, those of their siblings and also of their forbearers. New circumstances as a result of both a larger family and a growing business move later generations to set clear rules restricting the involvement of new family members in order to contribute to the FF's sustainability rather than simply guaranteeing employment for family members. It is clear for them that the FF's leadership implies specific skills and capabilities not always found among present family members.

Another association between virtues and choices that changes with newer generations is the one between prudence (character strength of temperance) and diversification. Founders undertake many risks when initiating businesses: they acquire knowledge via trial and error. Their self-confidence rests on their knowledge and experience. Over time and with their businesses growing, new generations and founders focus on keeping the existing FF viable as well as starting up other ventures. In most cases, we observed that the former does so with greater prudence and calculation than the latter. Later generations draw on the successful and unsuccessful experiences of the founders together with a larger information base provided by technological tools.

Two cases contrast with this finding. The Rincón family's founder worked his entire life around a well-managed educational initiative, while Junior is interested in diversifying far beyond that of the pioneering family venture, as well as out of the FF. He claims to be willing to take risks without fearing growth. The Caballero family's founders developed their business based on experience and rapport with clients; now a handful of second-generation members feel they should move into businesses based on speculation. This shows that the association between prudence and diversification may change between generations and that it is necessary to deepen the understanding of this dynamic in future research.

Finally, the Colombian cases show changes in the association between generosity (character strength associated with humanity) and others' welfare. Founders of these eight firms provided well-being to employees in the form of above-average salaries and stable employment; some also received bonuses. An 'open door policy' and fair treatment continue being part of relationships with staff. However, the mechanism to support generous deeds from the FF towards others has gained structure and focus.

CONCLUSIONS AND FINAL INSIGHTS

Our analysis and argument support four ideas: first, that FFs are places fit for cultivating and developing virtues such as Aronoff and Ward maintain (2000: 37); second, virtues are valuable capabilities for FFs since they can be related to specific outcomes; third, the ways in which virtues manifest themselves may change through generations. Finally, character strengths are an appropriate framework to identify the role of virtues within families and FFs.

Previous quantitative research has linked perceived virtues with outcomes at the company level (Cameron et al., 2004). Without focusing on a specific type of firm they found positive relationships among virtuousness and innovation, customer retention, quality and profitability, and a negative relationship between virtuousness and turnover. Our analysis differs from Cameron and colleagues (2004) in that we argue that the additional family component makes FFs a particularly appropriate place for the development of virtues. The spheres of actions identified by Habbershon and colleagues (2003) allow the sharing of experiences and reinforcing of virtues amongst FFs in a common path for the cases we considered. In addition, our analysis addressed the set of virtues that emerged in discourses whose interviews were not oriented to identifying virtues. It is significant that character strengths spontaneously emerged in the interviews of both family members and non-family members. This finding reinforces our proposal that family businesses and enterprising families and individuals in mutual interaction are breeding grounds for virtues.

Our findings suggest important lines for future research that may contribute to a better understanding of virtues in FFs as valuable capabilities. First, we did not focus on the differences between some virtues that seemed important in our cases and others that did not, which may relate both to the economic activities of FFs and their leaders' specific characteristics. For instance, temperance seems to be more important for some families but, in general, its practice has been one of the key elements enabling FFs to be sustainable. Likewise, wisdom and knowledge have different levels of influence according to Figure 1.1, being also important for the sustainability of FFs.

Second, the fact that the practice of some virtues shows significant changes over time (temperance and humanity) while the practice of others (integrity as part of the virtue courage) does not, sheds light on reasons behind this differentiation and acknowledges their contribution to enhancing transgenerational potential in current FFs. We noted that FFs' experience, family size, the level of engagement of new members and technological changes may influence the practice of said virtues. Technological changes, for instance, make information more available; also, more control generates a higher capacity to assume risks and that can influence prudence negatively. In addition, it is important to delineate the consequences of this dynamic for FFs in terms of succession and other issues.

A limitation of our research is our focus on the most successful family enterprises. To understand factors that enable longevity of family enterprises, a good starting point is to decipher the patterns common in the most successful enterprises. Once reliable measures for virtues are established then research efforts can expand to comparing the variances between firms of different timespans and other measures of success.

The practical implications of our findings stem from the fact that speaking about virtues goes beyond ideals (values) and establishing codes of ethics, although these are a valid starting point. For FFs and families to realize they are a breeding ground for virtues could prove advantageous if it results in cultivating these virtues in order to preserve the transgenerational potential of the FFs. Both for family and non-family enterprises, the continuous challenge lies in living the values established as principles, that is, walking the talk.

NOTES

1. A sample being: utilitarian (which holds that an action is right if it produces the greatest amount of good for the greatest number of people); deontological (which claims that duty, justice and rights are not reducible to considerations of utility).
2. Interview on 4 April 2007.

REFERENCES

Adams, J.S., A. Taschian and T.H. Shore (1996), 'Ethics in family and nonfamily owned firms: an exploratory study', *Family Business Review*, **9** (2), 157–70.

Amit, R. and P.J.H. Schoemaker (1993), 'Strategic assets and organizational rent', *Strategic Management Journal*, **14** (1), 33–46.

Aristotle (1984), 'Nicomachean ethics', in J. Barnes (ed.), *The Complete Works of Aristotle*, Princeton, NJ: Princeton University Press, pp. 1745–6.

Aronoff, C.E. and J.L. Ward (2000), *Family Business Values: How to Assure a Legacy of Continuity and Success*, Marietta, GA: Family Enterprise Publishers.

Barker, R.T., G.W. Rimler, E. Moreno and T.E. Kaplan (2004), 'Family business members' narrative perceptions: values, succession, and commitment', *Journal of Technical Writing and Communication*, **34** (4), 291–320.

Barney, J. (1991), 'Firm resources and sustained competitive advantage', *Journal of Management*, **17** (1), 99.

Baumeister, R.F. and J. Tierney (ed.) (2011), *Willpower: Rediscovering the Greatest Human Strength*, New York: Penguin Press.

Cameron, K.S., D. Bright and A. Caza (2004), 'Exploring the relationships between organizational virtuousness and performance', *American Behavioral Scientist*, **47** (6), 766–90.

Collins, J.C. (2011), *How the Mighty Fall: And Why Some Companies Never Give In*, New York: Jim Collins.

De George, R.T. (2005), 'A history of business ethics', Business Ethics Conference, Santa Clara, CA.

Dierickx, I. and K. Cool (1989), 'Asset stock accumulation and the sustainability of competitive advantage', *Management Science*, **35**, 1504–11.

Distelberg, B. and A. Blow (2010), 'The role of values and unity in family businesses', *Journal of Family and Economic Issues*, **31** (4), 427–41.

Donaldson, S. and I. Ko (2010), 'Positive organizational psychology, behavior, and scholarship: a review of the emerging literature and evidence base', *The Journal of Positive Psychology*, **5** (3), 14.

Dumas, C. and M. Blodgett (1999), 'Articulating values to inform decision making: lessons from family firms around the world', *International Journal of Value-Based Management*, **12** (3), 209–21.

Eisenhardt, K.M. and J.A. Martin (2000), 'Dynamic capabilities: what are they?', *Strategic Management Journal*, **21**, 1105–21.

Gomez-Mejía, L.R., C. Cruz, P. Berrone and J. De Castro (2011), 'The bind that ties: socioemotional wealth preservation in family firms', *Academy of Management Annals*, **5**, 653–707.

Habbershon, T.G. and M.L. Williams (1999), 'A resource-based framework for assessing the strategic advantages of family firms', *Family Business Review*, **12** (1), 1–25.

Habbershon, T.G., M. Williams and I.C. MacMillan (2003), 'A unified systems perspective of family firm performance', *Journal of Business Venturing*, **18** (4), 451–65.

Luthans, F. (2002), 'Positive organizational behavior. Developing and managing psychological strengths', *Academy of Management Executive*, **16**, 16.

Peterson, C. and N. Park (2006), 'Character strengths in organizations', *Journal of Organizational Behavior*, **27**, 5.

Peterson, C. and M.E.P. Seligman (2004), *Character Strengths and Virtues, a Handbook and Classification*, New York: American Psychological Association.

Sieger, P., T. Zellweger, R.S. Nason and E. Clinton (2011), 'Portfolio entrepreneurship in family firms, a resource-based perspective', *Strategic Entrepreneurship Journal*, **5** (4), 327–51.

Tapies, J. and J.L. Ward (2008), *Family Values and Value Creation, the Fostering of*

Enduring Values Within the Family Owned Business, Basingstoke, UK: Palgrave Macmillan Publishers.

Yu, A., G.T. Lumpkin, R.L. Sorenson and K.H. Brigham (2012), 'The landscape of family business outcomes. A summary and numerical taxonomy of dependent variables', *Family Business Review*, **25** (1), 25.

3. Professionalization of the family business: decision-making domains*

Alberto Gimeno and Maria José Parada

PROFESSIONALIZING THE UPPER CASE 'CONSTRUCT CO.' FAMILY BUSINESS

> I don't understand why you make your own decisions without sharing them with the board. It is the only way we can make strategic decisions with lower margins of error. What is so obvious to you is not so obvious to us. (Rafael Kohl says to his father Bernardo)

Rafael, Bernardo's second child, studied engineering and has always worked in the family business. After working with his father for 20 years, he realized the long and challenging path that lay ahead for him and his two brothers. Until now, all decisions, especially the strategic ones, were made quickly by his father who followed his intuition. Unlike their father however, Rafael and his brothers did not feel they had the same 'ability' to grasp the right opportunity intuitively.

Bernardo Kohl was the son of a miller and a housewife and the youngest of eight siblings. He had a hard childhood as his father died when he was a baby. His family made their living from farming and when resources were scarce they turned to selling plots of family land. He shouldered the responsibility of caring for his family and left school at a very young age in order to work on the family farm.

With little formal education, he started his business from scratch, taking the risk of mortgaging his house to buy a tractor. He used the tractor and his agricultural expertise to till his neighbors' fields. His business grew quickly, and eventually he began to rent tractors from entrepreneurs in other towns to meet the demands of his own market. Mr Kohl seized new opportunities with the advent of modern machinery. He launched the earth removal business that became the foundation for his construction company.

His great intuition helped him realize that the company's future lay in being a contractor rather than a subcontractor. As such, in early 1960 he founded a construction company. Mr Kohl knew which opportunities to exploit and which ones to pass on. This was evident in the decisive moments that led to continued growth, business reorientation and changes to the company's business model.

The 1990s saw increasing competition for winning construction project bids for the Barcelona Olympic Games. Instead Mr Kohl centered his attention on another segment – public works, positioning himself within the market as a solid and solvent contractor. When winning the tenders for public works became more competitive after the Olympic Games, he focused on offering quality and reasonable deadlines. He soon realized his clients needed something else. So, he offered shorter completion times and met the contracted standards of quality.

Today Construct Co. is a diversified family business with a main business unit focusing on construction and two smaller business units dealing with real estate and renewable energy. It is currently one of the leading companies on the Catalan market. Up to now, the driving force behind the company's growth has been the founder's enterprising spirit. The founder's resources, skills and ability to take advantage of the opportunities have led to the firm's diversification. He hardly shared any decisions and all of the knowledge he acquired during his long years of work is stored in his mind. In the industry, Bernardo Kohl is highly respected and known for his capacity to do business and network.

Mario, Rafael and Diego joined the company as soon as they finished their MBAs (master of business administration) at prestigious business schools. The second generation has taken managerial positions, each running different business units. Mario, the eldest son, took over the real estate division, which had great potential for growth. Mr Kohl deeply believed that 'value is in the land', and this led to a tendency to invest in property. Besides, thanks to his extensive knowledge of earth removal, and the group's solvency, he was able to dedicate resources to recovering and leveling these lands. Therefore, this division relied on a vast array of properties and land to use as the basis for its development. Interested in urban management, Mario focused on building shopping malls, a novel concept at the time.

Some years later, Mr Kohl became aware of the need to redirect the business in order to compete in difficult scenarios. Therefore, he hired an external chief executive officer (CEO), the most qualified engineer he could find. The new CEO introduced important changes within the company, the most noteworthy being the massive professionalization of the company, both at operational and executive levels. He developed processes for systematizing information, and empowered lower levels of management in order to improve decision-making processes.

At the same time, Rafael joined the family business. He started in the main division. Several years later he took over the energy division that had been created by Mr Kohl to supply fuel to his own fleet of machines. Mr Kohl allied himself with other independent gasoline station owners to form a large conglomerate that became the first liquid combustibles distributor in Spain not associated with an oil company. Rafael developed the energy division, quadruplicating gas stations and using renewable energies.

For 40 years the decision-making processes at Construct Co. were dominated by the founder's intuitive leadership style. Governance structures were simple, as everything relied on the founder. Rafael explains:

> My father is such a visionary, and the businesses he created have been successful. He smells it. For us it is more difficult and takes longer. We need to see numbers, have indicators to see real potential. This is why we need to build formal structures, develop a strategy together, to have support from others, to create a learning culture . . .

Recently, Mr Kohl saw the need to create a board of directors, consisting of himself, his three executive sons and two highly respected external board members. Despite best intentions, the struggle to move from a founder leader intuitive style to a more professional style is evident, as reflected in the comments below. 'This is not possible! You should share your thoughts and plans with the board. Where are we going? What is our plan for future growth? You cannot decide without taking the numbers into consideration! How do you know this will work if you have not really analyzed it?' says Rafael to his father, astonished at the fact that his father wants to internationalize into a region where they have no economies of scale or ways to compete advantageously. 'Why do we need so many numbers and analyses? You can see the potential just like that!' responds Mr Kohl.

DISCUSSION QUESTIONS

1. To what extent has the company been professionalized? Why do you think so?
2. What should the next steps be for professionalizing the company further?

INTRODUCTION

In this chapter we focus on the level of professionalization in decision-making and the roles played by external and internal managers in this process. Family business scholars have emphasized the inclusion of external non-family CEOs and managers in professionalization, inadvertently assuming that family managers are not professional (Bennedsen et al., 2007; Hall and Nordqvist, 2008).

Professionalization has been viewed as a move away from founder-centric organization to the inclusion of non-family managers (Chittoor and Das, 2007). These authors suggest that such a transition is smoother when family members have a planned exit path; non-family managers have previous experience working in the family business; when the key non-family managers are included on the board; and when the successor has some shares at stake.

Broadening the scope of professionalization, Stewart and Hitt (2012) use a contingent approach to argue that professionalization modes are linked to the mental models of the family leaders and what they envision for their businesses. Moreover, these authors suggest that the family leaders' capabilities will influence the way they decide to professionalize the company. Their paper sheds light on important elements of the professionalization processes and modes. In line with Stewart and Hitt (2012), Hall and Nordqvist (2008) challenge the assumption that family firms are not professional if managed by family members and only become professional when they incorporate non-family managers. Moreover, they also highlight the lack of discussion about the meaning of professionalization.

Generational transition affects decision-making processes. While decision-making by the founders has been widely studied, there is minimal research on what happens when successors come on board. It has been suggested that ineffective decision-making causes failed successions (Shepherd and Zacharakis, 2000; Ward, 1997). Decision-making processes beyond the founder's life cycle are usually approached as part of leadership and/or succession issues (Bird et al., 2002; Cabrera-Suárez et al., 2001; Chrisman et al., 1996, Chrisman et al., 2003; Sharma, 2004; Zahra and Sharma, 2004). Very seldom have they been understood from a professionalization perspective. Chittoor and Das's (2007) study is one of the few exceptions, linking succession performance with the professionalization of management. This approach, however, is restricted to passing the baton from a family member to a non-family manager.

Curiously, although most studies deal with decision-making within the context of professionalization, it is only tackled implicitly. In their review, Stewart and Hitt (2012) present different dimensions dealing with professionalization and the dichotomies between family and non-family businesses. For instance, they contrast analytical and intuitive management, formalized and organic management, leaders' backgrounds and ownership or governance issues. We propose that professionalization is related to decision-making processes where top managers face ill-structured problems and uncertain dynamic environments, blending ill-defined or competing goals with time stress (Orasanu and Connolly, 1993). This decision-making process is complex, and resembles 'the process of fermentation in biochemistry rather than an industrial assembly line' (Pfiffner 1960).

We highlight the dearth of understanding of exactly what it means to professionalize a company (Hall and Nordqvist, 2008). One of the main issues in studying the topic is the lack of consensus in defining professionalization (Stewart and Hitt, 2012). We view professionalization as a process of organizational transformation characterized by the codification of knowledge, clarification in role definition and the creation of different decision-making domains (cf., Charan et al., 1980[1]; Songini, 2006[2]; Stewart and Hitt, 2012; Weber[3], 1921 [1968]).

This chapter aims to study how family businesses are professionalized in terms of decision-making domains. The struggles faced during this process are evident in the Construct Co. case, as the company attempts to reduce its dependency on the founder's intuitive decision-making style. Later in this chapter, we analyze another, more mature, Spanish pharmaceutical firm, to illustrate how a family business professionalizes different decision-making domains. The Spanish pharmaceutical firm is large in size, with the fifth generation in control.

Our study contributes to the field of family businesses in at least two ways: by explaining the professionalization process in terms of decision-making; and taking into consideration contingency variables as key elements of professionalization. The chapter is structured as follows. We start with a general framework on professionalization and decision-making. Then we explain the methodology used and follow it with the case analysis. We finish by looking at the results and conclusions.

PROFESSIONALIZATION IN FAMILY BUSINESSES

Stewart and Hitt (2012) suggest that professionalization is contingent on the leader's mental model, capabilities and vision, and that it occurs in different levels or dimensions such as ownership, governance, returns, rewards, networks, leadership, careers and management.

Some authors argue the need to professionalize management, as well as governance structures, to overcome opportunism, nepotism, the lack of professionalism of family managers, and to maximize their strengths (for example, Martínez et al., 2007; Rondøy et al., 2009; Schulze et al., 2001; Sciascia and Mazzola, 2008; Westhead and Howorth, 2006). Yet, decision-making is ignored and what is really behind professionalization is still unknown.

As noted in the Construct Co. case, founders tend to develop their businesses using intuitive decision-making. Hence, organizations become highly dependent on their founders (Feltham et al., 2005). Family business literature has studied this phenomenon extensively under the rubric of controlling owners who create founder-centric organizations (Davis and Harveston, 1991). Such dependency results in successive generations having to deal with decisions they are not prepared for if the founder disappears (Dyer, 1986). For instance, Feltham et al. (2005) found that in 75 percent of the cases in a sample of more than 700 businesses, decisions were in the hands of a single decision-maker.

Many scholars highlight the difficulty or failure in succession processes arising from the successor's inability to acquire the knowledge and skills of the predecessor, or from a lack of leadership skills (for example, Bird et al., 2002; Cabrera-Suárez et al., 2001; Chrisman et al., 1996, 2003; Sharma, 2004; Zahra and Sharma, 2004). We contend that as a business evolves from the founder to the next generation of leadership and the nature of the business changes, different combinations of intuitive and analytical decision-making are needed. In fact, entrepreneurs' strategic decisions are based far more on intuition, while managers' decisions are mainly analytical (Busenitz and Barney, 1997). Incorporating successful managers may require managing the blend of intuitive and analytical decision-making (Mintzberg and McHugh, 1985). Thus, professionalization is closely related to decision-making processes and decision-making is a complex phenomenon. This central topic in any organization requires attention and is especially important within the context of family businesses where generational transitions occur and decision-making processes may need to change. Moreover, as noted by Stewart and Hitt (2012), professionalization is not a dichotomous construct; instead it is a process that incorporates different levels and domains of professionalization.

DECISION-MAKING DOMAINS

Understanding professionalization as a process requires identifying the domains of the organization that are being professionalized. Professionalizing different domains has diverse implications. Based on the level of complexity and unpredictability (Gimeno et al., 2010), we propose three domains of decision-making: administrative, operational and strategic. Complexity does not mean complicated. For example, anticipating the route of a hurricane is complex, but the orbit of a planet is not, although both are complicated. The administrative domain deals with low complexity issues. It refers to coding and articulating data and information[4] related to accounting, management control, finance, supply, operations, sales, and so on. The operational domain deals with higher complexity process issues that require human interaction inside all areas of the organization. The strategy orientation deals with the highest level of complexity, involving the interaction of an organization with different stakeholders in its environment to anticipate their expected movements.

Decision-making is a combination of analysis and intuition (Kahneman, 2011; Klein, 1999; Gigerenzer, 2007), in a way that decision-making processes can refer to a specific position in a continuum ranging from analysis to intuition (Kahneman and Frederick, 2004), based on individual levels of expertise and the nature of the problem.

Low-complexity problems are easy to structure and therefore can be addressed through analytical decision-making processes (Gigerenzer, 2007). When analytical decision-making processes are bypassed for problems that are difficult, novel or extremely entangled, expert managers incorporate intuitive problem-solving approaches (Isenberg, 1986).

Complex problems have to be approached in an eclectic way, accepting the ambiguity and contradictions therein, allowing expert decision-makers to look for solutions with a suitable combination of analysis and intuition (Tetlock, 2005).

Professionalizing the three domains represents a different type of problem. The administrative domain implies introducing analytical order, where predictability is present and therefore facts can be codified easily. The operational domain requires a certain degree of intuition to develop managers' expertise and relationships, given that human interaction involves subjectivity. The strategic domain is not only about being able to understand the organization's current situation and a multitude of external variables, but also anticipating their future evolution. It requires a combination of both intuition and analysis not only on an individual basis, but also at the top management team level, given the high degree of uncertainty. Therefore, the characteristics of the different levels require specific decision-making patterns (see Table 3.1).

METHODS

Following the STEP (Successful Transgenerational Entrepreneurship Practices) methodology, this study is informed by an in-depth analysis of a Spanish pharmaceutical company as we needed a context with a history that was long enough for us to be able to identify changes in

Table 3.1 Domains of professionalization

	Domains Administrative	Operational	Strategic
Characteristics	Codification of facts Predictability	Human interaction Subjectivity	Interaction with the environment Ambiguity and uncertainty
Decision-making	Analytical	Analytical with intuitive skills	Analytical with strong individual and group intuition

professionalization over time. Over 25 hours of in-depth interviews with eight individuals inform the case. The interviewees ranged in age from 40–75, and were a mix of family and non-family members. While some interviewed family members were actively involved in the business, others were not. To maintain the confidentiality of the case, pseudonyms were used. We used multiple sources of evidence from different family and non-family members and observation, and also checked secondary data such as news in media and internal reports. When in doubt, we relied on the key informants to answer questions and verify our understanding of the case facts. Such access to the interviewees helped improve the construct validity of our study (Yin, 2003).

THE PHARMA CO.

Founded in 1838, Pharma Co. is under the control of the founding family. The company has 600 employees and a turnover of €120 million. It is one of the largest pharmaceutical companies in Spain and among the oldest in Europe. The company has been transformed from a drugstore that carried food products, to a pharmaceutical business, which includes a high quality research and design (R&D) center. Currently the business is managed by an external CEO and is reinforced by a vast array of structures, systems and processes to support the top management team's decision-making. To reach this high level of professionalization, many changes were made along the way, especially between the fourth and fifth generations. Pharma passed from a 'founder' to a next generation top management team with four siblings. In terms of governance, the family created a two-tier model: the 'family council' that was presided by the 'founder'; and a 'board of directors' with external members that replaced the former 'advisory board'. Similarly, the management team is now divided into seven general managerial areas reporting to the CEO, with five business units and two support areas. How did Pharma achieve this high level of professionalization?

First Stage: The Family Occupying Key Operational Positions

Pharma Co. started as a business with very low complexity in the 1830s. Mr Pharma, the first generation, bought the drugstore from his former employer in 1838 and created an alliance with a pharmaceutical company. His oldest child started working at Pharma Co. at an early age, gaining experience and building his expertise. The two younger sons received complementary training to help their older brother. With the blessing of their father, the three sons grew the business and diversified it to incorporate a laboratory. The three brothers made key decisions collectively. In the third generation, nine children were born, four boys and five girls. The oldest sibling had only one son, who became the '*hereu*[5]'. He maintained a dominant position in terms of stock during the third generation. Mr Pharma III studied management, preparing to run the business. In addition to his formal education, he worked at Pharma Co. from a very young age, starting at the bottom.

Second Stage: Systematizing the Business

The joining of the fourth generation marked an inflection point in the family business, particularly evident in terms of decision-making. Mr Pharma IV, the only son of Mr Pharma III, had a PhD in Pharmacy. His scientific orientation played a key role in the promotion of R&D as a mainstream area within the family business. Although a lab had been created 50 years earlier, he was the one who gave impulse to carrying out their research. As indicated by the statement below, this was not an easy decision.

> It was very hard for me to convince my father how important R&D was. My father did not believe in it. In my case it was different; I was very clear about it and dedicated a lot of effort to developing the R&D division. It was not until R&D showed positive results that he supported me. (Mr Pharma IV)

Tasks were clearly divided. While the father (III generation) remained in charge of running the business, Mr Pharma IV was in charge of R&D and laboratory production.

> In the lab, my father gave me plenty of room, but where he didn't was in the administrative area; he didn't let me into the commercial area. Little by little this situation changed. (Mr Pharma IV)

Over time, Mr Pharma IV bought out his second cousins' shares, making him the sole stockholder. The business was growing and internationalizing. At that time Mr Pharma IV decided to create an advisory board composed of his friends to help him make important decisions. The business continued to grow and the four male children from the fifth generation joined the family business after completing their formal education at prestigious universities.

In the early 1980s, the eldest son, James, went through various areas: R&D, then production and purchasing. The second and third sons also studied business administration, thereafter joining at opportune times. Mr Pharma IV invited his sons to join the company one by one, when they were needed.

> I remember my father was all by himself at that time and, although he had trustworthy employees, they were not family members. He maybe thought it could be useful to ask me to give him my opinion about the possible purchase of two laboratories and get feedback from another source . . . Possibly his advisor told him to buy and my father replied, 'let's see what my son says'. (Jules)

Ethan, the third son, began his professional career working for a consulting firm.

> . . . a business situation developed here, which made them think that it was time for me to join the company. There was a vacancy; there was a problem and a series of actions had to be taken. They gave me a managerial role as head of organization and systems responsible for all the information systems and organization. Later on I started to take on responsibility for some administrative and financial matters too. (Ethan)

The youngest brother studied law and followed a similar path, gaining outside experience first.

> My father wanted to have all four of us here. After those five years I decided to reorient my professional life towards the company, so I decided to do an MBA at a prestigious business school. At that moment I joined the family business. (Mike)

The advisory board helped in the process of organizing the areas for the incoming children, and the children became four general managers. The brothers focused on the business' operations: James on sales and institutional relationships, Jules on the production plant, logistics, engineering and environmental issues, Ethan on administration and the commercial area, and Mike on corporate law and human resources.

The advisory board also encouraged succession planning and the design of the family constitution and family council. This body also highlighted the need for a strategic plan. The children took responsibility for the elaboration of a strategic plan, since they felt that the dominant managerial practices within the company had to change. These practices were based on the trust Mr Pharma IV had in the different managers, especially those in strategic positions, and their ability to coordinate themselves internally as a management team.

Third Stage: Further Professionalization of the Company

In the early 2000s, the siblings hired a prestigious consultancy group to help in the design and rethink of the strategy of the group.

> We identified collectively the need to ask a consultant for a plan; we could see storm clouds on the horizon and the plan that we had prepared was too status quo. (Jules)

The new strategic plan led to a concentration of power and leadership in two main visible heads, one for the pharmaceutical unit and one for the chemical business unit. The four brothers discussed and agreed on the profile required for each position. These decisions led to changes in the internal structure of the company. The advisory board was substituted by a board of directors composed of Mr Pharma IV and the four Pharma V brothers, with three additional independent members.

> We've surrounded ourselves by a board capable of making decisions. They are not the type of people who are going to tell us what they think we want to hear. They are not 'yes men'. They're here because they like the project. (Mike)

Another difficult issue was the need to replace Mr Pharma IV's trusted employees with new external managers, as Mike explained: 'It was a challenge for us to convince my father we wanted to replace his trusted people, as we had to build our own network of trusted employees.'

Observing that the co-CEO format was not effective enough, the brothers decided to choose one sibling as CEO as they believed that someone from the family had to cover that position. He was supposed to change the structure, develop the new strategy and face the upcoming challenges.

> . . . It was a time for strategic change, which required someone with experience. We were advised throughout by the Board of Directors. Later, the fact that it was a family member made us feel that he would be more committed, and had enough knowledge of the company. This was seen as an intermediate step

> towards hiring an external CEO when the situation was more mature, more defined, and the strategy more established and we could look for new formulae. (Mike)

At the same time, Mr Pharma IV stepped down from the board to occupy the presidency of the family council. This process was accompanied by a key strategic decision made by the board, the spin-out of the R&D activities and the participation of external investors in this unit. 'For the first time, the company is looking for external investors to participate successfully in the R&D development' (Dr Rafin, R&D Manager).

The last move in the professionalization process was the hiring of an external CEO.

> We have made many changes and we have finally incorporated an external CEO. Unfortunately, we are struggling with many issues, and we see that the CEO does not have the entrepreneurial mindset we need at this time. We have probably become slow at making decisions. (Mike)

The Pharma Co. Group has been very successful in professionalizing the family business. This process consisted of introducing formality into the decision-making processes, which led to a certain degree of paralysis. The whole process entailed moving along an intuitive-analytical continuum.

Table 3.2 depicts Pharma Co.'s professionalization process in terms of decision-making, starting from the creation of administrative order in the company, the development of better management in the areas between them and, finally, the creation of the capacity to redefine the corporate strategy.

In the first three generations of Pharma Co., the family business largely relied on intuitive decision-making. The vision of the '*hereu*', who had known the business since they were very young, guided the company. Professionalization was concentrated at the administrative level with a focus on formal accounting systems, stock management and sales administration.

In the fourth and fifth generations, professionalization was developed at the operation level, especially with the entrance of the four fifth-generation children. Business units were created, the industrial plants were managed more systematically and an executive committee was created to align the different operations. The middle management was empowered. Whilst generation four continued to make the strategic decisions with the support of an advisory board, the execution was left to the four fifth-generation family members.

When the fifth generation had gained experience and confidence they replaced the advisory board with a board of directors. It signaled the professionalization of the strategy domain. Through the board the strategy changed, divesting in the Pharma units and investing in over-the-counter products (OTC) and consumer goods. One of the siblings was appointed CEO and later a non-family CEO was hired.

DISCUSSION

In our opinion professionalization has been narrowly studied, because it is mainly seen as a succession issue between the founder or the family CEO and a non-family CEO. Therefore, the focus has been on the competences and life cycle of one individual – the founder – and how best to replace him/her across generations. In this chapter we focused on the process of professionalization at the organizational level. Two cases of firms at different stages and their evolution helped shed light on this process.

The Construct Co. case presents a situation where the company has been run intuitively by the founder's generation, while some domains are being partially professionalized. Now the challenge is to continue professionalizing and determine how the next generation can work in different domains with the appropriate combination of analysis and intuition. In the Pharma Co. case, we identify a more sophisticated process, focused on transformation in the decision-making process at different levels or domains of the organization.

The professionalization of a domain requires decision-making patterns that demand a specific set of skills and capabilities, a leader at a particular level in the hierarchy and a well-established relationship with the dominant family member. Pharma Co. carried out a successful professionalization process because it affected systems and processes, as well as individual and team capabilities. Table 3.2 reflects how the three different domains were professionalized and how they represent different steps in the 'professionalization ladder'. Professionalization of the administrative domain deals with creating control and order in the legal, economic and financial flows. This requires applying analytical systems within and perhaps engaging methodologies, by using internal resources or external service providers. A 'trusted employee' of the dominant family member – usually the chief financial officer (CFO) – may handle this.

At the operational level, professionalization requires the development of processes, knowledge, competent teams, management skills and professional culture. This means applying analytical decision-making to the processes and intuitive decision-making to the interpersonal dynamics. The person responsible for this level of professionalization is the figure of the chief operating officer (COO), who ought to have a strong alliance and frequent communication with the dominant family member in order to involve him/her and receive his/her support.

At the strategic domain level, professionalization means addressing ill-structured problems, uncertain dynamic environments, shifting, ill-defined or competing goals, action feedback loops and time stress (Orasanu and Connolly, 1993). This requires developing a committed and cohesive top management team, an effective governance structure and specific organizational values and culture. Responsibility lies in the CEO, who is trusted by the controlling family member. The roles are clearly defined to allow sufficient management through the board of directors or through formal meetings between them. The CEO has enough management discretion.

Pharma Co. developed the administrative domain of professionalization during the first three generations. It was the '*hereu*' (heir) who dominated the management of and key decisions made by the company. The fourth generation started the professionalization of the operational domain. The fifth generation continued the professionalization of the strategy domain. This process has led to the transfer of decision-making in different domains of professionalization. Climbing up the professionalization ladder requires the development of a management team, with individual and collective intuitive decision-making capabilities, changing the role of the dominant family members and establishing an appropriate relationship between family and non-family members at all levels in the company.

Advisors are crucial in the professionalization process. In the Pharma Co. case the advisory board supported the operational professionalization. The board of directors, which included three external advisors, led the professionalization of the strategic domain.

The Pharma Co. case shows the intense relationship between professionalization and successions. During the first three succession processes, many elements that are present in the succession literature appeared. Examples include the development and selection of a successor at an opportune time, and resistance to passing on the baton, and so on. Professionalization drove the last succession, as Mr Pharma IV was replaced by the creation of systems and structures that aided the development of knowledge and competences in the next generation of family members, and the incorporation of non-family members from the outside.

Table 3.2 Professionalization domain

	Domain		
	Administrative	Operational	Strategic
Characteristics	Codification of facts Predictability 'The administrative part was taken care of by my father' (Mr Pharma IV)	Human interaction Subjectivity 'My four sons entered the business and they took over different areas of the company' (Mr Pharma IV) 'We disembarked and we did cover the areas that were not covered by my father, which was a good way of avoiding overlapping and of leaving my father his space' (Mike)	Interaction with the environment Ambiguity and uncertainty 'The business has undergone three–four strategic business plans over the course of the last 20 years. In a highly uncertain industry, the need to define the strategic lines became evident with the arrival of the fifth generation' (Mike)
Decision-making	Analytical 'My father studied business administration at a prestigious business school. This is where he met many of his good friends who later on formed part of the advisory board' (Mike)	Analytical with intuitive skills 'We all studied and came on board with high qualifications, ready to apply our knowledge to the company' (Mike) 'We have incorporated new ways of doing things' (Mike)	Analytical with strong individual and group intuition 'We made three to four strategic plans, because we needed help to reorient the company. Unlike my father, we really need figures and more analysis to know where to go' (Mike)

Resources	Easy to incorporate (buy in) or outsource	Operational, formal knowledge, processes, teams, culture, management Effective leadership	Culture, values, top management team, commitment, learning capabilities, flexibility, mental leadership
'Professional' level	CFO, CIO '. . .My father hired a finance director who became his right hand' (Mike)	COO 'We had two siblings serving as CEO. Then we named my third brother as CEO, who took the lead supported by and in coordination with all of us' (Mike)	CEO '. . .to one family CEO and afterwards an external CEO with a professional and independent board of directors . . .' (Mike)
Relationship with the president	Trusted employee	Embedded, shared goals, frequent and informal communication, alliance	Trust, mainly through the board, formal follow-up meetings
	'. . . He had trustworthy employees who were not family members' (Jules) 'A challenge for us was to convince my father we wanted to replace his trusted people as we had to build our own network of trusted employees' (Mike)		'We have a formal board of directors with externals. We also have completely retired from management and are only present at the board (some of us) and at the family council (all of us)' (Mike)

CONCLUSIONS

This study aimed to gain an understanding of the professionalization process from a decision-making perspective. Variation in the temporality of professionalization in different decision-making domains based on the complexity of issues is highlighted. While previous studies highlighted professionalization as involving the hiring of non-family managers (for example, Chittoor and Das, 2007), we focus our attention on what is being professionalized and how it is carried out. The Pharma Co. case shows clearly that professionalization is a process. Decisions on the level of professionalization are made by the top management team (TMT) or by the board (Aronoff and Astrachan, 1996).

This study contributes to the field of management in various ways. To start with, research on decision-making is mainly conducted in the field of psychology and is developed through lab experiments. We are using the context of family firms and carrying out an in-depth case study to understand the professionalization of decision-making domains. Usually the research sample is composed of students (Klein and Klinger, 1991), who are not faced with a real decision-making process as in the case of family businesses where top managers constantly struggle with these issues. Finally, decision-making in organizations has mainly been approached as a lineal process or as a sequence of circular processes that follow a specific route or routes. Here we suggest that decision-making appears at various levels and the mix between intuitive and analytic decision-making is especially important.

This study also contributes to the family business field in at least two ways. It increases our knowledge of the professionalization of family firms by highlighting how the process unfolds over time as different domains of an organization are professionalized, reducing dependency on the owner manager and relying on a team of family and non-family experts.

The limitations of this study indicate opportunities for further research. The chapter is based on one empirical case study, which shows a single way of professionalizing the business. A multiple-case study could follow in order to see if there are several pathways to professionalizing decision-making domains. Our case illustrates the importance of consultation, consensus and team work in professionalizing a company, yet this topic could be further studied in greater depth in order to gain a better understanding of what facilitates professionalization. We do not explicitly address the role different generations play in professionalizing the company, and this would be worth investigating further so as to help family businesses in their professionalization processes.

NOTES

* We are sincerely thankful to the editors of the book, Pramodita Sharma and Kavil Ramachandran, for their highly valuable comments and insights. They have been very helpful in developing and presenting our ideas.

1. Charan et al. (1980) expose increased data and information systematization and quantification.
2. Songini (2006) highlights the need to introduce formalized systems.
3. Weber suggests that professional organization is based on rational decision-making.
4. What Charan et al. (1980) describe as increased data and information systematization and quantification.
5. Traditionally the first born, the '*hereu*', inherits all or the majority of the ownership.

REFERENCES

Aronoff, C.E. and J.H. Astrachan (1996), 'How to make better decisions', *Nation Business*, **84** (1), 39.

Bennedsen, M., K.M. Nielsen, F. Pérez-González and D. Wolfenzon (2007), 'Inside the family firm: the role of families in succession decisions and performance', *Quarterly Journal of Economics*, **122**, 647–91.

Bird, B., H. Welsch, J.H. Astrachan and D. Pistrui (2002), 'Family business research: the evolution of an academic field', *Family Business Review*, **15** (4), 337–50.

Busenitz, L.W. and J.B. Barney (1997), 'Differences between entrepreneurs and managers in large organizations: biases and heuristics in strategic decision-making', *Journal of Business Venturing*, **12** (1), 9–30.

Cabrera-Suárez, K., P. De Saá-Pérez and D. García-Almeida (2001), 'The succession process from a resource- and knowledge-based view of the family firm', *Family Business Review*, **14** (1), 37–48.

Charan, R., C.W. Hofer and J.F. Mahon (1980), 'From entrepreneurial to professional management: a set of guidelines', *Journal of Small Business Management*, **18** (1), 1–10.

Chittoor, R. and R. Das (2007), 'Professionalization of management and succession performance: a vital linkage', *Family Business Review*, **20**, 65–79.

Chrisman, J.J., J.H. Chua and P. Sharma (1996), *A Review and Annotated Bibliography of Family Business Studies*, Norwell: MA: Kluwer Academic Publishers.

Chrisman, J.J., J.H. Chua and S.A. Zahra (2003), 'Creating wealth in family firms through managing resources: comments and extensions', *Entrepreneurship Theory and Practice*, **27** (4), 359–65.

Davis, P. and P. Harveston (1999), 'In the founder's shadow: conflict in the family firm', *Family Business Review*, **12** (4), 311–23.

Dyer, W.C. Jr. (1986), *Cultural Change in Family Firms: Anticipating and Managing Business and Family Transitions*, San Francisco, CA: Jossey-Bass.

Feltham, T., G. Feltham and J. Barnett (2005), 'The dependence of family businesses on a single decision-maker', *Journal of Small Business Management*, **43**, 1–15.

Gigerenzer, G. (2007), *Gut Feelings*, London: Penguin Books.

Gimeno, A., G. Baulenas and J. Comacros (2010), *Family Business Models: Practical Solutions for the Business Family*, London: Palgrave Macmillan.

Hall, A. and M. Nordqvist (2008), 'Professional management in family businesses: toward an extended understanding', *Family Business Review*, **21**, 51–69.

Isenberg, D.J. (1986), 'Thinking and managing: a verbal protocol analysis of managerial problem solving', *Academy of Management Journal*, **29** (4), 775–88.

Kahneman, D. (2011), *Thinking Fast and Slow*, New York: Farrar, Strauss and Giroux.

Kahneman, D. and S. Frederick (2004), 'Attribute substitution in intuitive judgment', in M. Augier and J.A. March (eds), *Models of a Man: Essays in Memory of Herbert A. Simon*, Cambridge, MA: The MIT Press, pp. 411–23.

Klein, G. (1999), *Sources of Power. How People Make Decisions*, Cambridge, MA: The MIT Press.

Klein, G. and D. Klinger (1991), 'Naturalistic decision making', *Human Systems IAC Gataway*, **XI** (3), 16–19.

Martínez, J.I., B.S. Stöhr and B.F. Quiroga (2007), 'Family ownership and firm performance: evidence from public companies in Chile', *Family Business Review*, **20**, 83–94.

Mintzberg, H. and A. McHugh (1985), 'Strategy formation in an ad-hocracy', *Administrative Science Quarterly*, **30**, 160–97.

Orasanu, J. and T. Connolly (1993), 'The reinvention of decision making', in G.A. Klein, J. Orasanu, R. Calderwoo and C. Zsambok (eds), *Decision Making in Action; Models and Methods*, Norwood, NJ: Ablex, pp. 3–20.

Pfiffner, J.M. (1960), 'Administrative rationality', *Public Administration Review*, **20** (3), 125–32.

Rondøy, T., C. Dibrell and J.B. Craig (2009), 'Founding family leadership and industry profitability', *Small Business Economics*, **32**, 397–407.

Schulze, W.S., M.H. Lubatkin, R.N. Dino and A.K. Buchholtz (2001), 'Agency relationships in family firms: theory and evidence', *Organization Science*, **12**, 99–116.

Sciascia, S. and P. Mazzola (2008), 'Family involvement in ownership and management: exploring nonlinear effects on performance', *Family Business Review*, **21**, 331–45.

Sharma, P. (2004), 'An overview of the field of family business studies: current status and directions for the future', *Family Business Review*, **17**, 1–36.

Shepherd, D.A. and A. Zacharakis (2000), 'Structuring family business succession: an analysis of the future leader's decision making', *Entrepreneurship: Theory and Practice*, **24** (4), 25–40.

Songini, L. (2006), 'The professionalization of family firms, theory and practice', in P. Poutziouris, K. Smyrnios and S. Klein (eds), *Handbook of Research on Family Businesses*, Cheltenham, UK and Northampton, MA, USA: Edward Elgar, pp. 269–97.

Stewart, A. and M.A. Hitt (2012), 'Why can't a family business be more like a non-family business?: Modes of professionalization in family firms', *Family Business Review*, **25** (1), 58–86.

Tetlock, P. (2005), *Expert Political Judgment: How Good Is It? How Can We Know?* Princeton, NJ: Princeton University Press.

Ward, J. (1997), 'Growing the family business: special challenges and best practices', *Family Business Review*, **10** (4), 323–38.

Weber (1921 [1968]), *Economy and Society*, Totown, NJ: Bedminister Press.

Westhead, P. and C. Howorth (2006), 'Ownership and management issues associated with family firm performance and company objectives', *Family Business Review*, **19**, 301–16.

Yin, R. (2003), *Case Study Research: Design and Methods*, Thousand Oaks, CA: Sage.

Zahra, S.A. and P. Sharma (2004), 'Family business research: a strategic reflection', *Family Business Review*, **17** (4), 331–46.

4. Transgenerational entrepreneurship and entrepreneurial learning: a case study of Associated Engineers Ltd in Hong Kong

Jeremy C.Y. Cheng,* Florence H.C. Ho and Kevin Au

'Should I promote Francis and assign him risky projects?' With the question in mind, Jude Chow (42) looked across the desk at his youngest brother, Francis (31), who had proven himself as a respected manager. The Chow family had rounds of discussions on Francis's promotion as general manager, but the decision was not simple. Jude wondered if promoting Francis and delegating risky projects to him would build his instincts, advancing his development as an entrepreneurial leader, or would crush his confidence, destroying his career instead. Yet from his own experiences, Jude understood all too well that leaders could only rise from tackling challenges.

Jude was the managing director of Associated Engineers Ltd (AEL), an engineering firm founded by his father, Ging Tak (80), in 1961. It started with engineering jobs at the late Kai Tak International Airport and then diversified to other sectors that required innovative solutions. He learnt from his father and many others to be an entrepreneur, and understood the importance of entrepreneurial learning to AEL. Without continual innovation and changes to its business model, this engineering firm could not have developed to its existing size and success. In 2012, with a prosperous company in hand, Jude found it harder and harder to develop enough good managers. Particularly tricky to nurture was the intuition behind entrepreneurial decisions. An increasing workload meant he had an urgent need to accelerate learning in the firm. Promoting Francis to a new role might help, but Jude was not sure if Francis was really ready.

Jude inherited Ging Tak's vision and his attitude towards risk from ordinary places like the family dinner table. He reflected how since childhood their dining table had been a place for business discussions. His interest in business and engineering was inspired and influenced by these conversations, as was his ability to see opportunities in uncertainty. Jude started his first business deal very early on: 'I like model racing cars. Every time I went back to Hong Kong during my term break, I would buy one. I discovered the arbitrage opportunity, buying the models in Hong Kong and selling them in Australia.' Ging Tak was fully supportive of his endeavor and even funded his first deal. 'I advertised the model in a newspaper with a 30% markup', continued Jude, 'I was so excited to sell it just overnight'. To the thrill of Ging Tak, Jude bought another dozen and sold them all.

Jude began his career as an engineer in Australia. The journey had a tough start. 'My immediate supervisor did not welcome me in the very beginning. He did not understand why the company employed a person with an engineering degree when he could do the work without a degree.' This lasted until there was a challenging assignment. Jude was asked to jump into a narrow metal tube to do some measurements. 'I was unable to leave the tube. My Aussie coworkers lifted me up with a crane, but only after they made fun of this! My supervisor saw my passion at work in this incidence and changed his attitude . . . The work experience there was a blessing that earned me the license to work for my family firm.'

In 2005 Ging Tak asked Jude to return to AEL. At that time, two of his older brothers were still working in the company. Both were over ten years older than Jude. The eldest was responsible for sales in China, and another brother served as the general manager in one of the subsidiaries in northeastern China. 'Over chit-chats, my brothers shared their views on how to improve the business with me and who I should be cautious about.' No longer with AEL, Jude's eldest brother ran a waste management firm and his second brother ran a firm manufacturing gas pumps. Although Jude did not see his brothers often, he was able to observe and learn from them. 'I did not bring in new senior managers when I first stepped into the business. While I knew I needed my own team, I felt I first needed to get some buy-in from the key stakeholders in the company.'

AEL faced a number of changes in the environment, but the Chows kept working as a team to navigate through the big challenges. Critical was the decision to gain full control of the firm from partners after Hong Kong was returned to China and opened its new airport. The two partners were large conglomerates and had invested dating back to the colonial era. Ging Tak saw the prospect of going solo in 2004, and the family was behind his decision. After AEL became a family firm, Ging Tak and Jude used family resources and transformed the crisis into opportunities. They reinvented AEL's business models and expanded their research and design (R&D) capabilities to focus more on value-added services. When Jude took over as general manager, he replaced the multi-layered organizational structure installed by Ging Tak with self-accountable units.

In 2008 Ging Tak stepped down from daily management to enjoy life with a dozen grandchildren, the eldest one being in her early 20s. Jude felt the onus to lead the family firm. He was supported by his younger brother Peter, a lawyer, who gave him good legal advice. Francis was in daily operations and could be the next cadre of leaders for AEL. Jude truly appreciated the value of entrepreneurial learning in AEL. His experience had been positive. But people were different. He was not sure if he should make other people, even his brother, walk the same path as his.

Jude was at a crossroads. He had offered a supportive environment at work and to let Francis fall prey to some inevitable 'traps' might be wrong, even if that might accelerate his growth. 'As an innovative enterprise, we cross the river by feeling the stone every day', wondered Jude. 'But we cannot afford to make a wrong move in a life or death decision. It could destroy a young person.' Jude pondered whether he should offer Francis the promotion and take up full responsibilities for decisions on risky projects. What could he do to assess if Francis was ready for this challenge? And, if so, how could he ensure it would be a positive learning experience for Francis?

CASE QUESTIONS

1. What do you see as the unique learning experience in Jude's development?
2. Should Jude promote Francis and assign risky projects to him? Would you develop Francis by letting him fall prey to the inevitable 'traps'?
3. What are the major challenges for Jude and the Chow family in grooming the next generation of entrepreneurs in AEL? What can they do to overcome them?

INTRODUCTION

Entrepreneurial learning (EL), the process of acquiring skills and knowledge to initiate, manage and grow a venture, is conducive to entrepreneurial success (Corbett, 2005; Politis, 2005). This dynamic process builds on one's experience and influences decisions, actions and behaviors (Cope, 2005). A key element of EL is to recognize, socialize and realize opportunities by pooling necessary resources. Research has suggested that strategic alignment of entrepreneurship with existing resources and capabilities creates competitive advantages to drive firm performance (Hitt et al., 2011). This linkage between strategic entrepreneurship and firm performance further heightens the role of learning in the entrepreneurial process.

While a stream of research has investigated EL, only a few studies are contextualized in family business (Zahra, 2012). Family firms may be viewed as a bundle of family-influenced resources (Habbershon et al., 2003). The family subsystem (Tagiuri and Davis, 1996) may have a significant impact on EL. For instance, a family may develop their own intrapreneurship program to groom their next generation members (Au et al., 2012). Features of EL in family firms may be different when compared to those in non-family firms. EL might transform resources and entrepreneurial attitude to entrepreneurial behavior. But this important role in driving firm success has not been closely examined. Analyzing EL in the family business context shall contribute new perspectives for research and practice.

This chapter examines transgenerational entrepreneurship and EL in the family business context. Drawing on a case study of Associated Engineers, Ltd (AEL), a Chinese family business, it analyses how EL takes place and its implications on transgenerational entrepreneurship and firm performance. Two observations can be made that shed light on the framework of the Successful Transgenerational Entrepreneurship Practices (STEP) project. They may even point towards modifications of this framework in the future. The first observation is the positive impact of entrepreneurial orientation and familiness on firm performance in the AEL case. The second and more important observation is that the intensity of these relations can either increase or decrease over generations depending on the effectiveness of EL of next generation members. That is to say, EL moderates the relationships between entrepreneurial orientation or familiness and firm performance, from one generation to the next.

This research contributes to the literature in a number of ways. First, it studies a distinctive firm to enrich research of EL in the Chinese family business context. Its success in dealing with challenges, particularly during the handover of Hong Kong from Britain to China in 1997, constitutes a 'natural experiment' (Yin, 1994) for studying how family businesses handle EL in turbulent times. Second, it draws attention to how EL moderates the nature of the relationship between entrepreneurial orientation, familiness and performance across generations. Third, it addresses the calls for a theoretical analysis of learning in family business research (Moores, 2009). Next, we provide a brief theoretical background of EL and transgenerational entrepreneurship before describing the case and explaining the findings of the analysis.

ENTREPRENEURIAL LEARNING IN FAMILY FIRMS

Learning in Systems Theory and the Resource-Based View

EL plays an implicit role in systems theory and the resource-based view (RBV). Tagiuri and Davis (1996) describe the family firm as a system with three interlocking subsystems (family, business and ownership). As an open system, family firms interact with their changing environment which presents a larger set of variations than the firm. Since only variety can destroy or absorb variety (Ashby, 1956), the family firm system must increase its requisite variety to avoid entropy and make survival possible (Poza, 2007). Learning is contracted naturally as a process for family members and the firm to destroy or absorb variations in the environment. Family entrepreneurs learn from the firm's immediate environment with suppliers, clients, other family members, non-family co-workers and other stakeholders, developing new products or services to fit what they need and abandoning what they do not. EL is needed to drive new variations for superior performance in a competitive environment.

The RBV embraces learning as a process to develop human and social capital. It states that an organization is a bundle of resources that are valuable, rare, imperfectly imitable and not substitutable to create competitive advantages (Barney et al., 2001). A business family may offer a unique stream of resources to its incoming generation (Habbershon et al., 2003). Through adaptive learning, family entrepreneurs combine existing resources to form unique capabilities and generate new knowledge for innovation. At the organizational level, EL may build resources and help align individual resources to form organizational capabilities fitting into the strategic goals of the firm (Hitt et al., 2011). For instance, Poza (2007) proposed that family values could be an idiosyncratic familiness resource that drives family intrapreneurship. The processes for family value creation, sharing, interpretation and storage seemingly bear a learning dimension (Huber, 1991). To allow intergenerational learning, the family firm should develop a learning orientation to help 'establish networks for future generations and safeguarding the vital institutional memory' (Moores, 2009: 177).

Transgenerational Entrepreneurship and Entrepreneurial Learning

Transgenerational entrepreneurship is 'the process through which a family uses and develops entrepreneurial mindsets . . . resources and capabilities to create new streams of entrepreneurial, financial and social value across generations' (Habbershon et al., 2010: 1). Survival of a family firm depends on its ability to build an entrepreneurial orientation amongst the incoming generation to foster the search for profitable opportunities (Habbershon and Pistrui, 2002). It also means the existence of a familiness resource pool.

EL may be one of the processes that develop the entrepreneurial orientation and enrich the familiness resource pool. Even with a strong entrepreneurial orientation and rich familial resources, the incoming generation still needs to learn how to cope with changes effectively. EL is thus central to transgenerational entrepreneurship, helping individuals acquire the knowledge and skills required for exploring and exploiting new opportunities for family firms (Sharma and Salvato, 2011). It appears that EL can be the thread that traverses several transgenerational entrepreneurial processes, enabling different stakeholders to develop in conjunction with their evolving environment, and develop new behavior to negotiate the management and continuous growth of family firms.

Hamilton (2011) proposed the *situated learning perspective*. She postulated that EL in family businesses is socially situated and embedded in everyday practice; that is, the family and the business are overlapping communities of practices. The incoming generation can gain legitimacy by serving as apprentices. This way, they first participate in peripheral roles before they are fully admitted to the communities. The incoming generation members are thus said to engage in a 'generative process of producing their own future' – a process that stresses continuity and enduring practice (Lave and Wenger, 1991: 57). She argued that situated learning is a useful perspective for understanding how EL naturally happens in family businesses.

Studying Chinese business families, Chen (2011) found that learning from family business networks by the incoming generation can increase transgenerational potential, echoing the suggestion from the situated learning perspective. She also discovered that transgenerational entrepreneurship was associated with entrepreneurial exposure. Moreover, her findings showed that contrary to common belief, formal education and work experience outside the family firm were not significantly associated with transgenerational entrepreneurship. Thus, her findings appeared to suggest that entrepreneurial exposure in a family firm constitutes different learning functions and bears different impacts on entrepreneurial development from formal education and work experience outside the family firm.

EL plays a pivotal but less understood role in systems theory, the RBV and transgenerational entrepreneurship research. Existing family business studies relying on systems theory and the RBV have not accorded EL with a significant theoretical position. Thus, there is a need to examine the nature and the roles of EL in transgenerational entrepreneurship studies. Two research questions guide the current study:

1. What kinds of EL activities may happen in a family firm? How does EL take place?
2. How does EL affect the processes of transgenerational entrepreneurship?

METHOD

A case presents a holistic description and analysis of a person, an institution or a bounded system (Yin, 1994). Inductive case research helps early-stage theory development and identifies processes which enable 'researchers to get closer to the action' (Steier, 2007: 1101). This study followed the case research protocol of STEP (Habbershon et al., 2010). Semi-structured interviews were conducted with five participants, the backgrounds of whom are shared in Table 4.1. All interviews were recorded and transcribed. Company websites and other relevant documents were reviewed. These materials were cross-referenced to ensure reliability. The business and the family backgrounds were examined to contextualize the EL activities of the case.

Based on the literature we have identified different methods of EL for the case analysis. Table 4.2 categorizes them according to their nature and defining activities. This categorization helps structure our analysis. In addition to the learning methods discussed in the literature, our analysis revealed another method used in AEL. Jude's upbringing represented a body of more complex learning opportunities over an extended period of time. As this learning method did not fit with any described in the literature, we added it under the new label – 'learning through immersion in family entrepreneurship'.

We analyzed the learning activities of AEL using EL methods. Two researchers read through the transcripts and other documents to identify EL activities and classified them independently. If the researchers could not agree on the categorization or whether to include an EL activity, the third researcher would step in and make the final decision after discussion. Different EL activities seemed to occur in AEL's four development phases, discussed in the next section.

Table 4.1 Profile of interviewees in AEL

Interviewee	Number of interviews	Family role	Business role Management	Board	Ownership role
Mr Chow Ging Tak	1	First generation; Patriarch	Founder	Chairman	Shareholder
Mr Chow Chee Ping Jude	3	Second generation; Ging Tak's fourth son	Managing Director	Director	Shareholder
Ms Ophelia Chan	1	Wife of second son	Group Finance Manager	–	–
Mr Oscar Kwan	1	–	–	Non-Executive Director	–
Mr Edmund Cheung	1	–	Manager (Engineering Services Unit)	–	–

Table 4.2 An overview of EL methods and activities

Method of learning	Major learning activities	Relevant publications
Learning by doing	Trial and error; explicit problem solving and discovery	Rae (2005)
Learning from self	Reflective thinking and introspection	Rae (2005)
Learning from others: Individuals	*Vicarious learning* Education, training, mentoring and coaching	Bandura (1986) Del Giudice (2011)
Learning from others: Groups	*Knowledge transfer* Community of practices; organizational learning	Del Giudice (2011) Lave and Wenger (1991) Senge (2006)
Learning from non-linear, discrete events	Salient learning episodes and critical learning events;	Cope (2005)
	crisis;	Cope (2005)
	failure	Cope (2011)
Learning from routine and habitual activities	Working in daily activities such as serving customers and bidding for projects	Cope (2005)
Learning through immersion in family entrepreneurship	Family gatherings and dinner talks	Observed by the authors in AEL

THE CASE OF AEL

Business and Family Background

AEL was founded by Mr Chow Ging Tak in 1961. From a single-site workshop providing maintenance services for ground vehicles at the late Kai Tak International Airport, AEL had grown to a corporation doing business in Hong Kong, China and other parts of the world. Figure 4.1 shows AEL's corporate structure in 2012. AEL ran a diverse portfolio of businesses, including systems for air cargo handling, aircraft maintenance docking, mechanical handling systems, construction and environmental engineering and industrial product trading. It hired over 1000 workers and even prepared for an initial public offering (IPO) in 2010.

The Chow family consisted of three generations, starting from Ging

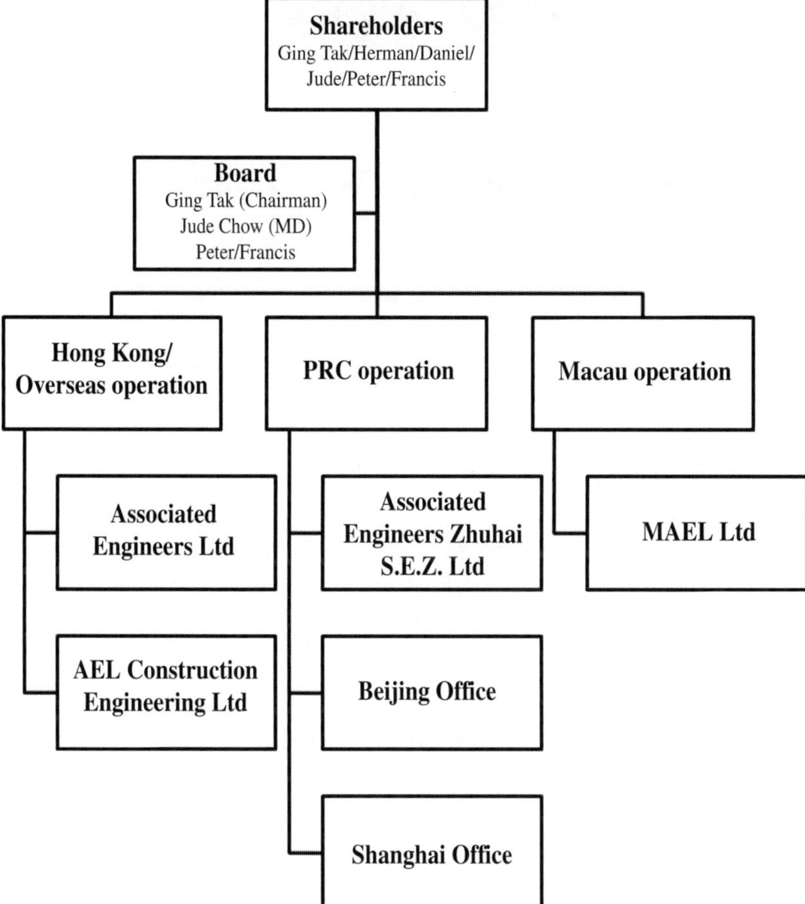

Figure 4.1 AEL corporate structure

Tak (see Figure 4.2). He had six sons with a large age gap. They were born in Hong Kong and attended high school and college overseas. Three second-generation members (Jude, Peter and Francis) were working in AEL. Roger (the eldest brother) and Herman (the second eldest brother) started their own businesses after they spent about ten years in AEL. Daniel (the third son) worked for an accounting firm. Ophelia, Herman's wife, was also serving in AEL. Ging Tak's father was an entrepreneur with a reputable paint factory in Shanghai, China.

Before taking the helm of AEL, Jude obtained a Bachelor in Mechanical Engineering, a Master in Engineering Management and an EMBA

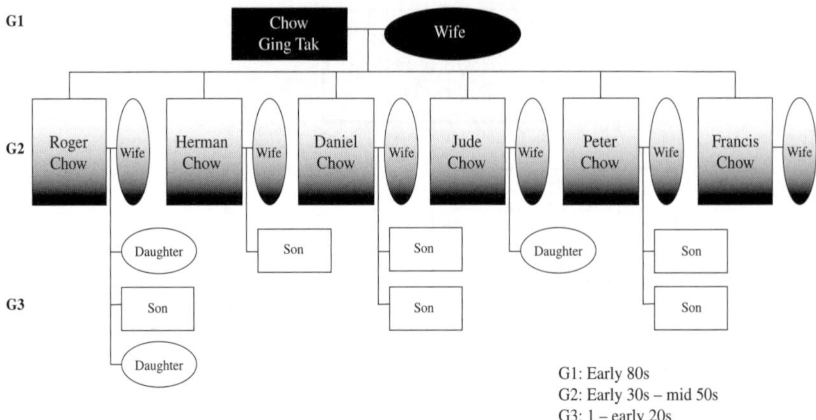

Figure 4.2 Chow family chart

(Executive Master of Business Administration) in which he studied organizational change and turnaround. In his early years in Australia, Jude was involved in large-scale engineering projects. Before joining AEL, he was a regional manager for customer services in a German medical technology firm located in Hong Kong. He returned to AEL as general manager in 2005 upon Ging Tak's request and assumed full responsibility as AEL's managing director in 2012. He owned shares of AEL together with his father and all of his brothers.

AEL presents distinctive features and is a valuable case. First, AEL was developed in the unique context of colonial Hong Kong when large trading conglomerates ruled the economy. Ging Tak and the company learnt best practices for management and engineering from the sophisticated trading houses. This unusual history facilitated AEL in developing into a knowledge-intensive firm which survived for the next generation. In addition, all second-generation members (except the third brother) learnt from working in AEL. But some chose to pursue their careers outside, potentially using the lessons learnt in the family firm. Ging Tak had worked with family and non-family members as successors. Jude happened to benefit from these transition experiences. Few families in Chinese societies are open enough to allow outside observers to study these experiences (Redding, 1990; Zheng, 2010).

Development Phases

The start-up phase (1961–70)

Ging Tak obtained his engineering certification for aircraft maintenance in the United Kingdom in 1951. After acquiring the necessary experience for his professional license, Ging Tak returned to Hong Kong and was appointed as a maintenance engineer with the Philippines Airline. Being industrious, Ging Tak helped his workmates out after hours, fixing different kinds of ground equipment at the airport. With an increasing demand for his services, Ging Tak set up his own business. This gave birth to AEL. He set up his workshop together with two close friends. Unfortunately they left the venture due to personal reasons. Ging Tak kept the business running. Despite his busy schedule, he went back home for dinner almost every night, spending time with his children, although business issues often became part of the conversation.

The expansion phase (1971–94)

As the airport expanded, their business grew steadily. The breakthrough came when two partners approached Ging Tak. They injected capital and became AEL's majority shareholders. Their networks and size offered AEL exclusive business opportunities. Leveraging their connections, Ging Tak managed to advance much-needed bank loans. The loans enabled AEL to purchase a two-storey factory for expansion.

The economy experienced a boom in the 1980s. AEL expanded their collaboration with other global partners in projects such as installing and extending cargo handling systems at the Kai Tak Airport. Ging Tak also acquired two Australian firms in 1988: A buy-out of a supplier of aerial maintenance parts and patent acquisition from a waste management firm. In addition, AEL China was founded in 1993, and the production base was moved to Zhuhai, China, in 1994.

The transition phase (1995–2005)

While everyone looked forward to good expansion with the new Chak Lap Kok Airport, opened when Hong Kong celebrated its sovereign return to China in 1997, the promising opportunity did not turn out to be as positive as expected. The robust economy drastically faded with the Asian financial crisis in 1997. The handover signified a game-changer: AEL forfeited its previous exclusive rights and had to join the race when all of the projects moved to an open-bidding system. AEL experienced the first loss in its history. As a result of the loss, AEL critically reviewed its business.

During the earlier phase, Jude's older brothers were closely involved in AEL. Roger solicited the first client in Shanghai in 1995 and set up a waste management station in Xiamen in 1997. Herman also led corporate development in northeastern China. Unlike Ging Tak, Roger preferred more autonomy in decision-making. It was not long before Roger decided to set up his own company, having stayed with AEL for over ten years.

In 2002, aged 70, Ging Tak retired from routine management. AEL appointed a non-family executive but the new leadership did not bring in the necessary business. The situation was complicated by the SARS outbreak (Severe Acute Respiratory Syndrome) in 2003. Mr Adrian Fan, a former AEL staff member, took over as the company's general manager in 2004.

Opting for greater autonomy and maintaining a strong belief in the business, Ging Tak made a difficult but quick decision to gain full control of the firm amid the crisis when SARS dragged the whole economy down in 2003. This decision was fully supported by his family. Ging Tak was keen to have a family member to steer the firm. Although he had not given much thought to succession, he believed that Jude might have the right background. In May 2005, Jude accepted the responsibility. While Ging Tak still held the title as chairman and managing director, the day-to-day operations were left to Jude and his two younger brothers, Peter and Francis. Jude shadowed Mr Fan and also learnt from the experiences of his elder brothers.

The revival phase (2005–present)

The patience to follow a natural learning curve was, however, barred by the global financial crisis in 2007. Jude had to expedite his learning when he took drastic steps in shaking up the firm. The workforce was downsized by 20 percent. To increase accountability, the existing functional units were replaced by self-managed business units. Capitalizing on their engineering expertise, Jude further diversified their product lines. Instead of a project-based business model, the firm switched to developing service-based products. By the end of 2009, the firm was back on track and made a profit. In addition to a steady expansion in China, AEL also established a network of research facilities and collaborated with scientists in Hong Kong and China to boost its technical competence. In 2012, Jude became the managing director and Ging Tak enjoyed his time serving only as the chairman.

ANALYSIS

The AEL case showed a rich portfolio of EL activities. We focused particularly on Ging Tak and Jude. Table 4.3 and Table 4.4 summarize their

Table 4.3 Ging Tak's EL journey

Period	Entrepreneurial learning methods	Entrepreneurial learning activities	Primary learning outcomes
1950s	Learning from others: Individuals	Education: License for aircraft maintenance (1951)	Technical skills
	Learning by doing	Discovery: Working overseas	International exposure
	Learning from others: Groups	Community of practice: Other engineers	Collaborative learning
1960s	Learning from non-linear discrete events	Critical learning event: Founding AEL with two partners (1961)	Start-up skills
		Salient learning episode: Withdrawal of partners (1968–69)	Business dynamics
1970s	Learning from others: Groups	Knowledge transfer: Partnership with two conglomerates (1970 and 1973)	Management foundation; financial governance; networking
	Learning by doing	Explicit problem-solving: Cargo terminal development (early 1970s)	Project management
1980s	Learning from others: Groups	Knowledge transfer: A multinational German firm (1985–89)	International partnership
	Learning from non-linear discrete events	Critical learning event: Acquisition of Australian suppliers (1988)	Supply chain integration
1990s	Learning from non-linear discrete events	Critical learning event: Expansion into China (since 1992)	Market diversification
		'Failure': The first losing investment (1995)	Stakeholder management
		Crisis: Sovereign handover and Asian financial crisis (1997)	Crisis management
2000s	Learning from non-linear discrete events	Salient learning episode: Retirement (2002)	Succession
		Crisis: Client issues with a non-family successor	Transition arrangement
		Crisis: SARS (2003)	Crisis management
		Salient learning episode: Partnership dissolution; successor reappointment (2004)	Ownership management
2010s	Learning from self	Reflective thinking	Letting go

Table 4.4 Jude's EL journey

Period	Entrepreneurial learning methods	Entrepreneurial learning activities	Primary learning outcomes
1970s	Learning through immersion in family entrepreneurship	Dinner talks	Business acumen
1980s	Learning from others: Individuals	Education: Bachelor in Mechanical Engineering	Engineering
1990s	Learning by doing	College function organization and 'arbitrage trade'	Entrepreneurial exposure
	Learning from others: Individuals	Formal education: Master of Engineering Management and EMBA	Engineering and general management
	Learning by doing	Discovery: Working outside	People skills
	Learning by doing	Managing family investments in Australia	Wealth management
2000s	Learning from others: Groups	Vicarious learning from Roger, Herman and Mr Fan	Decision-making within the family firm
	Learning from others: Individuals	Mentoring from Ging Tak	Gaining recognition from colleagues
	Learning from others: Groups	Another multinational German firm	Partnership development
	Learning from non-linear discrete events	Critical learning episode: Going back to AEL and taking charge; learning by doing (2005)	Understanding AEL
		Critical learning episode: Corporate restructuring with the Global financial crisis (2007–08)	HR management
	Learning from others: Groups	Organizational learning	Culture
2010s	Learning from others: Groups	Knowledge transfer: Universities	R&D
	Learning from others: Groups	Organizational learning: Corporate social responsibility	Culture development
	Learning from non-linear discrete events	Critical learning event: IPO preparation	Business modeling
	Learning by doing	Trial and error; discovery	Knowledge sharing with senior management including his brothers

EL methods and relevant EL activities in their learning journeys, with reference to the classification framework in Table 4.2. Ging Tak and Jude were both keen learners. They learnt by doing and critically reflected on their own experiences (Rae, 2005). They learnt from others, including family members, non-family co-workers and from other companies who collaborated with them (Del Giudice, 2011; Lave and Wenger, 1991). They learnt through changes, crises, failures and other critical events (Cope, 2005, 2011). The outcomes of these EL activities ranged from acquisition of engineering knowledge to start-up skills, understanding of business dynamics, partnership management, market diversification and people management. In the following section we describe different EL activities that occurred in different corporate development phases.

The Start-Up Phase: Dominance of Learning by Doing

This phase was characterized by the establishment of the business. The focal point was Ging Tak and how he survived the hardship of start-up via learning by doing. This also included going independent after the two founding partners (his old friends) withdrew from the business. EL was more or less on an individual basis and related to start-up skills and dealing with business dynamics. EL was not relevant for transgenerational entrepreneurship in this phase.

The Expansion Phase: Seeding Transgenerational Entrepreneurship via Immersion and Learning by Doing

This phase was characterized by the growing business and the immersion of the second generation into the family firm. The situation became more complicated. While Ging Tak continued his learning by doing, the significance of business partnership increased in his learning journey. The presence of the business began to influence family habits and the childhood of the next generation. Jude learnt about entrepreneurial acumen from his upbringing, which informed his education and career choice – apparently planting a seed for transgenerational entrepreneurship. EL was not only an individual matter but also a familial and business issue. Specific EL activities and their relations with entrepreneurial development were explained as follows:

Dinner talks to grow the entrepreneurial mindset

Jude was immersed in an entrepreneurial environment which offered routine but unnoticed learning opportunities. He repeatedly mentioned a few 'learning points' he gained from Ging Tak, such as risk-taking, vision, decision-making and working hard. Jude acquired these 'ingrained' entrepreneurial attitudes in genuine social settings such as at the dinner table. Jude's entrepreneurial identity was developed as a personal and social emergence (Hamilton, 2011). As Jude described:

> Since childhood, the dining table is a place for business. This greatly influences me. I was inspired to become interested in business and engineering.

The dinner talks partly shaped his self-awareness and career aspirations. Jude gradually picked up how to spot entrepreneurial opportunities and the steps required to mobilize familial resources. This ability was evident from the early appearance of his first successful entrepreneurial deal involving remote racing cars which was supported by Ging Tak.

Discovery from working outside the family firm

Other than the experience gained from his Australian colleagues in his first job, Jude was also exposed to other unique occasions:

> Before entering into my firm, I worked in a German firm responsible for Asia Pacific client support. That was a medical device company, which I had no experience at all. I had to work with a Japanese subordinate 40 years of age, highly qualified, and technically strong. I was young but I needed to manage him.

The knowledge and skills Jude developed through external work prepared him to handle similar situations in the family firm (Ward, 2011). This EL experience was especially important in the Chinese context where mistakes could mean a loss of face and long-lasting grudges (Zheng, 2010). Working outside could also allow experimentation and the development of self-efficacy. This enables the incoming generation to try their wings before assuming decision-making responsibility in their own family firms (Au et al., 2012).

In addition, working in different but complementary disciplines (in Jude's case medical technology) may diversify the skill set of the successor. Successors may 'combine family-firm specific human capital built through experience within the family firm with general human capital built through education and other work experience to generate new ideas leading to the entrepreneurial opportunity perception' (Sardeshmukh and Corbett, 2011: 111). In other words, transferring external working experience to the family firm environment could help identify entrepreneurial opportunities within the family firm. Facilitated by the deep transfer of sympathetic knowledge (Nonaka and Takeuchi, 1995), working outside should improve familiness.

Knowledge transfer from the multinationals
Ging Tak kept learning from others, especially from AEL's multinational partners, suppliers and clients. These external stakeholders presented great complexity to AEL (Ashby, 1956). To absorb the varieties the environment presented, Ging Tak and the whole of AEL learnt aggressively. The continuous learning gained from the multinationals brought financial capital, social networks and advanced knowledge. Jude recalled how Ging Tak learnt corporate governance and management practices from the partners:

> After the collaboration with the partners, we have to follow a lot of strict procedures. My father forced himself to learn how to read financial reports, which he knew nothing about before.

The second-generation members could access these resources indirectly through Ging Tak. Jude also followed this learning strategy in his own development.

The Transition Phase: Learning From and Together With the Family

This phase was characterized by several seismic events in AEL. AEL's first loss in major investment, forfeiture of the firm's exclusive rights at the new airport (due to the handover of Hong Kong back to China) and the financial crises threatened its survival. Ging Tak's retirement and the entry of new non-family and family leaders complicated the situation. Yet it presented a unique learning episode for Jude and the other Chows. Two specific EL activities related to entrepreneurial development were identified in this phase:

Vicarious learning from the elder brothers in business transition
Vicarious learning refers to learning by observing consequences of others' behavior (Bandura, 1986). No one can fully understand the intricate dynamics and 'taboos' of succeeding a business from his father unless they have experienced the case themselves (Ward, 1997). Jude enjoyed the sought-after opportunities of observing and learning from his elder brothers in the transition. As mentioned in the opening vignette, he learnt to avoid actions that could potentially offend Ging Tak or other senior management:

> Do not try out new initiatives when first stepping into the business. Do not bring up your own 'troops'.

Jude also vicariously learnt from the non-family successors, but this learning was more about management skills than the expectations originating from a blood relationship. Vicarious learning from family members coming from the same generation, working in the business, and doing so with an early intention to succeed the firm, offered necessary contextual knowledge and references for effective decision-making. This can increase the chances of a smoother transition that preserves the firm's financial values.

Crises to mobilize familial resources

Despite the adverse situation, Ging Tak deployed family resources to gain complete control of AEL and engaged the whole family in navigating through the turbulence. This was a huge risk but AEL gained the autonomy it needed to support new ventures in China, which generated a respectable profit later. It appeared that the Chow family learnt together to overcome the crises by utilizing family capital and making quick, consensual decisions to support opportunities for entrepreneurial and financial performance. Changing tack quickly and decisively could have saved AEL from the Asian financial crisis in the late 1990s.

The Revival Phase: Institutionalizing Different EL Methods for Performance

This phase envisaged how EL was institutionalized and was conducive to entrepreneurial performance. After settling down as general manager, Jude became fully engaged and accomplished impressive entrepreneurial performance. While EL related to organizational development was obviously important, he started learning to assume family leadership.

Crisis to catalyze transformation

Crises apparently catalyzed internal changes to unlearn the routines set up originally by the patriarch. Facing critical challenges, Jude moved fast to restructure the company:

> In 2008, I cannot find our way out slowly. Our clients suffered from the financial crisis and they had no money to invest. I cut down the number of departments from five to three . . . reverting the traditional model to some small companies where department heads are responsible for their entire team . . .

Jude took the chance to replace the multi-layered organizational structure installed by Ging Tak with self-accountable teams and units. How to gradually unlearn 'the old' to create 'the new' appears to be an art for the succeeding family entrepreneur. The crises presented both a learning opportunity and a change platform, allowing Jude's development as a 'family change champion' (Salvato et al., 2010). EL facilitated the change in governance structure and its underlining corporate culture to advance both financial and entrepreneurial performance.

Organizational learning for innovation

Jude engaged his teams in the learning process. He built a strong belief in empowered calculated risk-taking. He expected that 'empowerment and risk taking go down several layers from the top management'. This largely converged with what Edmund, project manager, recounted in building his team:

> Seeing the challenge of talent retention, I have made a deliberate attempt to recruit fresh school graduates, providing them with necessary training and incentives. I would spend time in listening to my team members, and getting them involved in the decision-making process. I am also convinced that my team should stay abreast with the latest technologies through using an off-the-shelf knowledge management system.

In this light, organizational learning appeared to link Jude's entrepreneurial mindset to firm innovation.

Failure to accelerate entrepreneurial growth

As mentioned in the opening vignette, Jude is inclined to groom Francis in a tough way. He himself benefitted from this daunting process. Yet, he understood that this path may not be suitable for everyone:

> I offer a supportive environment at work but I intentionally let Francis fall prey to necessary 'traps' to accelerate his growth.

His practice of engineering learning from failure has been discussed in the research. Cope (2011: 604) argued that 'recovery and re-emergence from failure is a function of distinctive learning processes that facilitate a range of higher-level learning outcomes'. Learning from failure appeared to increase Francis's entrepreneurial preparedness, equipping him with the ability to lead innovative projects at AEL.

DISCUSSION

Our overall analysis reveals that different EL activities appeared to produce different impacts on the transgenerational entrepreneurial processes in different development phases in AEL. For the sake of explanation, we summarize the findings in Table 4.5. In the *start-up phase*, the individual learning activities of Ging Tak were observed but they were not related to transgenerational entrepreneurship. In the *expansion phase*, EL took an active role in growing entrepreneurial orientation and familiness. The second generation developed their risk-taking and innovative attitudes by immersing themselves in an entrepreneurial environment. This strengthened the entrepreneurial orientation amongst the second-generation members. The family also nurtured resources for future business deployment, including the next cadre of entrepreneurial leaders, networks with multinationals, financial capital, decision-making repertoires, culture and knowledge in financial management and corporate governance. All of these enriched the familiness dimension (Habbershon et al., 2010). In the *transition phase*, EL activities linked familiness to both the financial and entrepreneurial performance of the firm. For instance, the Chows used its cash reserve to gain full control of the firm so that they had the autonomy required to explore the Chinese market. In the *revival phase*, EL linked entrepreneurial orientation to firm performance. A key observation is that Jude's philosophy of empowered risk-taking facilitated innovation throughout the whole organization. In this phase familiness was also utilized to drive financial and entrepreneurial performance, as evident in how Jude redefined the corporate structure and culture to survive the hardship during the global financial crisis.

In all phases, EL was crucial in developing entrepreneurial orientation and familiness. These two constructs also showed a positive impact on firm performance. In addition, the effectiveness of EL appeared to moderate the nature of relations between entrepreneurial orientation or familiness and entrepreneurial behavior. Increasing EL effectiveness promoted the use of entrepreneurial orientation and familiness to drive firm performance. In the earlier business life cycle, EL may have been based relatively on individuals and did not have a pervasive influence on the family. Entrepreneurial orientation and familiness were only loosely linked to firm performance. But as AEL developed, EL became more broad-based and effectively influenced both the family and the business.

These observations may have implications for the STEP framework. We propose, as shown in Figure 4.3, that EL moderates the relationship between entrepreneurial orientation or familiness and firm performance. This suggestion is an attempt to enrich the present understanding of the relationships between the constructs in the framework, which have been rarely discussed in the literature. As shown in the AEL case, EL effectiveness may be related to transgenerational pervasiveness of the EL activities and the ability to learn from multiple methods. It is hoped that our

Table 4.5 EL activities and impacts on transgenerational entrepreneurship in different development phases

Development Phase	Entrepreneurial learning activities	Impacts on transgenerational entrepreneurship
The start-up phase	Individual entrepreneurial learning activities observed but not related to transgenerational entrepreneurship	
The expansion phase	Dinner talks to grow the entrepreneurial mindset	Growing entrepreneurial orientation (risk-taking and innovativeness)
	Discovery from working outside the family firm	Growing familiness (decision-making and knowledge)
	Knowledge transfer from the multinationals	Growing familiness (capital, networks and knowledge)
The transition phase	Vicarious learning from elder brothers in business transition	Linking familiness (decision-making and knowledge) to performance (financial)
	Crises to mobilize familial resources	Linking familiness (capital and decision-making) to performance (financial and entrepreneurial)
The revival phase	Crisis to catalyze transformation	Linking familiness (governance and culture) to performance (financial and entrepreneurial)
	Organizational learning for innovation	Linking entrepreneurial orientation (risk-taking) to performance (entrepreneurial)
	Failure to accelerate entrepreneurial growth	Linking entrepreneurial orientation (risk-taking) to performance (entrepreneurial)

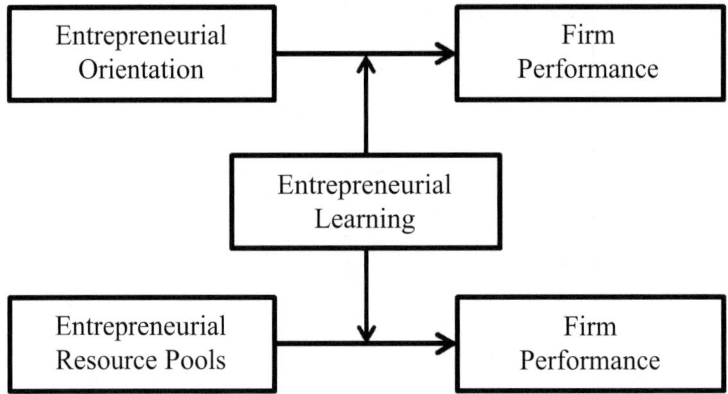

Figure 4.3 A proposed model of entrepreneurial learning in transgenerational entrepreneurship

analysis can stimulate future research to examine the exact nature of EL effectiveness in the family business context.

A wealth of EL experiences was identified which involved not only the Chows but also other actors in the case. In hindsight, the analysis suggests that the *situated learning perspective* can shed light on EL in family businesses. First, family involvement in the entrepreneurial processes was observed and this could have had an early influence on the entrepreneurial development due to immersion. The family and the business offered an overlapping community of practice (Hamilton, 2011). Also, Jude gradually gained legitimacy as Ging Tak's 'apprentice', succeeding in his entrepreneurial quest with his can-do attitude. The sibling partnership between Jude, Peter and Francis further reinforced the fact that the family members formed a tight working circle. Other than family members, non-family employees, business partners and even employers of the incoming generations could contribute to the EL processes. This converged with the understanding that the family and the business subsystems interact with their immediate environment given a permeable system boundary (Tagiuri and Davis, 1996). EL helped the Chows to absorb new varieties and destroyed unfit ones to survive and thrive in the competitive landscape. Eventually, Jude and his brothers appeared to develop a productive process of creating their own future.

The AEL case illustrates that the situated learning occurred in multiple and complex ways. EL took place in various contexts to achieve different learning outcomes. Ging Tak and Jude learnt from practical lessons, by trial and error, and through extensive interactions or vicarious experiences. The business and the family learnt together to overcome crises. From these EL activities, individual family members built skills and knowledge required for initiating, managing and growing ventures. Future research may continue to find the *situated learning perspective* useful for understanding EL in relation to transgenerational entrepreneurship beyond the present understanding (Hamilton, 2011).

CONCLUSION

Learning to be a family entrepreneur is a lengthy journey, if not lifelong. At different life stages, different EL processes may be needed to inspire and sustain transgenerational entrepreneurship systems (Le Breton-Miller et al., 2004). The learning journey for each family entrepreneur is different as no one can determine what crises, critical events or salient episodes will happen in their lifetime. While fate is uncertain, EL prepares family entrepreneurs even in the toughest conditions (Carayannis, 2011; Schuman and Ward, 2011), advancing the chance of survival and success in succession.

NOTE

* The authors would like to thank the Chow family and AEL for supporting this STEP project. Some information in this chapter has been hidden or altered to protect confidentiality. We also thank the editors for their feedback and guidance. The first two authors contributed the same to this chapter. Address all communications to Kevin Au, Centre for Family Business, The Chinese University of Hong Kong, Shatin, Hong Kong (email: kevinau@cuhk.edu.hk).

REFERENCES

Ashby, W.R. (1956), *An Introduction to Cybernetics*, London: Methuen.

Au, K., F.F.T. Chiang, T.A. Birtch and Z. Ding (2012), 'Incubating the next generation to venture: the case of a family business in Hong Kong', *Asia Pacific Journal of Management*. doi: 10.1007/s10490-012-931-7.

Bandura, A. (1986), *Social Foundations of Thought and Action: A Social-Cognitive Theory*, Englewood Cliffs, NJ: Prentice-Hall.

Barney, J., M. Wright and D.J. Ketchen (2001), 'The resource-based view of the firm: ten years after 1991', *Journal of Management*, **27** (6), 625–41.

Carayannis, E.G. (2011), 'Definition of terms and concepts', in M. Del Giudice, M.R.D. Peruta and E.G. Carayannis (eds), *Knowledge and the Family Business: The Governance and Management of Family Firms in the New Knowledge Economy*, London: Springer, pp. 189–228.

Chen, W.T. (2011), 'Entrepreneurial learning and entrepreneurship choice of transgenerational entrepreneurs in Chinese family firms', *Economic Management*, **33**

(8), 38–50. [Originally in Chinese: 陈文婷 (2011), '创业学习与家族企业跨代企业家的创业选择', 经济管理, **33** (8)期, 38–50.]

Cope, J. (2005), 'Toward a dynamic learning perspective of entrepreneurship', *Entrepreneurship Theory & Practice*, **29** (4), 373–97.

Cope, J. (2011), 'Entrepreneurial learning from failure: an interpretative phenomenological analysis', *Journal of Business Venturing*, **26** (6), 604–23.

Corbett, A. (2005), 'Experiential learning within the process of opportunity identification and exploitation', *Entrepreneurship Theory & Practice*, **29** (4), 473–91.

Del Giudice, M. (2011), 'Knowledge management and family business', in M. Del Giudice, M.R.D. Peruta and E.G. Carayannis (eds), *Knowledge and the Family Business: The Governance and Management of Family Firms in the New Knowledge Economy*, London: Springer, pp. 11–46.

Habbershon, T. and J. Pistrui (2002), 'Enterprising families domain: family-influenced ownership groups in pursuit of transgenerational wealth', *Family Business Review*, **15** (3), 223–38.

Habbershon, T.G., M. Nordqvist and T. Zellweger (2010), 'Transgenerational entrepreneurship', in M. Nordqvist and T. Zellweger (eds), *Transgenerational Entrepreneurship: Exploring Growth and Performance in Family Firms across Generations*, Cheltenham, UK and Northampton, MA, USA: Edward Elgar, pp. 1–38.

Habbershon, T.G., M. Williams and I.C. MacMillan (2003), 'A unified systems perspective of family firm performance', *Journal of Business Venturing*, **18** (4), 451–65.

Hamilton, E. (2011), 'Entrepreneurial learning in family business: a situated learning perspective', *Journal of Small Business and Enterprise Development*, **18** (1), 8–26.

Hitt, M.A., R.D. Ireland, D.G. Sirmon and C.A. Trahms (2011), 'Strategic entrepreneurship: creating value for individuals, organizations, and society', *Academy of Management Perspectives*, **25** (2), 57–75.

Huber, G.P. (1991), 'Organizational learning: the contributing processes and the literatures', *Organization Science*, **2** (1), 88–113.

Lave, J. and E. Wenger (1991), *Situated Learning: Legitimate Peripheral Participation*, Cambridge: Cambridge University Press.

Le Breton-Miller, I., D. Miller and L.P. Steier (2004), 'Towards an integrative model of effective FOB succession', *Entrepreneurship Theory and Practice*, **28** (4), 305–28.

Moores, K. (2009), 'Paradigms and theory building in the domain of business families', *Family Business Review*, **22** (2), 167–80.

Nonaka, I. and H. Takeuchi (1995), *The Knowledge-Creating Company*, New York: Oxford University Press.

Politis, D. (2005), 'The process of entrepreneurial learning: a conceptual framework', *Entrepreneurship Theory and Practice*, **29** (4), 399–424.

Poza, E.J. (2007), *Family Business*, Mason, OH: Thomson South-Western.

Rae, D. (2005), 'Entrepreneurial learning: a narrative-based conceptual model', *Journal of Small Business and Enterprise Development*, **12** (3), 323–35.

Redding, G.S. (1990), *The Spirit of Chinese Capitalism*, New York: De Gruyter.

Salvato, C., F. Chirico and P. Sharma (2010), 'A farewell to the business: championing exit and continuity in entrepreneurial family firms', *Entrepreneurship & Regional Development*, **22** (3–4), 321–48.

Sardeshmukh, S.R. and A.C. Corbett (2011), 'The duality of internal and external

development of successors: opportunity recognition in family firms', *Family Business Review*, **24** (2), 111–25.
Schuman, A.M. and J.L. Ward (2011), *Family Education for Business-Owning Families: Strengthening Bonds by Learning Together*, New York: Palgrave Macmillan.
Senge, P.M. (2006), *The Fifth Discipline: The Art and Practice of the Learning Organization*, New York: Doubleday.
Sharma, P. and C. Salvato (2011), 'Commentary: exploiting and exploring new opportunities over life cycle stages of family firms', *Entrepreneurship Theory and Practice*, **35** (6), 1199–205.
Steier, L. (2007), 'New venture creation and organization: a familial sub-narrative', *Journal of Business Research*, **60** (10), 1099–107.
Tagiuri, R. and J.A. Davis (1996), 'Bivalent attributes of the family firm', *Family Business Review*, **9** (2), 199–208.
Ward, J.L. (1997), 'Growing the family business: special challenges and best practices', *Family Business Review*, **10** (4), 323–37.
Ward, J.L. (2011), *Keeping the Family Business Healthy*, New York: Palgrave Macmillan.
Yin, R. (1994), *Case Study Research*, Thousand Oaks, CA: Sage Publishing.
Zahra, S.A. (2012), 'Organizational learning and entrepreneurship in family firms: exploring the moderating effect of ownership and cohesion', *Small Business Economics*, **38**, 51–65.
Zheng, V. (2010), *Chinese Family Business and the Equal Inheritance System*, New York: Routledge.

5. Successful family business ownership transitions: leveraging tacit knowledge

Rocki-Lee DeWitt and Ana Cristina González L.

DROPPO'S CURTIS PACKAGING

Don Droppo Jr, new vice president of marketing was deep in thought. The reality of joining his father, Don Droppo Sr, owner and chief executive officer (CEO) of Curtis Packaging, had set in. The pleasant memory of their special après-ski conversation still resonated; his father had revealed the competitive potential he had built in Curtis over the years and the role that Don Jr could play in realizing that potential. The addition of John Giusto, a highly experienced paper-based packaging leader as senior vice president of manufacturing, soon after Don Jr's hiring, meant that he would not be expected to realize Curtis's promise alone.

Don Jr knew his father had done something special in changing from an accomplished partner in an accounting firm whose clientele included Curtis to being Curtis's owner. Don Sr had enhanced the presence of a proud business and trusted employer, successfully weathering business and personal challenges. Capacity had been added through the acquisition of another troubled paper-based packaging company. Subsequent investments and employee engagement underpinned a business where proposals of 'how to make Curtis better' were now increasingly driven by the shop floor. Though Curtis still focused on commodity-based paper packaging, it now competed through investment in the future rather than through reliance on old facilities and ways. Don Sr's acquisition and leadership of Curtis had helped it become a stronger, more efficient competitor. Table 5.1 summarizes key transition events in Curtis's history.

Don Jr's enthusiastic ski house response, 'Let's blow the roof off Curtis!' was tempered with his recognition that he had a lot to learn. Some of Curtis's employees, customers and competitors would be watching to see just what the addition of both Don Jr and John Giusto would mean for

Table 5.1 Timeline – Curtis

Time	Attributes
1845	Curtis founded to make buttons and combs out of cow hooves and horns
1850s	Diversifies into wooden box making to provide containers for shipping, begins selling wooden boxes to others
Next four Curtis family generations	Evolves from manufacturing wooden boxes to commodity paperboard folding box business serving the consumer packaged goods sector
1980	Fails to effect a fifth-generation transition, non-family management team takes over ownership
1989	Non-family owners sell controlling interest to Don Droppo Sr, the accounting partner handling Curtis. He takes on a multi-million dollar note secured by the business' assets and a personal guarantee while handcuffing the now minority owners with an iron-clad buy-sell agreement and non-compete clauses
1992	Don Sr acquires financially struggling box maker to add capacity to Curtis in lieu of buying new machines; spends most of his time at the struggling box maker while top managers run Curtis
1995	150th anniversary of Curtis, new state-of-the-art, only-one-of-its-kind printing press installed. Curtis family invited to participate in celebration
1998	Buyout of former managers completed
2003	Don Droppo Jr and John Giusto join Curtis

Curtis. Only Don Jr and John Giusto were aware that Don Sr's intention was to leverage Curtis's foundation through Don and John's capabilities to migrate the company to the more attractive, luxury products paper-based packaging segment. This segment required greater collaboration between customers and Curtis to create unique designs through paper-based packaging.

Don Jr knew a road of discovery lay ahead as he and John Giusto helped realize Don Sr's vision. He wondered, 'What did I get myself into? How do I contribute to Curtis's success? How do I help Curtis move into a new market segment?'

INTRODUCTION

The market evidences respect for long-lived family businesses that play upon their heritage. Not surprisingly, some of these businesses have not been owned and operated by the same family over their lifetime. Though longevity across generations is the usual family business objective, this can be unreasonable. Ownership and leadership continuity, family involvement and governance are just the tip of the decision-making iceberg confronting family businesses. With business complexity and family dynamics juxtaposed with the potential for economic returns to heritage, it is not surprising that some family businesses continue under the ownership and leadership of someone other than the founding family.

To go forward without a merger or acquisition into a corporate portfolio a family business that can continue as a stand-alone going concern must be underpinned by well-established operating routines and supplier and buyer relationships. 'Insiders', those most familiar with the nature of the resources and capabilities of the business, are in the best position to become the next owners. They are aware of the economic potential embedded in how the company does business (Royer et al., 2008). Even though the family's departure poses knowledge loss risk, those willing to finance new owners may assume that 'insiders' have the next best insight into the operations of the business and its value.

In this context of ownership and leadership change, where some knowledge stocks disappear, we focus on efforts to apply knowledge derived from other experience to fill the knowledge void. Our research question is: Despite changes in ownership and leadership, how can the tacit knowledge (TK) stock of a family business be leveraged to achieve family business longevity?

We analyze the process of ownership, leadership and organizational change in Curtis to examine how the influx of knowledge resources (at the owner/leader level) affects family firm development. Since individuals play a significant role in TK as a firm resource, ownership/leadership disruptions should pose a major threat. Yet, they also offer much promise as a source of insight. Since the collective knowledge of the business remains, that is knowledge embedded in its routines and culture (Spender, 1996), a key to family business longevity is leveraging individual and business TK. We study the influence of this dynamic on organizational change as it contributes to the longevity of Curtis, a family business; albeit technically a family business interrupted then re-established.

The chapter is organized as follows. We briefly review the knowledge literature in order to define TK, its development and its relationship with family business ownership and leadership. Then we consider the processes by which TK is created and leveraged. Our analysis focuses on key decisions and accounts of interpersonal interaction captured in the interviews used to develop the Curtis case. In the conclusion, we offer implications for practice and research by using the 'lessons learned' as suggestions for how Don Jr might approach his transition into Curtis. In sum, our analysis of the evolution of intangible resources in one family business offers insight into the role of TK in family business longevity.

LITERATURE REVIEW

The knowledge-based view (KBV) of business, an outgrowth of the resource-based view (RBV), considers knowledge as the most strategically important resource to a business' competitive advantage (Grant, 1996). Knowledge within the business is embedded in and carried through organizational culture and identity, routines, systems and employees (Nelson and Winter, 1982). The KBV recognizes that individuals create and hold knowledge and that a business is a knowledge-integrating institution that exists to create conditions under which individuals integrate and apply knowledge.

Spender (1996) offers a matrix of organizational knowledge types derived from Nelson and Winter (1982) and Nonaka and Takeuchi (1995). Distinguishing between two levels, social and individual, he considers explicit and implicit knowledge at each level. Implicit knowledge is most akin to Polanyi's TK (1966). At the social level, knowledge is classified as objectified knowledge (explicit), publicly available for all firms, and collective knowledge (implicit), that is embedded in firms' routines and culture (Spender, 1996). At the individual knowledge level, distinctions are drawn between conscious (explicit) and automatic (implicit). Family businesses are illustrative of businesses that may facilitate the influx of implicit or tacit knowledge (Chirico, 2008; Chirico and Salvato, 2008; Royer et al., 2008). We examine interactions that occur among Spender's (1996) types of knowledge, especially between explicit and implicit types in family businesses.

Tacit Knowledge in a Family Business

TK is the human capacity to acquire knowledge beyond what we are able to communicate; that is, Michael Polanyi's classic statement 'we know more than we can tell' (Polanyi, 1966: 4). Derived from experience, TK is procedural and not openly stated (Sternberg et al., 1995). An individual's experience of working alone and with others informs what they pay attention to, how they behave and adapt to outcomes. When attached to the purpose of a specific business for long periods of time, it is an enduring intangible resource that may be further leveraged for the benefit of the business.

An individual's experience with defining elements of business organization, that is, decision-making, sensitivity to authority and coordination, begins in the family. This formative experience provides a cognitive frame in which experiences of being associated with, leading and owning a family business deepen and broaden the individual's understanding of 'family' and 'family business'. Experiential variety engenders a more complex idiosyncratic TK stock (Nonaka, 1994). When attending to one particular contextual aspect of a situation, seemingly far removed from 'family' consideration, a rich set of cognitive connections can be pulled into decision-making.

Patterns of professional and organizational know-how distinguish experts from novices (Wagner and Sternberg, 1985). Experts apply appropriate pieces of knowledge to a situation. For example, those who have worked with family businesses have an understanding of the interplay of family and business. Working within a particular family business, or even attending to dinnertime accounts of the day's doings, contributes to a deeper appreciation of the logic of family and non-family interaction unique to that business (Chirico, 2008). Through general and more specific family business experience, individuals develop the capacity to contextualize relationships across family and non-family members, a broader set of business routines (Cabrera-Suárez et al., 2001), as well as a larger stakeholder context.

In family businesses, this multi-level TK resource, especially when underpinned by a capacity to create it and transfer it, is a source of competitive advantage (Royer et al., 2008). The competition has difficulty replicating its unique family aspect (Cabrera-Suárez et al., 2001). Chirico and Salvato (2008) identify three aspects of the role of TK in the competitive advantage of family businesses. First, the purposive nature of TK (Sternberg et al., 1995), when attached to a concept that is societally construed as enduring, for example, family, builds a stock of internal social capital available to a controlling family. Individual and group efforts are attached to valued outcomes and family, thereby allowing incumbents, family and non-family to perceive stability and a long-term vision.

Second, the inability to codify TK when coupled with a motive to apply it also engenders enduring benefit. The value of business-unique TK remains as long as those who possess it remain, are personally engaged and desire to learn. Like an individual's earliest family experiences with positive reinforcement of learning, the opportunity to acquire and apply knowledge can foster attachment. Its retrieval and enhancement are strongest when individuals are affectively committed to and identify with the business; that is, 'I value what this business stands for' (Allen and John, 1990). When the owners and leaders of the business reciprocate commitment, by relying upon and utilizing others' TK, a routine of knowledge deployment and knowledge acquisition is supported.

Finally, potentially disruptive effects balance these positive effects. If conflict occurs, either between family members or between family and non-family members, TK transfer may face an obstacle. An individual's experience with conflict in the context of trusted relationships, like family, informs the extent to which conflict impedes the ability to develop TK.

Leveraging TK to Pursue Longevity

Changes in family business ownership and leadership are assumed to be disruptive. They can create a knowledge void and/or inject new ideas that are at odds with the capacity to process ideas or the willingness to engage in the learning required to change. Yet, Sharma and Salvato (in press) argue that both continuity and change are integral to family business longevity. This suggests that the appropriate stock of TK and its application can play a vital role in family business longevity. To address our research question about the influence of TK on business longevity in the face of ownership and leadership change, we consider the broader system of business and individual influences on preservation and change in the context of a family underpinning.

The family business owner/leader's challenge is to direct the acquisition, development and utilization of TK through family and non-family employee involvement in building and leveraging a multi-level mix of knowledge applied alongside tangible business resources to capture their best value in use. Hiring individuals, either family or non-family, with expertise developed through formal instruction and/or experience supports a business' acquisition of knowledge resources. Formal training and instruction may be used to further develop and scale the firm's general and business-specific knowledge with codification of the business' routines used to support dissemination (Krogh et al., 2000). Where knowledge complexity makes capture difficult, more experienced employees instruct less experienced employees to develop TK. As some individuals are more capable of encoding and combining information to develop knowledge (Sternberg et al., 1995), their retention plays a key role in the business' success.

Chirico (2008) provides evidence that knowledge can also be acquired by utilizing business resources, in particular, non-family members, who are employees or have strong relationships with the firm. In addition, Royer et al. (2008) affirm that TK's correct utilization, not just having the knowledge but knowing how to use it, can contribute to enduring success. In sum, we use the Curtis case to understand how a new owner and leader's TK offers new perspectives and engenders new approaches. This influx may help overcome a lack of internal social capital and more instrumental perspectives on family business involvement (Chirico and Salvato, 2008).

ANALYSIS AND DISCUSSION

Curtis progressed through ownership changes similar to, yet different from, those found in classic family business models (Gersick et al., 1997). Its early history reflects more traditional family business evolution. Four generations of Curtis family succession followed a founder-controlling owner (Lansberg, 1999) leaving the business to his children, and each subsequent generation leaving the business to the next. Two rounds of non-family ownership transitions, a management buy-out (MBO) followed by Don Droppo Sr's acquisition, occurred before it again became a traditional family business. This provides the variation needed to examine the roles of family and non-family experience and TK in family business longevity.

Our analysis focused on Curtis's recent evolution. Applying punctuated equilibrium logic (Lant and Mezias, 1992; Tushman and Romanelli, 1985), we compared and contrasted the roles of individual and business influence on types of organizational change to isolate relationship patterns. Four distinct stages were identified: (1) ownership transition from MBO to non-family 'insider', (2) new owner's early leadership experiences, (3) addition of TK required to add to the long-term viability of the business and (4) application of that additional TK. Our analysis of the first three stages, where Don Sr, the non-family 'insider', is owner and leader, provides the basis for the recommendations we offer Don Jr regarding how to apply his TK to best contribute to Curtis's business longevity. A summary of the knowledge at play, sources and indicators of that influence, as well as their contributions to longevity in the first three stages are presented in Table 5.2. Our recommendations follow our analysis.

Stage 1 (1989–91): Curtis Transitions from MBO to Non-Family 'Insider' Owner

During this stage Don Sr avoided radical changes that could disrupt the knowledge, culture and routines at Curtis. He wanted to limit Curtis's

Table 5.2 Application of TK to family business longevity at Curtis

Tacit knowledge influences	(Preservation) Current stock of knowledge		(Change and adaptation) Influx of new knowledge		Contributions to longevity
	Individual	Business	Individual	Business	
STAGE 1 Conscious and automatic knowledge to transition from an MBO to a non-family 'insider' owner 'Family' part of TK	• Don Sr becomes and behaves as an 'owner' • His accounting knowledge and experience interacting with other business owners informs his understanding of owner challenges and fiduciary responsibility	• He doesn't focus on change in ownership • 'They wanted to stay a family company. They didn't want a larger corporation buying it.' • 'They had worked here so long, they knew the people and they really cared about the people, they wanted to make sure they had jobs.' • Employees perceive Don Sr cares	• Don Sr: 'I wouldn't have wanted my father to work in a place like that.' • Makes decisions to emphasize his 'ownership right' and fosters mindset of a 'nice workplace'	• 'You don't know Don, you see we are in the box making business' • 'There wasn't much professionalism, we started working together, instituting things'	• Avoids disruptions to keep Curtis a 'going concern'

Table 5.2 (continued)

Tacit knowledge influences	(Preservation) Current stock of knowledge		(Change and adaptation) Influx of new knowledge		Contributions to longevity
	Individual	Business	Individual	Business	
STAGE 2 Business conscious and automatic knowledge through experience with stronger objectified and collective knowledge 'Family' part of conscious knowledge as divorce leaves him only with Curtis	• Don Sr combines 'owner' and 'leader' roles • Emphasizes returns to investment to pay debts • Don Sr knows he needs to improve facilities • Divorce leaves Don Sr only with Curtis • Don Sr asks employees: 'What can we do to make Curtis better?' and 'How will we pay for it?'	• He listens when experts tell him 'You've got ancient equipment' • 'Old' owners help keep the business 'steady' with Don Sr's tweaks during the acquisition • Employees stay	• Acquires a troubled business after Curtis • Spends more time on acquired business which increases reliance on others • Becomes aware of differences between the commodity and differentiated box business • Begins capital investment in Curtis with incorporation of unknown capacity in equipment	• Business difficulties necessitate growth in Don Sr's understanding. • 'Don pushed us to think outside the box. We bought a new piece of equipment. What can we do that our competition isn't doing?' • 'And they do have that open door policy. I think everyone pretty much feels like family.'	• Fosters enduring capacity, recognizes threats to that capacity and need of adaptation, employees begin to use his 'how we will pay' logic, foregoes selling

			• 'I kept the account with XYZ company because I wanted to keep a foot in the door.' • Don Sr realizes he needs marketing people to pursue new business segment	• Employees offer ideas and begin to think 'cash flow' rather than 'margin' • Employees understand changes without Don Sr prompting them on what to do	
STAGE 3 Void in knowledge creates solutions Recognition of 'family' potential in conscious and automatic knowledge	• Don Sr feels responsible for business • Don Jr has few recollections of Curtis from when he worked there earlier	• Previous owners/ managers leave when payment finishes, placing weight on Don Sr • Search for replacement after departure of head of operations • 'We're going to stay a family business'. (Key employee)	• 'I would be selfish if I didn't give my son a chance.' • 'The sun, moon and stars all aligned.' (Don Sr)	• 'I always wanted to work with my father.' (Don Jr) • Don Jr's motivation: he and his wife's desires • As his father, Don Jr recognizes how much he has to learn • John enters the business with industry knowledge	• Recognizes son's potential to contribute to future success but recognizes he can't do it alone.

clients' perceptions that this change would affect its products. Despite being a controlling owner who could have implemented substantive change (Gersick et al., 1997), Don Sr focused on preservation, learning and understanding the business. The incremental workplace changes he introduced were built upon empathy for the employees' working conditions, as his father had been a manufacturing laborer. These limited changes increased employees' and clients' commitment.

Tacit knowledge influences

Don Sr brought his experience and relationship as Curtis's accountant to the firm, as well as his personal motives. An accomplished accounting firm partner, where professional expectation mirrors that of a commercial banker (Wagner and Sternberg, 1985), the accountant is expected to secure enduring client relationships within the context of the legal code (Marchant and Robinson, 1999). He understood there was no obligation to announce an ownership change to avoid uncertainty for Curtis's clients.

Don Sr's pre-Curtis career also suggests that he appreciated business owner challenges and the fiduciary responsibilities of the business. His professional underpinning made him attend to the broader environment of business financing and the interpersonal conflicts that contributed to business failures. New accounting business referrals came from bankers and satisfied clients. Reputational advantage came from distinguishing between task and relationship conflicts (Kellermanns and Eddleston, 2004).

His experience with Curtis as a client offered him insight into that business, opining on its financial soundness. Yet, as but one of his many clients, he focused on the numbers, as assessed by his audit team. He stated, 'I know they've always made money.' He did not go beyond the confines of his professional lens to explore how they made money.

The potential to acquire Curtis also played upon thinking that appeared to have a stronger emotional appeal. He explained, 'I had started exploring business opportunities. I had always wanted to run my own business.' The mention of his clients' interest in selling aligned with Don Sr's emerging entrepreneurial interest which was coupled with knowledge of how to use the business' assets as loan collateral. Able to acquire the business with limited savings, the repayment obligation kept him focused on balancing preservation and change; cash and liquidity equated to business longevity. Although Don Sr controlled Curtis (51 percent initial ownership), he knew that until he completed buying out the former MBO team, they would offer their knowledge for better or worse, as members of Curtis's board.

Contributions to longevity

The minority owners contributed to structural inertia, characteristic of preservation (Hannan and Freeman, 1984). Their desire to have the business remain a 'family business' and not to sell to a corporation made them amenable to the deal's structure. They continually reminded Don Sr that he was in the box making business. They questioned his choices through the lens of their narrow understanding of box making, largely derived from their experience at Curtis.

In addition to taking on ownership, minor changes implemented by Don Sr signaled to employees that he cared about them. This was critical as a group of long-tenured employees had the knowledge required to obtain production from Curtis's assets. While many routines could have been codified, Curtis's previous owners had not done so. Instead, they relied on a lack of employee turnover to sustain knowledge stocks. He also learned that common professional business practices were missing.

Business preservation was the hallmark of this stage. Don Sr made an individual decision that can unambiguously be classified as change. He left a lucrative professional position, became a business owner and took on significant financial obligations. But, that substantive individual change, effected through his early ownership behaviors at Curtis, reflected an appreciation for moderation's role in business continuity. His early risky moves coupled with his positive emotional connection to business ownership with the commitment to further build his and others' Curtis-specific TK. Similarly, the previous owners, employees, clients, as well as lending community, were also committed to Curtis's preservation. While the ownership change could have been disruptive, individual and business influencers had the wisdom to take a longer-term perspective. They evidenced the leadership skills and ownership motivation, action and behaviors that reflect a long-term perspective important for business continuity (Le Breton-Miller et al., 2004).

Stage 2 (1992–2002): Don Sr Strengthens the Business

Don Sr continued to focus his attention on strengthening the longer-term viability of Curtis. But, he appeared to be less concerned about disruption of key external relationships and more focused on leveraging employee knowledge while addressing the demands posed by the turnaround of the acquired business. As an overview, this stage evidences the recursive interplay of him learning more about the industry and Curtis from outside sources and direct experience. He applied his knowledge to the direction and control of Curtis, with the subsequent increase in employee knowledge and capacity providing a foundation for his commitment of additional support. At the same time, he became aware of other industry opportunities which influenced his resource allocation decisions. These choices provided Curtis options that Don Sr would ultimately value more.

Tacit knowledge influences

A conversation with an outside expert caused Don Sr to realize that upgrades to the firm's production assets were needed. Don knowing that 'he doesn't know' coupled with the importance of his knowing triggered a never-ending search for improvement. Changes were driven by his recognition that updates to Curtis's equipment were needed to meet his repayment obligations. A classic 'make or buy' analysis informed the decision to acquire another troubled business.

The financial obligations related to acquiring the business were brought into sharper relief as Don's divorce left him with Curtis as his only asset. While the increased dependence on Curtis might have caused him to behave in a threat-rigid manner and be more directive of employee behavior (Staw et al., 1981), he recognized he needed to rely upon employees' knowledge to drive performance. Non-family members were present within the business for support.

Drawing upon his experience of how to engage people, he involved employees in the identification and implementation of 'making Curtis better'. He used the term 'we' rather than 'you' or 'I', reflecting shared involvement, and used the term 'Curtis' to reinforce their attachment to the family business. He reinforced this perspective and created credibility when he implemented ideas. Don increasingly developed his TK about Curtis's capabilities. This shift from the previous leadership's 'top down' to a 'bottom input' approach was accompanied by a change in the metric used to justify investment from 'positive variances' to cash flow; that is, 'How are we going to pay for this?'

Contributions to longevity

Don Sr noted that the confluence of Curtis, the newly acquired business and his personal life made this 'the worst time of his life'. Yet, his understanding of employee engagement in combination with his and their dependence on Curtis allowed him to build upon Curtis's foundation as a going concern and enhance its ability to compete.

Employee involvement further deepened the firm's TK and built Don's confidence that his business had the capacity to continue to grow. Time demands for the turnaround of the acquired business early in this period caused employees to recognize that they were responsible for Curtis's performance and their employment. Employees' engagement was also evidence that they understood what he was doing. Their contributions further reinforced his commitment and the promise of the business.

Don Sr's investments in Curtis were future-oriented. As he learned more about the business and the industry and wanted to 'be able to do something that competition could not', he included some unspecified capacity in capital expenditures. He also retained a business relationship that might have otherwise been let go. It kept 'Curtis' foot in the door' of an industry segment that appealed to him. These changes helped provide a foundation for future ones while avoiding disruption. Employees were asked to apply their ideas to the existing line.

The most important decision relative to Curtis's longevity during this period was Don Sr's rejection of offers to purchase the business. During this stage, like the first stage, Curtis continued to exhibit characteristics of a 'family business' where TK at the individual level and close interpersonal ties at the business level contributed to its success. But, this 'family business' intangible resource was embedded in employees and their interactions with Don Sr. It did not appear to go the other way.

Don Sr was even less attuned to family than in the beginning. While entertaining a purchase offer for the business, he decided not to sell because the offer failed to account for the value of equipment he had recently added. No mention of a sale's effect on employees was made. Connections between the business and Don Sr's family were also weak. Though employees were aware of his family as his children had come to company picnics, their involvement was limited to Don Jr working in the business one summer. He had dissuaded him from getting into the business during the middle of this stage because of concerns about its viability. To Don Sr, at this stage, Curtis was just a business and his focus remained on its viability.

Stage 3 (2002–03): Don Sr Recognizes Curtis's Potential as a Family Business

In contrast to the previous stage, Don Sr now had the time for deeper thinking about his business and personal situation as he was not pressured by his co-owners or the turnaround demands of the acquired business. In reflecting upon foregoing the purchase offer, Don Sr said, 'What would I have done? Played more golf? Drank more wine?' While he knew that some wondered about his son's lack of involvement, two aspects of the business caused him to seriously consider a role for him. First, he reflected, 'I would be selfish if I didn't give my son a chance to be involved in the business.' Second, in harkening back to a conversation about the value of skilled marketing and sales professionals with a respected business professional, he recognized that his son could actually fill this knowledge void. He also needed to fill a vacancy caused by the departure of the head of operations. His recurrent disenchantment with the company's sales professionals caused him to think more expansively about the business' talent mix. Don Sr was in a predicament, but his experience gained handling other businesses contributed to his ability to focus on Curtis's strategy and the role of the experience of others in Curtis's future.

Tacit knowledge influences

Don Sr's conversations with two individuals, Don Jr and John Giusto, gave momentum to his next business moves. After a day of skiing with his son followed by a long conversation, he recognized that there was potential for his son to contribute. Not only did he confirm that Don Jr applied creative thinking to business problems, he learned that a change in employment would allow Don Jr and his wife to realize personal goals.

Following his father's guidance to 'find his own way', Don Jr realized early career success as a financial services sales and marketing professional. After a few years, Don Jr obtained a more responsible and rewarding position with another well-regarded financial services firm. He was very skilled at broaching 'cold call' conversations with individuals who paid close attention to their personal and business wealth and was highly resilient in the face of adversity. According to his father, 'Don Jr never had a bad day. If I had been confronted with some of what he has dealt with, I would have been down; but, not Don.' Don Sr's negotiations with his son for a 'signing bonus', enhanced his respect for his son's deal-making skills. Don Jr's comment, 'I had always wanted to work with my Dad', reflected a desire based upon affective commitment (Sharma and Irving, 2005).

Regarding John Giusto, Don Sr overcame his trepidation about offering him employment based upon his assumption that Curtis could not afford his experience. But a conversation with John revealed that he was ready to leave a more remunerative position to work in a situation with more socio-emotional benefits (cf., Gomez-Mejia et al., 2007). John was drawn to Curtis because of his desire to travel less and play an important role in the pursuit of new markets. The creative challenge appealed to his intuitive understanding of what mattered to him and his family at this stage of his life. The equipment and capabilities at Curtis complemented his talent. Opportunities for outsiders like John are realized not only because family businesses are more willing to bring in outsiders (Chirico, 2008) but because the outsider recognizes an opportunity present in the employer's TK stock and its physical and social capital.

Contributions to longevity

While Curtis was preserved because Don Sr decided not to sell, the entrance of Don Jr and John contributed a TK stock that Don Sr expected would be leveraged to change and reposition the company. Through this process, like classic succession in a family business, Don Sr would develop the capacity of the business, allowing him to let go as a leader, paying more attention to its oversight while building others' strategic decision-making capabilities (Le Breton-Miller and Miller, 2006).

Implications

We address the practical implications of our analysis for sons who bring outside expertise to their father's businesses by answering Don Jr's questions in the case vignette.

What did I get myself into?

Don Jr is in a situation far better than what his father initially found at Curtis. Don Sr had no direct family connection or owners who were predisposed to discovery. Don Sr was reliant on the previous owners' commitment to the status quo, outside experts, and his own capacity to learn. Yet, Don Sr knew that his influence alone was not enough. He believes that the convergence of his work and the entrance of his son and John Giusto represent 'the sun, the moon and the stars all coming together' and demarcate his efforts to contribute to the longevity of Curtis.

Don Jr lacked accounting experience and he had to learn the packaging business; his summer working at Curtis was not enough. He would need additional business and industry specific types of knowledge. Don Sr put in place a robust financial reporting system and hired an experienced and creative operations leader who could do more than keep Curtis operating as it was. John was hired to more than fill the void left by the departure of Curtis's head of operations. Don Sr wanted Don Jr to 'own' this initiative by being attentive to the unique requirements of luxury packaging, seeing it through his own eyes as a sales and marketing professional, as well as through the eyes of experienced others.

How do I contribute to Curtis' success?

Following the example set by his father, Don Jr's most important first step is to learn the business. To leverage his marketing and sales TK in the context of others' knowledge about Curtis and the paper-based packaging industry requires at least two types of learning. First, Don Jr must learn from listening to others, within and outside the business. Second, he must offer what he thinks he knows in order to discover what he does not know, especially as it pertains to Curtis's competitive advantage. Being predisposed to listening and sharing is key to effecting change (Gioia and Chittipeddi, 1991).

To learn a new business and its position within an industry requires attention to the value-adding sequence that begins with raw materials through their transformation into finished goods (Porter, 1985). Learning is more likely when there is a readily available context, expertise that can be used to make sense of that context, and when there are consequences for failing to learn. Curtis's shop floor, John Guisto and Don Sr provide such a context for Don Jr. Consequences for failing to learn abound. While Don Sr was motivated to learn the business due to financial obligations, Don Jr is motivated because he has committed to help his father take Curtis forward and support his family through the success of the business.

In managing his relationship between clients and the business, he needs to focus on understanding what Curtis does and how that matches with client's needs. He has a limited time to learn as employees will be paying attention to what he does. Their relief that the 'business is going to remain a family business' with Don Jr's appearance will provide but a brief period for learning. Getting on the 'shop floor' will help him learn what Curtis does and convey to employees that like his father before him he is interested in and respects the TK that resides within the business.

John's entrance and his engagement of Don Jr and other employees will help draw employees' attention to their role in production. John's experience in paper-based packaging makes it easier for him to engage employees in identifying unique advantages. Because John's schooling had a heavy 'hands-on' learning approach he is predisposed to use that same approach. Don Jr can learn how various steps work in the business while John engages operators in a conversation about equipment's functioning, its role in the process and how it compares to competitors.

Don Jr also needs to debrief what he has learned with John and his father. John's experience with multiple employers provides him with an understanding of the relative competitor advantages derived from hard assets and organizational structures. As his role reignites his passion for creating packaging solutions rather than managing packaging businesses, his conversations with Don Jr and Don Sr subsequent to the shop floor visits will clarify how Curtis can distinguish itself. This provides a venue for Don Jr to ask questions and for the answers to be incorporated in business initiatives.

How do I help Curtis move into a new market segment?

Experimentation with a willing client is critical to Curtis's efforts to break into a new segment. Like the acquisition of a troubled company was to

Curtis's addition of capacity and Don Sr's enhanced industry understanding, a first trial is requisite. While Don Sr, Don Jr and John may believe that Curtis's capabilities and history of undertaking some customization for other customers is a basis for pursuing a client from the luxury goods segment, only when they undertake a move into this segment will they learn lessons that cannot be anticipated.

They will rely upon John's familiarity with luxury packaging and Don Jr's customer sense in the selection of their first client. Significant attention by all involved will be required. Explicit client communication about normal pricing and a 'trial discount' should help drive shared learning and the development of business-to-business relationship-specific TK. This approach could be at odds with the business' routine of answering the question, 'How will we pay for it?' unless payback is viewed with an explicit consideration of the investment in learning.

To provide the basis for repositioning that is expected to contribute to longevity, the experiment needs to be collectively driven and owned by Don Sr, Don Jr, John and their employees. While Don Jr clearly feels personally responsible, at the same time his language reflects a role of 'helping' as opposed to directing the move into the new market segment. Like his father, Don Jr evidences an appreciation for the role of others in business success.

Discussion

In the case of a family business where the founding family departs from ownership and leadership, one is left to consider both TK attached to non-family individuals within the business and TK brought by the new owner/leader. It is this focus that draws attention to the significance of TK held by long-tenured non-family insiders involved in and committed to the business.

Some studies affirm that family businesses realize the importance of employee knowledge and invest more than non-family businesses in human resources (Le Breton-Miller and Miller, 2006). However, understanding the value of people does not always mean that family businesses manage TK as a resource. This study emphasizes the enduring nature of a family business' TK embedded in long-tenured employees and leveraged with new TK from ownership and leadership changes.

From a resource-based perspective, because TK is 'disorganized, informal and relatively inaccessible' (Wagner and Sternberg, 1985: 439), it is inimitable. Sustained advantage comes from the recurrent creation and application of knowledge. Le Breton-Miller and Miller (2006) state that family businesses have higher levels of patents, customer loyalty and quality, and thus deeper core competencies. But, like their non-family counterparts, a family business built around consistency and reliability, that is, structural inertia (Hannan and Freeman, 1984), has little motive to pursue new lines of business. They are unlikely to do so unless it is clear that change is required.

A new owner/leader brings his/her own TK to the evaluation of the acquired business. But, his/her TK must be carefully applied. Business continuity requires effecting the appropriate change by leveraging the existing knowledge and investing in new knowledge creation (Abell, 1993; Hamel and Prahalad, 1994). For family businesses these knowledge management challenges differ from non-family businesses. A family business' advantage may come from an informal approach to knowledge management, of non-codified or explicit knowledge. Any structural change may endanger this stock.

Our case, incorporating the potential for both persistence and change due to non-family ownership and leadership changes in a long-lived family business, provides insight into the enduring influence of family business-generated TK and the introduction of new non-family TK to business longevity. From his takeover of Curtis, Don Sr was aware of his strengths and weaknesses regarding business knowledge. He did not begin his ownership by abruptly changing routines. Instead he introduced incremental changes allowing him the time to learn and giving the continuing owner and employees the time to adjust to the new leader. When the time came to make a radical change, he did it with guidance and openness by allowing current employees and outsiders to bring their TK, thereby balancing preservation and change.

Implications for research

First, 'knowing about not knowing' is critical to learning. When Don Sr was made aware of his erroneous assumptions about Curtis he quickly realized he did not know about important aspects of the business and set about learning. Don Jr knows that one summer's experience does not translate into leadership and that he will be surprised as he begins working at Curtis. Both Don Sr and Don Jr appropriately respond to inevitable knowledge gaps by learning.

Second, a family upbringing where empathy is valued enhances sensitivity to the motives of others working in close proximity. This coincides with what Chirico and Salvato (2008) state about the importance of social capital and affective commitment in TK transfer in family businesses.

Finally, broader experience working in and with family businesses provides a cognitive foundation for understanding a family business decision-making context and leveraging one's capabilities in that context.

This aligns with what Royer et al. (2008) conclude regarding succession, that is, in specific situations where family business-specific experiential knowledge is relevant, family members or close non-family employees are preferred as successors.

In sum, sensitivity coupled with experience outside the family business in or with other family businesses facilitates the sense-making and sense-giving (Gioia and Chittipeddi, 1991) needed to successfully navigate ownership and leadership change in a family business. When family business TK is coupled with broader business experience, it provides the professional and industry context that underpins successful strategic change to leverage family business advantage, even if that family business is one that is not originally yours.

Research on family business succession addresses the question of whether a family successor or someone outside the family should run the business (Royer et al., 2008). After 150 years of operation, Curtis once again became a family business with the perspective of first-generation ownership and the wisdom of multiple decades of outside experience. Curtis's ownership and leadership transitions gave them the best of two worlds. On the energetic, engaged novice side, it obtained a controlling owner with a long-term commitment to make the investments necessary for success. On the wise, experienced business leader side, it gained an individual with leadership skills who understood that letting go and engaging followers in doing what they knew best, and better than him, was appropriate. And, like a classic first-generation family business, it obtained this in a combined role, enhancing alignment and coordination of these roles.

CONCLUSION

In sum, TK is embedded through multiple entities. The primary task of leadership is establishing the coordination necessary for knowledge integration (Grant, 1996). The ability of family leaders to place the efforts of the business in the context of a marketplace derived from a multi-level mix of knowledge informs their understanding of the potential need to reposition the business versus improve the business' efforts within a given position. Their understanding of the knowledge and skills necessary to gain a competitive position derived from years of experience within the business informs their assessment about the appropriateness of tangible and intangible resources relative to that position. Failures to effect external and internal alignment and establish a culture threaten family business success.

The analysis of Curtis suggests that TK is a key intangible resource that contributes to a firm's longevity. Our analysis suggests that despite the risks inherent in ownership and leadership change as it affects the balance between preservation and adaptation, TK sourced from outside and embedded within the family business, when appropriately leveraged, can contribute to family business longevity.

REFERENCES

Abell, D.F. (1993), *Managing with Dual Strategies*, 1st ed., New York: Free Press.

Allen, N.J. and P.M. John (1990), 'The measurement and antecedents of affective, continuance and normative commitment to the organization', *Journal of Occupational Psychology*, **63** (1), 1–18.

Cabrera-Suárez, K., P. De Saá-Pérez and D. García-Almeida (2001), 'The succession process from a resource- and knowledge-based view of the family firm', *Family Business Review*, **14**, 37–46.

Chirico, F. (2008), 'The creation, sharing and transfer of knowledge in family business', *Journal of Small Business & Entrepreneurship*, **21** (4), 413–33.

Chirico, F. and C. Salvato (2008), 'Knowledge integration and dynamic organizational adaptation in family firms', *Family Business Review*, **21** (2), 169–81.

Gersick, K.E., J.A. Davis, M. McCollom Hampton and I. Lansberg (1997), *Generation to Generation: Life Cycles of the Family Business*, Boston, MA: Harvard Business School Press.

Gioia, D.A. and K. Chittipeddi (1991), 'Sensemaking and sensegiving in strategic change initiation', *Strategic Management Journal*, **12**, 433–88.

Gomez-Mejia, L.R., K.T. Haynes, M. Nunez-Nickel, K.J.L. Jacobson and J. Moyano-Fuentes (2007), 'Socioemotional wealth and business risks in family-controlled firms: evidence from Spanish olive oil mills', *Administrative Science Quarterly*, **52**, 106–37.

Grant, R.M. (1996), 'Toward a knowledge-based theory of the firm', *Strategic Management Journal*, **17** (Winter Special Issue), 109–22.

Hamel, G. and C.K. Prahalad (1994), *Competing for the Future*, Boston, MA: Harvard Business School Press.

Hannan, M.T. and J. Freeman (1984), 'Structural inertia and organizational change', *American Sociological Review*, **49** (2), 149–64.

Kellermanns, F.W. and K.A. Eddleston (2004), 'Feuding families: when conflict does a family firm good', *Entrepreneurship: Theory & Practice*, **28** (3), 209–28.

Krogh, G.V., K. Ichijo and I. Nonaka (2000), *Enabling Knowledge Creation: How to Unlock the Mystery of TK and Release the Power of Innovation*, 1st ed., New York: Oxford University Press.

Lansberg, I. (1999), *Succeeding Generations: Realizing the Dream of Families in Business*, Boston, MA: Harvard Business School Press.

Lant, T.K. and S.J. Mezias (1992), 'An organizational learning model of convergence and reorientation', *Organization Science*, **3** (1), 47–71.

Le Breton-Miller, I. and D. Miller (2006), 'Why do some family businesses outcompete? Governance, long-term orientations, and sustainable capability', *Entrepreneurship: Theory & Practice*, **30** (6), 731–46.

Le Breton-Miller, I., D. Miller and L.P. Steier (2004), 'Toward an integrative model of effective FOB succession', *Entrepreneurship: Theory & Practice*, **28** (4), 305–28.

Marchant, G. and J. Robinson (1999), 'Is knowing the tax code all it takes to be a tax expert? On the developemnt of legal expertise', in R.J. Sternberg and J. Hovarth (eds), *Tacit Knowledge in Professional Practice*, 1st ed., Mahwah, NJ: Lawrence Erlbaum Associates, 3–20.

Nelson, R.R. and S.G. Winter (1982), *An Evolutionary Theory of Economic Change*, Cambridge, MA: Harvard University Press.

Nonaka, I. (1994), 'A dynamic theory of organizational knowledge creation', *Organization Science*, **5** (1), 14–37.

Nonaka, I. and H. Takeuchi (1995), *The Knowledge-Creating Company: How Japanese Companies Create the Dynamics of Innovation*, 1st ed., New York: Oxford University Press.

Polanyi, M. (1966), *The Tacit Dimension*, Gloucester: Peter Smith.

Porter, M.E. (1985), *Competitive Advantage: Creating and Sustaining Superior Performance*, New York: Free Press.

Royer, S., R. Simons, B. Boyd and A. Rafferty (2008), 'Promoting family: a contingency model of family business succession', *Family Business Review*, **21** (1), 15–30.

Sharma, P. and P.G. Irving (2005), 'Four bases of family business successor commitment: antecedents and consequences', *Entrepreneurship: Theory & Practice*, **29** (1), 13–33.

Sharma, P. and C. Salvato (2014), 'Family firm longevity: a balancing act between continuity and change', in P. Fernandez-Perez and A. Colli (eds), *The Endurance of Family Business: A Global Overview*, Cambridge, UK: Cambridge University Press, in press.

Spender, J.C. (1996), 'Making knowledge the basis of the dynamic theory of the firm', *Strategic Management Journal*, **17** (Winter Special Issue), 45–62.

Staw, B.M., L.E. Sandelands and J.E. Dutton (1981), 'Threat-rigidity effects in organizational behavior: a multilevel analysis', *Administrative Science Quarterly*, **26** (4), 24.

Sternberg, R.J., R.K. Wagner, W.M. Williams and J.A. Horvath (1995), 'Testing common sense', *American Psychologist*, **50** (11), 912–27.

Tushman, M. and E. Romanelli (1985), 'Organizational evolution: a metamorphosis model of convergence and reorientation', *Research in Organizational Behavior*, **7**, 171–222.

Wagner, R.K. and R.J. Sternberg (1985), 'Practical intelligence in real world pursuits: the role of TK', *Journal of Personality and Social Psychology*, **49** (2), 436–58.

6. The role of social capital in succession from controlling owners to sibling teams

Luis Cisneros, Mircea-Gabriel Chirita and Bérangère Deschamps

THE TREMBLAY CASE: SUCCESSION SCENARIOS AND THE PREDECESSOR'S DILEMMA

Returning from dinner with his younger son on a spring day, Martin Tremblay[1] could not stop thinking about his dilemma. Until a few days earlier, he had thought he had devised a good succession plan that would allow his family business to continue to grow after his departure. One of his sons would be in charge of the family business, while the other would back him up. It would be like when he started his company, Tremblay Services Financiers Inc., back in 1976 with his long-time friend, Guy Dupont, as an equal partner. Martin was responsible for the company's strategic decisions and Guy took care of the day-to-day management. Drawing upon his own first-hand experience as a business founder, Martin was considering transferring the company to his younger son, who had already expressed his willingness and commitment to playing the role of family firm leader.

However, Martin soon learned that the implications of his succession plan transcended the frontiers of business into the realm of family life. In the space of one day, he made a complete reversal of his decision and decided to transfer the company to his older son, who had worked in the company longer than his younger son, and who was well-known and respected by the business community. However, this change of plans understandably upset his younger son, who threatened to leave the business.

Martin never thought that retiring from his business and passing the torch would be the most difficult decision he ever had to make. Although it had been a tremendous challenge to found the financial services company, things had seemed simpler back then. Martin and Guy started small; however, their company grew rapidly, climbing into the top ten of the financial services providers in Quebec. As the company expanded they required additional forces to support its growth. Ten years after founding their firm, the co-founders invited Martin's older son, Philippe, to join the company, and agreed to give him free reign to expand the business.

At this time, Philippe already had six years' experience in the financial services industry. With his prior experience and his network of contacts, he quickly started developing an effective strategy to capture market share. He hired more people, creating teams that he then led. He focused on new markets and within ten years the company needed another person on the same level as him.

Martin and Philippe decided to ask Antoine, Martin's younger son (Philippe's brother), who was at that time an insurer in Toronto, to come back to Montreal and work for the family business. Antoine agreed but asked to become a shareholder in return. The business continued to grow because of the brothers' dynamic and complementary skills. The resourcefulness and business savvy of his sons made Martin realize that they were well prepared to succeed him.

In 1997, Guy Dupont experienced health problems and decided to sell his shares. As the company had grown and had an excellent reputation, Philippe and Antoine were able to obtain a joint personal loan to acquire 50 per cent of the company's shares from Guy Dupont for $2 million dollars. Following Guy's departure, Philippe and Antoine rapidly took on more responsibility. Philippe became the vice president of marketing and sales and Antoine became the vice president of human resources and operations.

In 2003, after deep reflection and several discussions, Martin considered transferring the leadership of Tremblay to Antoine, especially as Philippe did not show much interest in the chief executive officer (CEO) position. As Martin observed: 'Philippe is a talented salesman. He would be happy if the only thing that he did was selling. Management bothers him.'

However, not only was Philippe the older son, he had worked at Tremblay longer than his brother Antoine. The financial services industry watches for symbols, and if Philippe was not appointed the CEO of Tremblay, it might be seen as an indication of his incompetence. Not surprisingly, Antoine was hurt by his father's change of heart and expressed his disappointment during dinner with him. Antoine expressed this sentiment as follows: 'My father had told me that I would be the President. He told me afterwards, during a meal, that it would be a co-lead. It was like giving candy to a child, and taking it back immediately after. Maybe my father felt obliged.'

Unsure what to do, Martin Tremblay started asking others for advice. He needed to answer two critical questions: as both his sons were working for the firm, to whom should he pass on the family business? How could he ensure that the company would be properly managed after his retirement, and that it would not lose its good reputation?

INTRODUCTION

The Tremblay case illustrates a frequent dilemma for incumbents: to choose a single successor or to transfer the business to several (or even all) children? The growing complexity of the business environment, the need for complementary skills and the time-consuming process of building social capital (SC) has made the pathway of transferring an enterprise from controlling owner to sibling partner leaders very desirable. Such a transfer of leadership to multiple family members within family enterprises has become common practice (Cater and Justis, 2010). According to a study conducted by MassMutual (2007) in the US, 42 per cent of family firm (FF) owners consider transferring their companies to a team of successors rather than to a single successor. Mazzola et al. (2008) observed that in an environment that is favourable to the transfer of leadership to a team of successors, tacit knowledge can be transmitted effectively because of affinities among family members.

This chapter aims to understand the process of the transfer of SC from controlling owners to sibling partners during the succession process. Six French-Canadian family firms that have experienced such transfers are examined. Results indicate that the transition from a controlling owner to a sibling team entails the alignment of individuals' responsibilities according to capabilities and interests as was done in the Tremblay case. The transition process also includes the transfer of internally focused *structural* SC. This is followed by the gradual transfer of externally focused *relational* SC, wherein the senior generation introduces the sibling partners to appropriate networks that relate to their responsibilities in the organization (cf., Nahapiet and Ghoshal, 1998).

Thus, the transfer of tacit knowledge, as an element of *structural capital*, was found to be a precursor to the collective succession creating the premise for the formation of a sibling team. The importance of networks and reputation, as essential elements of *relational capital*, had a trigger effect on the sibling team succession. This study indicates that sibling team succession may be a promising solution to retain and augment the SC of a FF as the company is passed to subsequent generations.

LITERATURE REVIEW

Family Succession to Several Heirs

Despite succession being one of the dominant topics in FF literature (Ward, 1987; Allouche and Amann, 2000; Sharma, 2004; Chua et al., 2003), family succession to several heirs has not been explored in-depth. Although models for the succession process present the issue from different perspectives, authors have ultimately shown that the succession process is a complex one. The complexity primarily arises from the numerous actors (family members, employees, shareholders, stakeholders) within the family and the organizational system (Cadieux, 2007; Le Breton-Miller et al., 2004; Brockhaus, 2004) impacted by the process, and also because of the dual transfer of leadership and ownership. However, most of the literature on FF succession only looks at the relationship between predecessor and successor from a one-to-one perspective, without considering the possibility of transferring the leadership from one predecessor to several heirs. Although there are a number of authors (Aronoff, 1998; Gersick et al., 1997; Cadieux et al., 2002; Sonfield et al., 2005; Cater and Justis, 2010) who do point out that there may be cases where more than one successor is involved, they do not explore this idea further.

To present the FF transfer from controlling owner to sibling partners, we adopt the four-phase model of family business succession proposed by Handler (1994) for transfers of leadership from a single predecessor to a single successor. According to Handler (1994) and Cadieux (2007), the succession process can be divided into four main phases, namely *incubation, implementation, joint management* and *new leadership and predecessor's disengagement*. (1) During the *incubation* phase, the predecessor is the dominant actor. He manages and controls the firm. The process of leadership transfer begins at home, where the successor (the heir) is conditioned in the family values and where the predecessor plays a key role in instilling in the successor an interest in the FF. It is during this first phase that the successor is initiated into the daily workings of the firm, and he/she then either does or does not show interest in the family business. (2) During the *implementation* phase, the successor officially joins the firm. The predecessor assigns him/her tasks and gives him/her operational and administrative responsibilities. It is at this point that the successor shows his/her willingness to take over the leadership of the company. Following an informal or formal evaluation of potential successors, the predecessor chooses the successor. (3) The *joint management* period is characterized by the development of an even closer relationship between successor and predecessor as they collaborate to lead the family business. The predecessor then designs potential career paths for the successor. Over time, important projects and responsibilities are assigned to the successor. A timetable is established for the transfer of leadership by the predecessor to the successor. In addition, the firm's leader begins the transfer of ownership to the successor and the SC (Arrègle et al., 2004). (4) Finally, during the last phase of *new leadership and disengagement*, the predecessor retires. Leadership and ownership transfers are complete. The successor takes over the leadership of the organization, signalling the end of the succession process.

Social Capital

(a) Social capital and the family firm

The family is a social system endorsed by rules and customs to take care of its members' needs (Kepner, 1983). Tradition, stability, loyalty, trust and interdependency are key elements to the functioning of the family and need to be explored to understand its operation. These elements maintain cohesion between family members over time and events. They are essential in interpersonal relationships based on emotion, affection and a sense of responsibility and loyalty. According to Arrègle et al. (2004), when family members are involved in a FF, the learning acquired within the family seeps through into the management of the company. As it strongly contributes to building the behaviour and thought patterns of its members, the family has a direct impact upon the formation of a firm's SC. In the same vein, Carr et al. (2011) considered that the SC of a FF is not simply a reflection of the organizational characteristics, processes, markets, products and services or customers, but represents unique and inimitable resources derived from the family system, in turn influencing and ultimately defining the FF itself.

Indeed, Salvato and Melin (2008) found that FFs create financial value over generations through their capacity to renew and redesign their social interactions inside and outside of the controlling family rather than through a specific resource or from higher-level combinative capabilities. Arrègle et al. (2004, 2007) then linked the competitive advantage of family businesses to the creation of SC and the ability to transmit it from one generation to another. However, the competitive advantage resulting from the SC of an FF tends to reverse when the founder retires (Coeurderoy and Lwango, 2008).

The SC transfer to following generations represents a critical challenge for FFs, as a growing number of them maintain their economic stability through intangibles such as personal business contacts and networks (De Freyman et al., 2007). Despite widespread agreement among scholars that SC represents the ultimate explanation of the competitive advantage of FFs, the crucial issue of the sustainability of this advantage is largely unstudied. Long and Chrisman (2013) inferred that research on FF succession would benefit from a closer look into the development of a successor's relational skills, credibility and SC.

(b) Forms of social capital

Nahapiet and Ghoshal (1998: 243) defined social capital as 'the sum of the actual and potential resources embedded within, available through, and derived from the network of relationships possessed by an individual or social unit' and proposed a model of organizational SC based on three distinct but highly interrelated dimensions. These dimensions are: (1) *structural* (knowledge, links and network configurations), (2) *relational* (trust, norms, obligations, identification with the group, relationships and contacts), and (3) *cognitive* (shared representations, interpretations and systems of meaning).

Based on their review of previous empirical studies focusing on the influence of intangibles in the success of companies, Durst and Güldenberg (2009) revisited the classification of SC by Nahapiet and Ghoshal (1998). They proposed a classification taxonomy that divides SC into three subgroups: *human*, *structural* and *relational capital. Human capital* includes the skills that employees acquire on the job, through training and experience. *Structural capital* refers to four aspects, which are innovative capabilities, company culture, knowledge management and organizational structure. *Relational capital* is divided into customers and networks (Durst and Güldenberg, 2009). We should also include here the perspective proposed in De Castro et al. (2004): they considered that *reputation* determines the configuration of relational capital of each firm and has a moderating role.

In this chapter we concentrate our attention on structural and relational capital: while structural capital emphasizes the quantity of relations, relational capital emphasizes the quality of relations in organizations (Granovetter, 1992). We focus on tacit knowledge (as part of *structural capital*) and networks and reputation (as part of *relational capital*).

Our decision to especially focus on tacit knowledge and networks for the purpose of this study is underpinned by the OECD[2] definition of SC as 'networks together with shared norms, values and understandings which facilitate cooperation within or among groups' (OECD, 2009: 103).

Knowledge is considered by many to be a company's most valuable strategic resource (Conner and Prahalad, 1996; Grant, 1996). Indeed, Grant (1996) advanced the 'knowledge-based view of the firm', recognizing it as the most significant source of competitive advantage.

Malecki (1997) captured the quintessence of knowledge when he defined it as *know-what* (facts), *know-how* (tacit knowledge), *know-why* (science) and *know-who* (networking). Tacit knowledge (know-how), which includes talents and skills, managerial systems and routines and values and norms, represents approximately 80 per cent of a company's valuable knowledge resources (Leonard-Barton, 1995). The concept of tacit knowing was introduced by the philosopher Michael Polanyi, who, in his famous book *The Tacit Dimension*, asserted that, 'we know more than we can tell' (1966: 4). Nonaka and Takeuchi (1995: 7) defined tacit knowledge as 'personal knowledge embedded in individual experience and involving intangible factors such as personal belief, perspective and value system'. They contrast this with the other kind of knowledge, 'explicit knowledge'. Contrary to explicit knowledge, which 'can be articulated in formal language including grammatical statements, mathematical expressions, specifications, manuals and so forth' (Nonaka and Takeuchi, 1995: 8), tacit knowledge is known for the difficulties encountered when sharing it with others. According to Nonaka and Takeuchi (1995), the process that transfers tacit knowledge from one person to another is socialization. Sandoval-Arzaga et al. (2011) considered that the family business represents a context favourable to knowledge transfer. Particular mention should be made of the model proposed by Cabrera-Suarez et al. (2001) regarding the integration of knowledge by the successors of a family business. For these authors, the competitive success of FFs is based on the '*tacitness of the knowledge*' embedded in their distinctive resources (commitment, networks, trust and reputation).

(c) The role of social capital in the family firm succession

Durst and Güldenberg (2009) reviewed empirical studies on the influence of SC components on companies' success and reached the assumption that if these intangibles have an impact on companies' success they may be relevant in terms of companies' succession. Pasi (2004) showed that the transfer of knowledge and networks plays a crucial role in FF succession. For Cabrera-Suarez et al. (2001), succession in modern-day FFs is largely a process of transfer of tacit knowledge. Furthermore, for many FFs, strategic advantages reside in the SC that has been developed over the years and is not easily traded or transferred (Steier, 2001).

According to Steier (2001), the importance of SC transfer and management is evident for FFs engaged in a succession process. Steier (2001) suggests that the transactional content of relational capital may change from one generation to another during and after the succession process, as the weak ties (those not strongly linked to resources) would fade. For Long and Chrisman (2013), a successor's SC and his/her willingness and commitment to assume the role of FF leader are critical to the succession process.

Using the conceptual lens offered by SC literature, we further examine the key role played by SC, and more specifically tacit knowledge, networks and reputation in the transfer from controlling owner to sibling partners in an FF.

METHODS

The methodology used to explore the transfer process of the FF from controlling owner to several sibling partners is qualitative, exploratory and based on multiple case studies. In addition to the Tremblay case, we examined five other family business succession cases of FFs located in the province of Quebec, Canada.

Exploratory Qualitative Research

As there is scant literature that looks at the transfer of FFs to sibling teams, this study's exploratory approach provides a better understanding of the issues involved (Sekaran, 2003). Indeed, the case study approach is particularly useful for generating new knowledge in such exploratory situations where there is no clear, single set of outcomes (Patton and Applebaum, 2003).

Eisenhardt (1989) stated that randomization is not necessary when selecting cases for study. On the contrary, cases need to be strategically selected in relation to the relevant theoretical background (Patton and Applebaum, 2003). We chose FFs located in the same region (Quebec, Canada) with the following characteristics: private enterprises where the capital was entirely held by the family running the business, were small to medium-sized enterprises (SMEs) and had experienced a successful succession. Within the context of this research, a successful succession means: (1) the harmonious transfer of intangible capital, leadership and ownership (that is, the arrival of the successors had a positive impact on the financial performance of the enterprise – growth, increase in revenues, innovations, new markets); (2) the successors hold a majority share of the FF's capital; (3) the other siblings are satisfied with the new distribution of roles within the FF; (4) and the shareholders (often confused with the members of the family) are satisfied with the outcome of the succession.

Data were collected through personal, semi-structured interviews (primary sources) and from workshops (secondary sources). Interviews were conducted during formal meetings. In each firm, the predecessor and all successors were interviewed. In addition, in all except one case, an additional stakeholder (a third-party adviser involved in the transfer of leader-

Table 6.1 Description of interviewees

	Sector of activity	Predecessor	Successors	Others
Firm B	Construction	Father	1 son, 1 daughter	External member of the board Succession adviser
Firm D	Plumbing and heating supplies	Father	3 sons	Succession adviser
Firm H	Hydrocarbon processing industry	Father	2 sons, 1 daughter	Accountant
Firm J	Construction	Father	2 sons, 1 daughter	Accountant
Firm M	Machining	Father	2 sons, 1 daughter	Succession adviser
Firm T	Financial services	Father	2 sons	*

Note: *Unfortunately, the adviser passed away at the time of our study into the succession.

ship) was also interviewed. Twenty-eight interviews, lasting an average of two hours, were conducted (see Table 6.1).

Six separate, extensive case studies were elaborated from the data gathered from primary and secondary sources. To improve internal validity, the analysis was presented to respondents for discussion purposes (interviews and workshops) and the data were then triangulated.

All six firms selected to complete the study are success stories in terms of turnover and staff growth. Four of them (firms D, J, M and T) have even won awards for the quality of their succession. Three companies are now managed by the second generation and the other three by the third generation.

ANALYSIS AND DISCUSSION

We present the results of our research using the framework provided by Handler's four-phase model of family business succession (1994).[3]

Family Business Succession Process

Incubation and transfer of tacit knowledge through socialization with the family firms

None of the successions we studied were initially planned as a succession to several family members in shared leadership. The child already involved in the firm was the initiator of the shared leadership, motivating his/her siblings to join the company. As we will see further, once the other sibling (or siblings) joined the FF and was socialized within the firm (and SC was transferred to him/her), the predecessor found it difficult to opt for a single successor and to then justify that choice.

For all of six firms, one of the most critical elements of the incubation phase was the beginning of the tacit knowledge transfer: the process of the successors learning how all elements of the firm were connected and coordinated. This phase was about socialization within the FF, being the primary process in the transfer of tacit knowledge to the potential successors. That said, in every case the successors' personal commitments were the determining factor for learning tasks and procedures within the FF.

Implementation and the transfer of networks

In this phase, the incumbent started to actively transfer knowledge and networks to the successors to train them to cope with the business environment of the FF. The predecessors gradually acquainted the successors with their business contacts and networks. There was a large degree of hands-on involvement of the incumbent and successor in the transfer of network contacts. In all six cases, the predecessor made sure that he passed on his network of contacts and gradually introduced his children to the most important stakeholders of the FF: 'My father introduced us, my brother and me, to the people we would be doing business with . . . the clients, the banker, the agents . . . he let us work with them gradually' (successor Philippe, Firm T).

It should be mentioned that the transfer of networks has been closely connected in the beginning with the transfer of managerial responsibility. This was particularly evident in cases D, J, M and T. In these cases, the network transfer to successors strengthened their sense of legitimacy and their recognition by the business community; thus, it provided the foundation for sibling team succession.

The transfer of tacit knowledge continued during the entire implementation phase as the successors began to take responsibility for the FF's operations.

Joint management: between leadership and letting go

The predecessors gradually delegated their functions, projects and responsibilities to their children. However, despite having handed over the firm leadership to their children, the incumbents kept controlling shares, and therefore their right to supervise the management of their successors. During this period, the fathers often felt that the children were going too fast. 'When my children started making purchases I was worried . . . I thought they were going too quickly and weren't taking into account the time you need to run several firms. I was tempted to make them reconsider their decision . . . even though I didn't actually do it' (predecessor, Firm B). The predecessors did, however, give their successors enough autonomy so that they felt that they could innovate and use their initiative: 'My father let us make decisions, even if we lost money a few times. Later, he confessed he had made provisions so that we could take risks, and he had planned to intervene if we lost more than the amount for which he had made provision' (successor Julia, Firm H).

The predecessor retained a measure of control for a time, allowing the transfer of SC (in terms of tacit knowledge and network contacts) to continue. In this phase of the succession process, the SC transfer was according to the roles and the responsibilities of successors within the FF. They took operational decisions individually according to each of their roles within the FF, while strategic decisions were taken together. In each case, the predecessors accompanied the successors to train them and to advise them in making strategic decisions. The incumbent played a mediator role between successors.

New leadership and predecessor disengagement

In this phase, the sibling succession teams assumed FF leadership. However, at the time of our research, the predecessors in firms B, J, T and H had not completely left the company. They were still physically present, even maintaining their initial offices. While they no longer directly participated in decision-making, they still wanted to be kept current with the business: 'I do insist that my children keep me regularly informed about how current projects are progressing, and about new projects. I can still give good advice, after all!' (predecessor, Firm J). The successors still consulted their predecessors regarding strategic decisions. The predecessors continued to play a mediating role between the successors and the firm's employees: 'I often go talk to our employees, or they come to talk to me. They tell me what they think about the firm or the way my children are running it. I listen to them, and I offer them advice before I go and talk to my sons' (predecessor, Firm T). In firms H and M, the predecessors had entirely disengaged. The management board (Firm M) and the advisers

(Firm H) substantially contributed to ensuring that the timing for disengagement was respected.

In this stage, the transfer of SC was completed in all six cases, and successors worked to further develop it. They especially considered networking as an entrepreneurial resource that requires continual development and management to maximize its effectiveness. In all six cases, the successors expanded the networks of the FF. Most successors became active members in organizations that support and bring together businesspeople; for example, one of the successors of Firm D is the former president of YPO Montreal.[4]

Summary of findings In all six cases, the transfer of the tacit knowledge started during the incubation period and was amplified during the implementation period; the transfer of networks mainly started during the implementation phase. The decision to transfer the FF to the sibling team occurred in all six cases in the third phase of the succession process, that is, the joint management phase. During this phase, the transfer of tacit knowledge and networks continued, but was according to the successors' roles within the FF. In the last phase of succession process (that is, new leadership and predecessor disengagement), the sibling succession teams fully assumed leadership and started expanding SC, while the predecessor retained a mentor's role.

A Model for Sibling Team Succession

This study illustrates how the early transmission of intangible capital to children working in an FF creates the premise for the transfer from controlling owner to a team of sibling partners. In the cases studied, the idea of transferring the firm to several successors came as a result of the strong performance of the children within the company and their appropriation of intangible capital (structural and relational). The predecessors subsequently felt that it was time to retire, as the next generation was ready to take over and continue their original mission. The family then got involved, with a gradual move towards a sibling team succession.

We can conclude that the FF transfer from controlling owner to sibling partners emerged as a response to: (1) the requirements of the predecessor who wished to designate one successor but had welcomed more than one of his children into his business; (2) the willingness of the child already in the firm to be supported by his/her sibling(s) as co-leaders of the firm; (3) the gradual appropriation of the structural capital by the successors working in the family business; and (4) the need to preserve and enhance relational capital. This trend is more obvious for FFs operating in the services sector that require significantly higher levels of relational capital, namely increased confidence in relationships and access to information and knowledge intrinsic in relationships.

The Role of Social Capital in Sibling Team Succession

Structural capital as a precursor of sibling team succession

As mentioned above, the sibling collective successions in our case studies were not planned. Either one child was already present in the firm and invited his/her sibling(s) to become involved, or several children previously worked in the firm, and some of them decided to manage it together. It is interesting to highlight here that these successions with several children emerged gradually. In almost all cases, the father wanted to share ownership equally among all of his children, and he wanted to designate one child to be the successor, which is similar to the work of Cater and Justis (2010). It should be noted that the successors, who were not sought by the incumbent for the leadership role, did not join the FF because there were tailor-made positions for them. Instead, they joined the FF to meet existing needs (there were vacant positions for which their competencies fit). They actively participated in the appropriation of knowledge and skills that they rendered mutually interdependent. They showed strong commitment and motivation to collectively face problems and challenges.

Finally, the members of the sibling succession team were competent and had complementary profiles (confirmed by psychometric testing) (Harper, 2008). Their complementary profiles contributed to the creation of a holistic and collective decision-making process. This is in contrast to the situation experienced by the predecessor. When the company was set up, the founder needed to be versatile and to play a number of roles, from salesman and bookkeeper to head marketer and bill collector. He was the one who established the business network. However, it is important to note that a FF's growth requires the development of networks and the assembling of both diverse and complementary skills. Thus, we found in the companies studied here that as the children joined the family business they were assigned different operational responsibilities and they made decisions as collegial teams.[5] This facilitated the transfer of tacit knowledge from predecessors to successors, and also between successors.

During the joint management phase, the management team constituted both predecessor and successors. The incumbent did not rein in innovative behaviour when he was acting in the capacity of mentor. While he retained control shares of the firm, he allowed his successors to act on their ideas and to take risks. He operated between controlling and letting go. This idea is important and has nuances of the proposition of Cater and Justis (2010); they state that the failure to release control by prior generation FF leaders inhibits the development of shared leadership. Here the predecessor, from his position in the background, stabilizes the processes.

Relational capital as a trigger for sibling team succession

Relational capital as part of family business SC covers several aspects, from relationships with suppliers and customers to image and reputation. This exploratory study confirms that relational capital is a fundamental asset for FFs. All six companies acknowledged the importance and necessity of properly transferring relational capital to the next generation. Moreover, our findings show that family succession teams increased existing relational capital in terms of networks.

In the studies referred to in this chapter, of all the elements of relational capital, reputation was mentioned most. Reputation (that is, stakeholder perceptions with regard to an organization's ability to deliver valued outcomes) provides the firm with an asset that influences subsequent performance (Rindova et al., 2010).[6] Thus, the transfer of leadership within the FF must neither bring prejudice to its reputation nor arouse the suspicions of stakeholders about the firm's new leaders.

In the case of Firm T,[7] the fear of losing the company's good reputation was a strong argument for Martin Tremblay to decide to transfer the companies to both his sons. Both sons had gradually appropriated the SC of the FF in terms of tacit knowledge and networks, and this facilitated the FF transfer to their sibling partnership.

Successors also gradually became accustomed to shared leadership. In the case of Firm J, the predecessor entrusted each of his children with different executive roles within the company, knowing that they had complementary profiles. The predecessor organized the transfer of leadership and SC (Arrègle et al., 2004), putting each child in contact with the stakeholders concerned. As successors were each introduced to different stakeholders, the process of sibling team succession was accelerated, and they could strengthen and further develop the existing networks independently.

LIMITATIONS

This research is not without limitations. The qualitative study of the six Canadian (Québec-based) FFs does not allow inferences to be made as to whether or not the results would also apply to family business successions in other countries. Furthermore, we only studied cases where the sibling team succession was successful, where the successors had increased the SC of the family firms, especially in terms of networks. We feel it would be worthwhile to study sibling team successions that were unsuccessful. In addition, to provide external validation of our results, it would be conceivable to formulate a questionnaire, based on the elements identified by the present study, to collect data from a statistically representative sample of successions in FFs. We could then turn our attention to hybrid collective successions (composed of both family members and FF employees).

CONCLUSION

The purpose of this study was to examine the role of SC in FF succession from controlling owners to sibling teams. One of the contributions of this study is the linking of the four phases of the succession process to the transfer of different types of SC and the role of incumbents and successors: (1) *incubation*, the beginning of the tacit knowledge transfer and successors' commitment to acquire such knowledge; (2) *implementation*, the beginning of network transfers and the continuation of tacit knowledge transfer, and the incumbent is actively involved in their transfer to successors; (3) *joint management*, the oriented transfer of tacit knowledge and network contacts towards successors according to their role and responsibilities within the FF and the incumbent takes a mediation role between successors; and (4) *new leadership and predecessor disengagement*, the transfer of SC is completed and successors start to expand it, and the incumbent retains the mentor role.

The introductory case highlights the fact that the transfer of SC to successors begins before either the transfer of ownership or leadership in the family business. Both of Martin Tremblay's sons gained credibility and legitimacy as potential successors through their integration of the FF's networks and their desire to enlarge it. Subsequently, their appropriation of the tacit knowledge of the FF and their willingness and commitment to assume its leadership constituted key elements for their sibling partnership.

The analysis of six cases of successful successions further allowed us to identify tacit knowledge as a precursor to sibling team succession, and to acknowledge the importance of networks and reputation, which have a trigger effect upon sibling team succession. Finally, this study suggests that sibling team successions are a promising solution to retain and strengthen the SC of a FF as the company is passed on to subsequent generations.

NOTES

1. Names have been changed for confidentiality reasons.
2. Organisation for Economic Cooperation and Development.
3. See 'Family succession to several heirs'.
4. The Young Presidents' Organization (YPO) is a global network of young CEOs, with approximately 18,000 members in more than 100 countries.
5. Except in the case of Firm B.
6. According to Rindova et al. (2010: 611), reputation is a sociocognitive construct, which is 'characterized by two dimensions – quality and prominence – that together determine its value as an intangible asset contributing to firm competitive advantage'.
7. The Tremblay case presented at the beginning of the chapter.

REFERENCES

Allouche, J. and B. Amann (2000), 'L'entreprise familiale un état de l'art', *Finance Contrôle Stratégie*, **3** (1), 33–79.

Aronoff, C.E. (1998), 'Megatrends in family business', *Family Business Review*, **9** (3), 181–5.

Arrègle, J.L., R. Durand and P. Very (2004), 'Origines du capital social et avantages concurrentiels des firmes familiales', *Management*, **7** (1), 13–36.

Arrègle, J.L., M.A. Hitt, D.G. Sirmon and P. Very (2007), 'The development of organizational social capital: attributes of family firms', *Journal of Management Studies*, **44** (1), 73–95.

Brockhaus, R.H. (2004), 'Family business succession: suggestions for future research', *Family Business Review*, **17** (2), 165–77.

Cabrera-Suarez, K., P. De Saa-Pérez and D. García-Almeida (2001), 'The succession process from a resource- and knowledge-based view of the family firm', *Family Business Review*, **14** (1), 37–46.

Cadieux, L. (2007), 'Succession in small and medium-sized family businesses: toward a typology of predecessor roles during and after instatement of the successor', *Family Business Review*, **20** (2), 95–109.

Cadieux, L., J. Lorrain and P. Hugron (2002), 'Succession in women-owned family businesses: a case study', *Family Business Review*, **15** (1), 17–30.

Carr, J.C., M.S. Cole, J.K. Ring and D.P. Blettner (2011), 'A measure of variations in internal social capital among family firms', *Entrepreneurship: Theory and Practice*, **35** (6), 1207–27.

Cater, J.J. and R.T. Justis (2010), 'The development and implementation of shared leadership in multi-generational family firms', *Management Research Review*, **33** (6), 563–85.

Chua, J.H., J.J. Chrisman and P. Sharma (2003), 'Succession and non-succession concerns of FFs and agency relationship with non-family managers', *Family Business Review*, **16** (2), 79–107.

Coeurderoy, R. and A. Lwango (2008), 'Capital social, coût de mesure et efficacité organisationnelles: y a-t-il un avantage spécifique à l'entreprise familiale?', Working Paper 04, Louvain School of Management.

Conner, K. and C. Prahalad (1996), 'A resource-based theory of the firm: knowledge versus opportunism', *Organization Science*, **7** (4), 477–501.

De Castro, G.M., P. López Sáez and J.E. Navas López (2004), 'The role of corporate reputation in developing relational capital', *Journal of Intellectual Capital*, **5** (4), 575–85.

De Freyman, J., K. Richomme-Huet and R. Paturel (2007), 'Social capital transfer and family business succession: a qualitative exploratory study', 3rd FERC, Mexico.

Durst, S. and S. Güldenberg (2009), 'The meaning of intangible assets: new insights into external company succession in SMEs', *Electronic Journal of Knowledge Management*, **7** (4), 437–46.

Eisenhardt, K.M. (1989), 'Building theories from case study research', *The Academy of Management Review*, **14** (4), 532–50.

Gersick, K., J. Davis, M. McCollon Hampton and I. Lansberg (1997), *Generation to Generation: Life Cycles of the Family Business*, Boston, MA: Harvard Business School Press.

Granovetter, M.S. (1992), 'Problems of explanation in economic sociology', in N. Nohria and R. Eccles (eds), *Networks and Organizations*, Boston, MA: HBS Press, pp. 25–56.

Grant, R. (1996), 'Toward a knowledge-based view of the firm', *Strategic Management Journal*, **17** (Winter Special Issue), 109–22.

Handler, W.C. (1994), 'Succession in family business: a review of the research', *Family Business Review*, **7** (2), 133–57.

Harper, D.A. (2008), 'Towards a theory of entrepreneurial teams', *Journal of Business Venturing*, **23**, 613–26.

Kepner, E. (1983), 'The family and the firm: a coevolutionary perspective', *Organizational Dynamics*, **12** (1), 57–70.

Le Breton-Miller, I., D. Miller and L.P. Steier (2004), 'Toward an integrative model of effective FOB succession', *Entrepreneurship Theory and Practice*, **28** (4), 305–28.

Leonard-Barton, D. (1995), *Wellsprings of Knowledge: Building and Sustaining the Sources of Innovation*, Urbana, IL: University of Illinois at Urbana-Champaign's Academy for Entrepreneurial Leadership Historical Research Reference in Entrepreneurship.

Long, R.G. and J.J. Chrisman (2013), 'Management succession in family business', in L. Melin, M. Nordqvist and P. Sharma (eds), *SAGE Handbook of Family Business*, Thousand Oaks, CA: Sage, in press.

Malecki, E. (1997), *Technology and Economic Development: The Dynamics of Local, Regional, and National Competitiveness*, Toronto, ON: Longman.

MassMutual (2007), *American Family Business Survey*, Atlanta, GA: Kennesaw State and Family Firm Institute.

Mazzola, P., G. Marchisio and J. Astrachan (2008), 'Strategic planning in family business: a powerful developmental tool for the next generation', *Family Business Review*, **21** (3), 239–58.

Nahapiet, J. and S. Ghoshal (1998), 'Social capital, intellectual capital, and the organizational advantage', *Academy of Management Review*, **23**, 242–66.

Nonaka, I. and H. Takeuchi (1995), *The Knowledge Creating Company: How Japanese Companies Create the Dynamics of Innovation*, New York: Oxford University Press.

OECD (2009), 'Insights: human capital. What is social capital?', accessed 14 March 2013 at www.oecd.org/insights/37966934.pdf.

Pasi, M. (2004), 'Problems in transfer of business experienced by Finnish entrepreneurs', *Journal of Small Business and Enterprise Development*, **11** (1), 130–39.

Patton, E. and S.H. Applebaum (2003), 'The case for case studies in management research', *Management Research News*, **26** (5), 60–72.

Polanyi, M. (1966), *The Tacit Dimension*, Gloucester, MA: Peter Smith.

Rindova, V., I. Williamson and A. Petkova (2010), 'Reputation as an intangible asset: reflections on theory and methods in two empirical studies of business school reputations', *Journal of Management*, **36** (3), 610–19.

Salvato, C. and L. Melin (2008), 'Creating value across generations in family-controlled businesses: the role of family social capital', *Family Business Review*, **21** (3), 259–76.

Sandoval-Arzaga, F., M. Ramírez-Pasillas and M. Fonseca-Paredes (2011), 'Knowledge integration in Latin American family firms', in *Understanding Entrepreneurial Family Businesses in Uncertain Environments Opportunities and Resources in Latin America*, Cheltenham, UK and Northampton, MA, USA: Edward Elgar, pp. 181–202.

Sekaran, U. (2003), *Research Methods for Business*, 4th ed., Hoboken, NJ: John Wiley and Sons.

Sharma, P. (2004), 'An overview of the field of family business studies: current status and direction for the future', *Family Business Review*, **17** (1), 1–36.

Sonfield, M.C., R.N. Lussier, S. Pfeifer, S. Manikutty, L. Maherault and L. Verdier (2005), 'A cross-national investigation of first-generation, second-generation and third-generation family businesses', *Journal of Small Business Strategy*, **16** (1), 9–26.

Steier, L. (2001), 'Next-generation entrepreneurs and succession: an exploratory study of modes and means of managing social capital', *Family Business Review*, **XIV** (3), 259–27.

Ward, J.L. (1987), *Keeping the Family Business Healthy: How to Plan for Continuing Growth, Profitability, and Family Leadership*, San Francisco, CA: Jossey-Bass.

7. Opportunities and dilemmas of social capital: insights from Uganda

Waswa Balunywa, Peter Rosa, Diana Nandagire Ntamu and Shakilah Nagujja

IGANGA GENERAL MERCHANDISE

Honourable Sarah Kwesiga, the Speaker of the National Parliament of Uganda and a friend of the Sentongo family, has known the family for many years. Mr Charles Sentongo is the current head of the family. One of his sons, Mr George Sentongo, works as an assistant clerk in the parliament. George invited Sarah to attend the graduation ceremony of his son. In addition, he asked her to use this opportunity to convince his father, Charles, to devote more time to the business in order to safeguard the future of both the business and the family. Sarah is reflecting on what to say to Charles.

As a local councillor for the last seven years, Mr Charles Sentongo has become more involved in politics, leaving him less time for his family's business. He has been the anchor of this business that he built over the years through his numerous contacts not only in Iganga town but also all over Uganda. It is these contacts that had enabled him and other family members to grow not only their core family business but also the other enterprises they started. At the peak of his involvement in the business, he would give it between 10 and 16 hours a day. Now, several days go by without him checking on the business. At times, he fails to attend meetings in which crucial decisions are to be made.

Uganda went through a period of dictatorship during Idi Amin's rule in the 1970s. It was in 1986 that a new government was formed which introduced political pluralism into the country. This attracted Charles to join politics. When he joined, the responsibilities were light and did not require a lot of his time. In recent years, however, he has increasingly spent more time in politics. Charles had talked to George about quitting the business. The consequence of spending less time in the business was a decline in sales. George felt that if his father quit the business, the oldest family business in Iganga town would collapse. Unfortunately, this would also affect the businesses run by Charles's brothers.

The Sentongo family has been in business since 1920 when Mr Fred Sentongo, Charles's grandfather, founded the business. Fred had been a farmer who bought produce from fellow farmers in the countryside and sold it to buyers in Iganga town located in the east of Uganda, on the highway from Mombasa in Kenya to Uganda's capital, Kampala. Iganga became famous for commercial production of cotton, coffee and food products introduced in the early 1900s. The British, who had arrived in Uganda in the late nineteenth century, had built the Uganda railway in the 1920s, primarily to ferry cotton to the sea. A large number of people from the Indian subcontinent came to Uganda as railway technicians and popularized trade in many parts of Uganda, including Iganga town.

Fred saw an opportunity to sell agricultural products in Iganga. He bought products from the countryside and sold them mainly to Indians in Iganga town. He was the head of a large African extended family with 30 children, though only 11 of them were alive when Fred died in 1950. Several years before his death, Fred had inducted one of his sons, Alphonso Mugerwa, into the business. Alphonso took over his father's business and the family responsibilities. He grew the business, making it more competitive. Like his father, Alphonso inducted his sons into the business, though it was his second eldest son, Charles Sentongo, who worked most closely with his father. By the time of Alphonso's death in 1969, Charles had become very knowledgeable about the business.

In 1971, two years after Charles's father's death, Idi Amin overthrew Milton Obote's elected government in a military coup. Amin decided to expel the Indians who had since the early 1920s been the key players in the growth of businesses in Uganda. The departure of the Indians created a vacuum and opportunity for expansion. Before the Indians left, Charles's shop was one of the biggest shops in town. With the departure of the Indians, the business grew further and continued to be one of the leading businesses in town. The Sentongo family business was unique. Charles operated a business that dealt with selling bicycles, bicycle parts and also repaired bicycles. However, in another part of the shop, his brothers sold different types of merchandise that they brought to Iganga from other parts of Uganda and neighbouring countries.

In 1979 Idi Amin was ousted, elections were held, and Milton Obote was re-elected. However, the elections were disputed and a civil war emerged in some parts of the country, eventually leading to the overthrow of the Obote government in 1986. Despite this civil strife, the Sentongo family business continued to thrive primarily because of Charles's network and contacts in the government. The new government introduced a popular local system that involved electing leaders that the community wanted. Charles was elected as chairman of the village Local Council (LC). Two of his brothers, Mr Edson Ssali and Mr John Lukwago, were also elected as chairpersons of LC in the respective areas where they resided. LC is the basic administrative unit in a locality and the chairperson of the locality has power over issues that affect the community. The chairperson provides references for those who want to acquire passports, register telephones and get electricity and water connections. S/he also witnesses contracts involving the sale of land and any other property; settles disputes and oversees the maintenance of the community's security, among other functions.

Charles was highly respected not only in the town, but also all around his district. He was consulted both on business and civic matters. He was known to be an honest and trustworthy person. Inheriting the business from his father, he also inherited his father's contacts. These contacts included customers, suppliers and friends. Over the years, Sentongo had acquired his own contacts that enabled his business to grow. Not only was he able to secure credit from his suppliers, he also secured supply orders from government and non-governmental organizations (NGOs).

Family members looked up to Charles for guidance and advice. In family matters, his word was final. While there was no written agreement on ownership of the business, Charles worked with his brothers as if they were owners. Most of them were employed in the shop and received a salary. Whoever wanted to establish a personal business, would seek Charles's permission and approval and he would provide the necessary capital. Those who left brought goods to Charles's shop to sell them from there. Having been recently elected to the LC, Charles's political responsibilities had increased. He was active on various committees of the council and his opinions had a significant impact on decisions made. He introduced transparency and credibility into the activities of the LC.

In recent years Charles spent more time attending to his duties as a councillor than he did at the family's business. In his late 60s, Charles felt he did not have the energy to give more attention to the business. Instead, he was more drawn to serve his community. He had indicated to his brothers his desire to get out of the business and concentrate on political work to serve the community. They had discussed the fact that his absence was affecting the business adversely.

In an earlier discussion between George and Sarah, he had impressed upon her that Charles needed to have a well-phased exit that would support the health of the business. She was not sure how to approach Charles, whom she had known for some time. Sarah wanted to recommend that Charles spend a little more time in the business, especially in the family business meetings, as it was clear to her that his absence would very likely lead to the collapse of this family business.

QUESTIONS

1. How did the Sentongo family create social capital?
2. What are the advantages and disadvantages of social capital to the Sentongo family?
3. How will Charles Sentongo's exit of the business affect the social capital of the family?

INTRODUCTION

Many resources and capabilities available to family firms emerge from family involvement and interactions (Habbershon and Williams, 1999; Chrisman et al., 2003). Such resources help the family business to succeed. Among these resources is social capital (Pearson et al., 2008), which confers unique competitive advantage to family firms. Arregle et al. (2007) describe social capital as the relationship between individuals and organizations that facilitates action and creates value in family firms. Bourdieu (1986) had earlier defined social capital as the aggregate of the actual and potential resources that are linked to possession of a durable network of more or less institutionalized relationships. Social capital arises from the social network and relations between individuals within an organization and outside it. Coleman (1988) asserts that social capital is productive because it facilitates the achievement of objectives. Social capital enables 'bonding' between individuals and in the process creates good relations and 'bridging' which permits organizations and individuals to connect to each other and benefit from one another.

Families are social units in which individuals relate to one another as a result of blood, marriage and other relations. These relationships create social capital that bonds the family members together. As family members relate to outsiders, they create bridges to other people. Social capital thus creates opportunities for the achievement of organizational goals and is invariably viewed as a positive resource. The possibility that, in some circumstances, social capital can have adverse effects has not been examined. The family business literature lacks discussion on too much social capital arising from social networks and social relations. This study presents a case of social capital in a family business that on the one hand creates opportunities for the family business but on the other hand also creates challenges that disadvantage the family business.

Iganga General Merchandise (IGM) is a family business that has been growing largely through bridging and bonding social capital built over three generations. Recently, however, social capital has disadvantaged the business as the head of the family started paying less attention to the business. The case presents the challenge of understanding how social capital can act as a disadvantage. Social capital resources are used to pursue the economic objectives of the firm. Arregle et al. (2007) put emphasis on the process of creation of social capital rather than its content. Nahapiet and Ghoshal (1998) argue that the process is more dynamic in nature than the content and the process is constituted by stability, interaction, interdependence and closure.

In this study, we begin by describing the African context in which this family enterprise exists. Thereafter, we review literature on social capital and family business, highlighting the social capital that arises from bonding and bridging relationships and how family firms create this capital and use it for family success. We then explore the theoretical advantages and disadvantages of social capital. Finally these issues are explored in the case of IGM and how social capital helped the success of the family firm. In so doing we address a more general research gap, how modern family businesses can emerge from complex traditional family systems in a developing country.

THE CONTEXT OF FAMILY BUSINESSES IN SUB-SAHARAN AFRICA

Whenever reference is made to Africa, what comes to mind is sub-Saharan Africa, that is, 'black' Africa. However, Africa is generally divided into Arab Africa in the north, sub-Saharan Africa and South Africa. These three regions have distinct cultures, economic histories and statuses. The African Arab north is generally seen as a middle-income area. It is predominantly Muslim. South Africa is more developed. It has a large black population that is largely poor and a white population that is largely wealthy. The white population migrated to South Africa in the seventeenth century. In contrast, sub-Saharan Africa consists largely of the black African countries that have many cultural, linguistic and economic similarities, yet are still very diverse. Sub-Saharan Africa is largely underdeveloped and with a large number of people living in the rural areas. According to the World Bank Development Report (2012), the average rural population in this region in 2010 was 63.6 per cent, compared to less than 5 per cent in Western Europe. In Uganda the figure is 85 per cent. They also have lower per capita incomes and large household sizes, implying bigger and more complex extended families. Thus, the African concept of family differs appreciably from that of the West where the smaller nuclear family prevails (Bohannan, 1963; Khavul et al., 2009).

Despite the impact of foreign influence, sub-Saharan African families continue to be large in size and are of the extended family type. Richmond and Gestrin (1998) state that in terms of African belief, life can be meaningful only in a community. In traditional African societies, it is widely believed that individual needs take second place. Blain Harden, cited in Richmond and Gestrin (1998), states that the extended family is called a day care, social security and welfare system. It babysits children of working parents, it keeps the elderly from feeling useless, feeds the unemployed and gives refuge to the disabled. The family thus takes care of everybody, creating a powerful social network (Khavul et al., 2009).

The extended family is also strong in North Africa. Achoui (2006) reports that Algerians also have extended families (see Table 7.1). On other hand, the South African family structure consists of the Western family system for the white community and the traditional black African family system for the black community.

While it appears that there are a lot of commonalities among Africans, studies by social anthropologists of traditional family and marriage systems in Africa have shown major differences. Examples include classic studies such as Levi-Strauss (1945), Radcliffe-Brown and Forde (1950), Evans-Pritchard (1951), Middleton (1958), and more recent research in the context of family firms by Stewart (2003). These studies have shown that kinship is the basis of social and economic organization (Mair, 1967). While matrilineal families are found in some countries in West Africa, Angola, southern Tanzania and Mozambique, Uganda and the rest of Africa are largely patrilineal societies. Despite these differences, African families are large and identified based on lineage. The extended family is partly created through the lineage system that creates a family and a community that is linked together. The lineage therefore defines the community and the strength of the community. Strong lineages have greater power to access resources. Therefore, having many children was historically vital for the strength of the family and the community.

Anthropologists, however, indicate that the strength of the ties among the community and family members reduce as the degree of kinship reduces (Evans-Pritchard, 1940; Dyson-Hudson, 1966). Kinship is therefore a basis for supporting an enterprise. The closer the individual, the more support he will give or get. These close links are weakened when tension develops between members of the family, usually due to sharing

Table 7.1 Key differences between North, South and sub-Saharan Africa (Uganda)

Item	Uganda (an example of a poor sub-Saharan country)	South Africa	Algeria (an example from North-Arab Africa)
Rural population	85%	42.2%	33.5%
Average family size	5 people	4.2 people	6.68 people
Income per capita	$506	$6100	$4500
Average number of children	6.7 children	2.38 children	3.1 children
Tradition, social change and the extended family.	Ethnically diverse with major ethnic and linguistic groups (Bantu, Nilotic, Cushitic) with large, diverse and complex lineage-based traditional family and political systems and large extended families. Social change important since the early twentieth century, accelerating since independence, but large rural population ensures retention of many features of traditional family system.	Ethnically relatively uniform, mostly Bantu speakers, but much more ethnically diverse in terms of non-African immigrant whites and Asians. Large extended families common in rural areas. Social change has been pronounced since early nineteenth century, and large number of rural-urban migrants have established distinctive urban communities with smaller families. Much less ethnically diverse.	Less ethnically diverse, Arabic and Berber speakers, predominantly Muslim (Muslim cultures). Extended families are large and important, but not as complex or diverse as in the rest of Africa. North Africa has been in close contact with Europe and Asia for centuries, and has experienced phases of European occupation since the Greco-Roman period, and has maintained extensive trade links.

Source: Generated from data collected.

of resources. In such cases, individual members tend to assert themselves (Long, 1977, 2001). It therefore takes a powerful leader to keep the family together. Besides, the degree of cohesiveness of communities was also determined by whether societies had evolved into kingdoms or not (Middleton, 1958). Areas with kingdoms tend to be more cohesive than those without. The Ashante in West Africa and Baganda in Uganda are examples of kingdom areas. The Kikuyu in Kenya and Talensi in Ghana are examples of areas without kingdoms.

With the influence of foreign religions and Western culture, a lot has changed in many parts of Africa. Families are becoming smaller. Many Africans moving to cities are becoming more individualistic and less prone to sharing resources. Gender roles are changing as women are becoming more independent (Robertson, 1976; Allman, 1991). These changes have brought about a blend of different family traditions. A typical Ugandan still has links with parents and grandparents and supports them. This has the potential to create social capital. Ugandans in family businesses still draw on their relationships with family members. Those in a rural setting with a traditional family structure have stronger relations and therefore more social capital. However, Elkan (1988) observed that extended family is an impediment to the development of modern family businesses because it draws away resources; however, where the family is bringing capabilities, it is a resource. The traditional African family system is an opportunity for the development of social capital and business growth though it may also be a handicap. This chapter examines the role of social capital in a family business in this interesting setting.

THEORETICAL CONSIDERATIONS

Families are social units constituted by a network of individuals bound together by blood relationships and marriage. This network has inherent social capital that is important in the success of the family business. Social capital is the resource that emerges from the capabilities of the individual members of the family and the advantages that emerge from the relationships between family members. Social capital creates bonds between individuals and improves interpersonal relationships. It also enables bridges which link one person or group to another. By interacting, people bond and have a sense of obligation towards one another. By bridging, more individuals or groups are linked. Both bonding and bridging lead to the development of resources and capabilities that a family can exploit.

Habbershon and Williams (1999) and Habbershon et al. (2003) call this familiness. They argue that familiness is the idiosyncratic resources and capabilities available in family firms that emerge from family involvement and interactions. Social capital is what these resources and capabilities are (Arregle et al., 2007; Hoffman et al., 2006; Pearson et al., 2008). Putnam (1993) viewed social capital as a resource that could improve the efficiency of society through social networks. Social capital is therefore a resource and capability a family firm can use to achieve its goals.

Arregle et al. (2007) emphasize the process of creating social capital rather than its content in highlighting its importance as a capability and resource for the family firm. The content perspective is the structural, relational and cognitive dimension of social capital. The process deals with how social capital is formed, it includes stability, interaction, interdependency and closure (Nahapiet and Ghoshal, 1998; Yli-Renko et al., 2001). Stability depends on how long the members of the family have been interacting, which leads to clarity and visibility of mutual obligations and also leads to development of trust and norms of cooperation (Putnam, 1993). The interactions between individuals help to develop and maintain the mutual obligation in a social network (Bourdieu, 1986). Interdependence, on the other hand, is the level by which the people in the network depend on one another. High levels of social capital will develop if there is interdependence (Nahapiet and Ghoshal, 1998). The relationship between family members creates social capital (Coleman, 1988).

Arregle et al. (2007) argue that organizational social capital in a family business is derived from family social capital and that family social capital is determined by membership, interactions and interdependence among members and closure. Familiness creates a unique bundle of resources used in a family firm. While social capital has a content aspect, it also takes other forms, including bonding and bridging social capital (Adler and Kwon, 2002). Sharma and Manikutty (2005) state that bonding capital enables the formation of dense networks within a collective unit such as a family or an organization. These networks in turn help build trust, internal cohesiveness and solidarity in pursuit for common goals (Coleman, 1988). Bridging capital on the other hand focuses on the external links an actor has with other actors. These may be individuals, groups, families or organizations. A bridge facilitates the achievement of the goals of a family unit or organization by providing information, identifying opportunities and being able to negotiate in contractual relationships with other individuals or groups (Adler and Kwon, 2002; Sharma and Manikutty, 2005).

Pearson et al. (2008) confirm that familiness results in organizational performance that transforms into economic performance and that value creation is closely aligned with family interaction and involvement in the business. Families with large numbers of members are expected to build a higher level of organizational social capital. Bonding capital emerges from that close interaction among family members and becomes a resource that gives the business the ability to compete. It is a family bond that acts to create the familiness (Sharma, 2008). Bridges occur when a relationship is established between an individual or business unit and an outsider such that the interaction of these two bodies creates a resource or a capability that enables the organization to exploit opportunities. The bridge also creates familiness, which enables the organization to succeed. Bonding and bridging social capital thus create resources and capabilities that enable a firm to achieve its goals.

ADVANTAGES AND DISADVANTAGES OF SOCIAL CAPITAL

The nature and size of family differs from community to community. In the sub-Saharan African context, in particular Uganda, social capital has unique advantages and disadvantages as discussed below:

Family Size: Bigger Extended Families and Lineages

The extended family as defined by the authors is any blood relationship from either paternal or maternal lineages that has a relationship of dependency on a specific family. Hence:

Proposition 1a: The extended family increases the potential family resources available in terms of larger networks, and offers more choice of family members to contribute to the business in terms of knowledge, labour and financial capital.

However the extended family increases the number of dependents and thus increases the number of people sharing the profit. Hence:

Proposition 1b: The large extended family can be a disadvantage and a drain on resources because of the increased number of dependents and obligations, and the increased potential for conflict as family size and depth increases.

Bonding: More Community Based Cohesion

The traditional African family as a community is very cohesive. This leads to closer bonding which enhances familiness. African societies have elaborate ceremonies which increase contact and social capital. This may reinforce family business. Hence:

Proposition 2a: The interactions of family members will produce even greater social capital benefits in African societies owing to strong community based cohesion.

However, cohesion depends not so much on 'community spirit' but more on the authority and influence of the head of the family. The head has the power to regulate family activities which may stifle initiatives in the business. Elaborate ceremonies can also be costly. Hence:

Proposition 2b: The community based cohesion may be counterbalanced by the disadvantages of patriarchy and the financial drain caused by ceremonies.

Also, social change, including migration to cities, is also reducing contact and cohesion among families. This can adversely affect family businesses. Hence:

Proposition 2c: Bonding and cohesion within African families are being eroded by social change, leading to a dilution of the beneficial social capital effects associated with a bonded and large extended family.

Bridging

Social change brought migrants to African countries, this developed new relationships, providing new networking and cooperation opportunities (Parkin, 1966). Successful families also network with government officials and politicians. This has created opportunities for bridging ties. Hence:

Proposition 3a: Social change has produced widespread opportunities for establishing bridging social capital in Africa to the potential benefit of family businesses.

But:

Proposition 3b: Social change has also provided increased opportunities to pursue social and political goals which can divert bridging social capital to the disadvantage of family businesses.

METHODS

Iganga district is one of the most densely populated districts in Uganda, and Iganga town is the administrative centre of the area. It is located on the Kampala to Mombasa highway. Indians who came to Uganda as traders in the early part of the twentieth century helped develop the town. The native people in the area are Basoga. Their traditional family system is based on lineage and clan-based villages, but within a more centralized authority under the rule of 11 local kings who elect one principal king, the Kyabazinga. The Busoga traditional political and family system has been studied extensively by Cohen (1972, 1977, 1982) and highlights the complex family system. The Basoga people were influenced by outside visitors, traders and religious missionaries. The introduction of modern cash crops, including cotton and coffee, dramatically changed their lives and led to the economic prosperity of the area. Today many Basoga have migrated to the large cities of Jinja and Kampala, with families having members both in the city and the rural areas. This is the context in which networking resources in family businesses are investigated.

In deciding on a family to study, inquiries were made of different business people in Iganga town to establish the oldest businesses in town. Two businesses were repeatedly said to be among the oldest. One of them was Iganga General Merchandise (IGM), owned by Mr Charles Sentongo. Mr Sentongo had witnessed different political generations starting from the 1960s. While the town has numerous family businesses, the Sentongo family business stood out as one that had experienced a change in ownership from parent to children.

A letter of introduction was obtained from the district commercial officer to Mr Charles Sentongo who found time for several interviews. Three in-depth and unstructured interviews were held with Mr Sentongo on different days. One interview lasted more than two hours while the other two were on average one and a half hours each. Subsequently, interviews were held with three of Charles's brothers. Two of the brothers were interviewed twice and one of the brothers was interviewed three times. Mr Charles Sentongo's son George was interviewed three times. All of these interviews lasted one and a half hours on average. A two-hour interview was held with the chairman of the LC, who worked with Charles very closely. An interview was held with Ms Sarah Kwesiga, the speaker of the Uganda parliament and a close friend of the family. The shops of the different family members and their family compounds were visited. Content analysis was used to analyse the collected data.

SOCIAL CAPITAL IN IGANGA GENERAL MERCHANDISE

In this section we analyse the case in relation to the propositions developed in the theoretical section:

The Large Extended Family and Social Capital

The Sentongo family is remarkably large. It includes four generations, Charles's grandfather Fred, his father Alphonso, himself and his children. The relatives of the wives who married into the family are also all part of the extended family. This has provided a wide pool of family labour to help develop and run the business, from casual to managerial categories. Alphonso selected his son Charles, an obedient and responsible child, to help him in the business. Charles acquired skills by working with his father and was selected as the heir even though he was not the eldest son. This could have potentially created conflict in the family. Mugerwa II, despite being the eldest son, was not preferred as the first choice to work with his father, though he eventually did. The large number of family members constituted a pool of dependants and the heir to the family fortune was responsible for school fees and other expenses. The heir also had the additional role of getting his brothers and children into new careers as they grew. This large number of dependants drains away the resources of the family business. However, Charles's brothers established separate businesses and retained links with the main family business. As members of the family, they collaborated and through frequent family meetings were able to expand the family business. In these meetings they would discuss how to improve the business and contribute to the success of IGM. By starting their own businesses and having a high degree of autonomy conflict was minimized and they could benefit from interaction and cooperation.

BONDING CAPITAL

As illustrated, there is considerable interaction and bonding in the Sentongo family, particularly in the way Charles and his brothers have cooperated to further their own interests and those of the family business. The expansion of Charles's main business, and that of his brothers' linked businesses, widened the range of social and business contacts that were able to be exploited for their mutual businesses. The general reputation of belonging to a wealthy and cohesive family was a particularly good asset.

Closer analysis, however, revealed that holding the family together was only possible with the influence of the head of the family, now Charles. It was reported that Charles had the final word on family issues. This personalized authority was likely to cause considerable problems once Charles's interest in the family business waned in favour of his political interests, as no one else had the power, knowledge and influence to manage the family business profitably, or to unite the family to work together. Charles's son's concern about his father absence from the business reflects this.

The Sentongo family holds numerous ceremonies, one example being the graduation ceremony that was reported. It attracted a large number of people and was a significant cost for the family. Additionally, with marriage ceremonies wealth is transferred to the girl's parents, but the family function is also still a cost. The large extended family can also therefore be a drain on the family business.

The increasing number of children being educated is also leading to migration of people from villages to towns. Charles's children and possibly those of his brothers have moved away from Iganga to larger cities to seek jobs. His brothers are also trading outside Iganga. While this widens opportunities for business and increases political and social contacts, it is reducing contact in the family. Charles's son now works in the national parliament in the country's capital, Kampala. It is an advantage for the family, in terms of bridging with outsiders, but reduces bonding social capital.

EFFECT OF SOCIAL CHANGE

Various changes that have taken place in Uganda have brought different advantages but also disadvantages. Fred Sentongo, who established the original business, did so as a result of his friendship with a local Asian trader. This was bridging capital. The political changes that took place in the country in the 1970s and 1980s not only enabled the business to grow but also enabled Charles to embrace politics and get elected as a council chairman in the mid-1980s. Charles became more popular and respectable, securing more contacts that improved the business. Charles's brothers travelled both within and outside Uganda in pursuit of business opportunities. This led to expansion of the business. Social change was thus providing an advantage for the business. However, Charles's increased participation in politics was reducing the time he spent attending to the family business. This was a disadvantage.

DISCUSSION

Nahapiet and Ghoshal (1998) proposed a number of dynamic factors that influence the development of social capital in a family business. These include stability, interaction, dependency and closure. Arregle et al. (2007) used these factors to develop his model for organizational social capital. The authors proceed to make propositions on which basis they conclude that social capital is the major force for development of the organizational social capital of a family business.

In IGM, we note that despite the large size of the family business there is trust among the different members. Charles who is a younger son collaborates with his elder brother Mugerwa II, which creates goodwill among the brothers. Charles also works with his younger brothers who deliver goods to his shop. Charles also provides funds to his younger brothers to start businesses. This confirms findings by Granovetter (2005), Hitt et al. (2002) and Putnam (1993) and also confirms that in the process of its formation, social capital is influenced by the stability of relationships between family members. IGM has endured through generations and there is family cohesion that contributes to social capital. It is important to note that African families differ significantly from Western ones. It is the extended family that creates social capital.

Bourdieu (1986) argued that increased interaction between actors helps the development and maintenance of mutual obligations in a social network. Interaction is another factor proposed by Nahapiet and Ghoshal (1998) as one of the factors that influences the formation of social capital in family firms. The Sentongo family appears to be close-knit. Alphonso's children would work together in the shop. Even when he took over, Charles let his brothers work with him in the shop. The family holds meetings at which business is discussed. These interactions help in the creation of social capital as they promote bonding among members. Nordqvist and Melin (2001) concluded that interaction among family members affected family firms' strategy formulation processes. Portes (1998) reported that this interaction promoted the formulation of norms and high levels of obligation. However, the anthropology literature challenges the notion of the African family being close-knit. Studies have shown that there are tensions in lineage systems which favour the split of extended families into units over time. Individuals may use the resources of the business for personal use (Long, 1977, 2001). The interdependence may, however, be limited if conflict arises in the family. In the Sentongo family, one strong leader kept other family members in check. Charles's decision was final.

Interdependence is the other factor affecting social capital formation in a family firm. Coleman (1990) argued that social capital evolves with people in a network who become more dependent on one another. Nahapiet and Ghoshal (1998) argued that higher levels of social capital are developed in a context with substantial mutual interdependence. The Sentongo family firm evolved based on the goodwill and contributions of different members of the family. To start his business, Mugerwa II was supported by his father. To start their own businesses, Charles gives seed money to his brothers. To be able to sell their goods, Charles's brothers use his shops as an outlet. This interdependence therefore contributes to the formation of social capital through the bond that exists between family members.

External influences have weakened the family system. Exposure to outside influences strengthens individual ambitions of family members. Charles's son George works in Kampala and does not depend on the family business income for his personal livelihood. The social change therefore reduces the closure factor because individuals develop personal ambitions that weaken the family. Adler and Kwon (2002) say that closure is the extent to which actors' contacts are interconnected. This interconnection, according to Portes (1998), affects the observance of the network's behavioural norms. This closure may include sanctions on an individual who violates the norms. The Sentongo family is reported to be a close-knit family, many of whom stay in one family compound. They are reported to have frequent family meetings and Charles reins in members. He is respected and has the final word on family issues.

Bonding social capital is influenced by these factors, as proposed by Nahapiet and Ghoshal (1998). This capital contributes to the performance of the organization. Indeed, the growth of IGM was a result of this capital. Bridging capital is also crucial in a family business and indeed explains the success of IGM. Bridging capital is external and it focuses on the links of an actor. Charles Sentongo is a key actor in the current family business who has linked the business and his brothers to different people. Bridges enable organizations to achieve their goals by providing information, enabling identification of opportunities, allowing favourable negotiations and enabling access to power (Adler and Kwon, 2002; Sharma, 2008). Bridging capital has been a key instrument of success. Charles's grandfather made a breakthrough, through a bridge to the Indian community. Charles is able to secure benefits for his business through contacts he establishes through the family business and through his political office. The advantages of this social capital flow backwards into the family business and to individual family members.

LIMITATIONS

This study enables us to understand the role of social capital in creating value in the family business in an African family. It enables us to explore the concept of the extended family in an African setting and how these families generate social capital. We are able to acquire insights into how closely linked family units can exploit the interactions within the family for success. Richmond and Gestrin (1998) report on the dark side of the extended family. They say that the distribution of family income over a large number of people is a constraint to savings. However, we now see social capital as creating an advantage for the family business. This study contributes to the theory formation process initiated by Arregle et al. (2007). The study does not consider matrilineal families in Africa and while it is said that there is a convergence of matrilineal and patrilineal family systems, how they operate has not been taken into consideration.

Methodologically, the study is limited by the fact that the work is done in one family, in one district and is qualitative. While it provides insights into social capital, it does not lend itself to generalization. More work should be done in this area both qualitatively and quantitatively. The theoretical framework created by Arregle et al. (2007) does not deal with bridging capital. In this case, bridging capital is seen to create value for the organization. For future research purposes, this may be modelled on the theory that Arregle et al. (2007) are attempting to build. At the time of the commencement of the study, it was not envisaged that there would be a case of too much social capital either from bonding or bridging.

The study clearly highlights the case of too much social capital. The effect of too much social capital is not dealt with. This is the dark side of social capital. This calls for additional studies on the work of Arregle et al. (2007). Questions are raised whether it has negative consequences, whether it will result in inertia and whether it poses the challenge of free-riding by certain members of the family (Adler and Kwon, 2002; Portes, 1998). This was not explored and is an area of future research. Of course it would be interesting to study whether countries like Algeria, an African country with an Arab population but with similar extended family patterns, are able to generate similar social capital.

CONCLUSION

Family businesses are unique institutions where family members and their participation in the business, or their lack thereof, affects the performance of the organization. Although large extended African families are often closely linked, changes in family systems can reduce interdependence and lead to splits in families. It is strong leadership that keeps families together. It is under those circumstances that the extended family can create social capital, arising out of the family social networks and the interaction among family members. It is assumed that family businesses are set up to cater to the needs of the family members and therefore individual family members have a role to play in the success of family businesses. By coming together and interacting, they create a resource that gives the business capabilities. The familiness theory that is being generated assumes that social capital will be generated depending on the time people spend together, the nature of the interaction, the degree of interdependence and how members of the family abide by the network norms. However, too much social capital has a dark side. It may create individual ambitions and reduce the resources created in the family business.

REFERENCES

Achoui, M.M. (2006), 'The Algerian family, change and solidarity', in J. Georgas, J.W. Berry, F.J.R. Vijver, C. Kagitcibasi and H.Y. Poortinga (eds), *Families across Cultures, a 30 Nation Psychological Study*, Cambridge: Cambridge University Press, pp. 243–50.

Adler, P.S. and S.W. Kwon (2002), 'Social capital: prospects for a new concept', *Academy of Management Review*, **27**, 17–40.

Allman, J. (1991), 'Of "spinsters", "concubines" and "wicked women": reflections on gender and social change in colonial Asante', *Gender & History*, **3** (2), 176–189.

Arregle, J., M.A. Hitt, D.G. Sirmon and P. Very (2007), 'The development of social capital: attributes of family firms', *Journal of Management Studies*, **44** (1), 73–95.

Bohannan, P. (1963), *Social Anthropology*, London: Holt, Rinehart and Winston.

Bourdieu, P. (1986), 'The forms of capital', in J.G. Richardson (ed.), *Handbook of Theory and Research for the Sociology of Education*, New York: Greenwood, pp. 241–58.

Chrisman, J., J. Chua and S. Zahra (2003), 'Creating wealth in family firms through managing resources: comments and extensions', *Entrepreneurship Theory and Practice*, **27** (4), 359–65.

Cohen, D. (1972), *The Historical Tradition of Busoga, Mukama and Kintu*, Oxford: Clarendon Press.

Cohen, D. (1977), *Womunafu's Bunafu*, Princeton, NJ: Princeton University Press.

Cohen, D. (1982), 'The political transformation of Northern Busoga, 1600–1900', *Cahiers d'Etudes Africaines*, 87–8, XXII-3-4, 465–88.

Coleman, J.S. (1988), 'Social capital in the creation of human capital', *American Journal of Sociology*, **94**, 95–120.

Coleman, J.S. (1990), *Foundations of Social Theory*, Cambridge, MA: Harvard University Press.

Dyson-Hudson, N. (1966), *Karimojong Politics*, Oxford: Clarendon Press.

Elkan, W. (1988), 'Entrepreneurs and entrepreneurship in Africa', *World Bank Research Observatory*, **3** (2), 171–188.

Evans-Pritchard, E.E. (1940), *The Nuer*, Oxford: Oxford University Press.

Evans-Pritchard, E.E. (1951), *Kinship and Marriage among the Nuer*, Oxford: Clarendon Press.

Granovetter, M. (2005), 'The impact of social structure on economic outcomes', *Journal of Economic Perspectives*, **19** (1), 33–50.

Habbershon, T.G. and M.L. Williams (1999), 'A resource-based framework for assessing the strategic advantages of family firms', *Family Business Review*, **12**, 1–15.

Habbershon, T.G., M.L. Williams and I.C. MacMillan (2003), 'A unified systems perspective of family firm performance', *Journal of Business Venturing*, **18**, 451–65.

Hitt, M.A., H. Lee and E. Yucel (2002), 'The importance of social capital to the management of multinational enterprises: relational networks among Asian and western firms', *Asia Pacific Journal of Management*, **19**, 353–72.

Hoffman, J., M. Hoelscher and R. Sorenson (2006), 'Achieving sustained competitive advantage: a family capital theory', *Family Business Review*, **19** (2), 135–45.

Khavul, S., G. Bruton and E. Wood (2009), 'Informal family business in Africa', *Entrepreneurship, Theory & Practice*, **33** (6), 1219–38.

Leana, C.R. and H.J. Van Buren (1999), 'Organizational social capital and employment practices', *Academy of Management Review*, **24**, 538–55.

Levi-Strauss, C. (1945), *The Elementary Structures of Kinship*, London: Beacon Press.

Long, N. (1977), *An Introduction to the Sociology of Rural Development*, London: Tavistock.

Long, N. (2001), *Development Sociology: Actor Perspectives*, London: Routledge.

Mair, L. (1967), *New Nations*, London: Weidenfeld and Nicholson.

Nahapiet, J. and S. Ghoshal (1998), 'Social capital, intellectual capital, and the organizational advantage', *Academy of Management Review*, **23**, 242–66.

Nordqvist, M. and L. Melin (2001), 'Exploring the dynamics of family firms: linking corporate governance to strategy change', Annual Conference of European Group for Organisational Studies, Lyon, France.

Parkin, D. (1966), *The Cultural Definition of Political Response: Lineal Destiny amongst the Luo*, London: Academic Press.

Pearson, A., J. Carr and J. Shaw (2008), 'Toward a theory of familiness: a social capital perspective', *Entrepreneurship Theory & Practice*, **32** (6), 949–69.

Portes, A. (1998), 'Social capital: its origins and applications in modern sociology', *Annual Review of Sociology*, **24**, 1–24.

Putnam, R.D. (1993), 'The prosperous community: social capital and public life', *American Prospect*, **4** (13), 1–11.

Radcliffe-Brown, A. and D. Forde (eds) (1950), *African Systems of Kinship and Marriage*, Oxford: Oxford University Press.

Richmond, Y. and P. Gestrin (1998), *Into Africa, Cultural Insights*, London: Nicholas Blearey.

Robertson, C.C. (1976), 'Women and socioeconomic change in Accra, Ghana', in *Women in Africa: Studies in Social and Economic Change*, Stanford, CA: Stanford University Press, pp. 111–35.

Sharma, P. (2008), 'Familiness: capital stocks and flaws between families and business', *Entrepreneurship Theory and Practice*, **32**, 971–7.

Sharma, P. and S. Manikutty (2005), 'Strategic divestments in family firms: role of family structure and community', *Entrepreneurship Theory & Practice*, **29** (3), 293–311.

Stewart, A. (2003), 'Help one another, use one another: toward an anthropology of family business', *Entrepreneurship, Theory & Practice*, **27** (4), 383–96.

World Bank Development Report (2012), accessed at wdronline.worldbank.org/.

Yli-Renko, H., E. Autio and H.J. Sapienza (2001), 'Social capital, knowledge acquisition and knowledge exploitation in young technology-based firms', *Strategic Management Journal*, **22** (6–7), 587–613.

8. Bridging for resilience: the role of family business social capital in coping with hostile environments

Aramis Rodriguez, Nunzia Auletta and Patricia Monteferrante

SÁNCHEZ & CO.: SURFING TOUGH ENVIRONMENTS

After a long and sleepless night, Juan Miguel Sánchez, Vice-President of Sánchez & Co., felt all the responsibility of the company's future on his shoulders. In less than an hour, he was to present his action plan for a major turnaround to the board of directors.

The company and the family were not new to changes and turmoil in their business and social environment. As his father and president of the board, Juan José, was proud to repeat: 'the history of Sánchez & Co. was evidence of the firm's considerable capacity for re-inventing itself. In over 90 years, the nature of the company's business had changed each time circumstances required it, shifting from coffee and cocoa exporters, to foodstuffs importers, to electronics retail and franchising, all without impairing the firm's progress'. In the last month, Juan Miguel and his managerial team had gone over different scenarios from radically innovating the franchising concept of Video Magic, the group's home video rental chain, to proceeding to a strong disinvestment strategy in Venezuela. Video Magic was facing major changes in the video rental industry: with the introduction of digital technology, movies became available on the internet, radically changing consumer habits. By 2008, Video Magic franchisees were closing one after the other, at an alarming pace. Hence, will Juan Miguel be able to continue the success story of his father and grandfather, or will he be the first to fail when facing a hostile environment?

A FAMILY HISTORY OF CHANGES

Sánchez & Co. was founded in Venezuela in 1921 by Jacobo Sánchez, a Spanish immigrant who started a trading activity to and from Europe, exporting coffee, cocoa, hides and spices, and importing foodstuffs, liquor and other consumer goods.

The company grew steadily from 1939 onwards, involving Jacobo's son, Jorge, in the operation. However, World War II strongly impacted trading activities by cutting the main sources of manufactured products and depressing consumer markets for agricultural goods in the countries at war. This pushed father and son to seek new lines of business in the USA, entering the home appliances trading market by importing different brands.

In 1950, Jorge, as company president, supported by his younger brother Diego, obtained a distributorship from General Electric (GE), making Sánchez & Co. the exclusive local distributor both for home appliances and more sophisticated industrial and medical equipment. Sales of GE appliances in Venezuela rose considerably. However, in 1972, GE decided to establish direct distribution operations in Venezuela, thus causing a setback for Sánchez & Co., which would thenceforth practically have to start from scratch. The brothers proceeded to create a new distributorship with four main product lines: home appliances, electronics, industrial and medical equipment, all from a variety of rising Japanese brands.

The growing Venezuelan economy, along with stable trade policies, facilitated not only the growth but also the downstream integration of the firm into a home appliance retail chain, House Supply (HS), with 17 stores throughout the country by 1982. Moreover, a joint venture with a German partner in 1980 moved the company into the manufacturing industry, running a factory, which by that time provided around 4 percent of the products sold in the HS stores. The growth also called for new generations of the family to become involved in the business, such as Juan José, Jorge's son, who joined the company after a long experience in a multinational retail company in the USA.

The 1980s unleashed a major economic crisis in Venezuela, due to a 30 percent drop in oil prices, thus strongly affecting the balance of trade in an oil-focused economy, with subsequent capital flights and the decline in foreign exchange reserves. By February 1983, the government had to take emergency economic measures on foreign exchange.

The crisis impacted a large number of Venezuelan companies, as well as multinationals operating in the country, many of which eventually closed operations. Germán Robles, HS's managing director, remembered: 'When this February came, we had to substantially downsize the company as letters of credit were not honored. We had to close down several stores and focus exclusively on a few domestic brands. It was an unexpected disaster.' Struggling to honor its debt with foreign providers, and abandoned by its German production partner, Sánchez & Co. had no other way to go on but to put money into their domestic production, and build a new network of domestic providers for their stores.

Fortunately, the family's strong ties with the Venezuelan business society and its leading role in the business association of home appliances manufacturers enabled their survival. As noted by Alejandro Sánchez, Juan Miguel's brother: 'One of the skills transmitted from my grandfather down was to know how to manage public relations. My father is a public relations champion, and my brother also does it very well.'

As Juan José Sánchez remembered: 'We learned our lesson, and pursued our diversification during the 90s, a decade in which we faced all kinds of challenges ranging from market liberalization, a huge bank crisis and the political and social turmoil which became part of the picture.' HS was no longer their crown jewel, and the group opened itself up to new opportunities such as sporting goods, professional graphics and leading medical equipment.

In 1992, Sánchez & Co. also decided to develop a new franchising concept of home video rentals, Video Magic, which was very soon recognized as one of the most successful new retail chains in the country, competing fairly against its multinational counterparts such as Blockbuster Video. Those were days of innovation for the company, always looking for the latest technology, and seeking the best commercial partners to grow further. At the same time, outside the company, family members anxious to diversify risk explored other investments, among which were shareholdings in a health and beauty products chain in Colombia, a home appliance factory and an abrasives factory in Peru. Commenting on those years of new venture opportunities pursued by the family, Juan Miguel said: 'We were perceived as cool people to do business with. There were always people who wanted to become our partners.'

Yet, the Venezuelan environment was about to change again, with a coup attempt against President Hugo Chávez in 2002, and a general strike in 2003. Following these events, early in 2003 the government once again chose to introduce exchange controls in order to curb capital flights stemming from the country's political uncertainty. In the following years, a major shift in economic policy implied business nationalization and a more restrictive legal framework, setting the foundations for a state-controlled economy.

FAMILY TRADITION OR STRATEGIC TURNAROUND?

By 2008, the Sánchez companies were still facing strong limitations to their operations in Venezuela, with a substantial decrease in revenues and benefits that called for a strategic turnaround. A further step in their internationalization strategy was a joint venture with MPR – a Venezuelan company owned by the Muller family to whom the Sanchez's were related. Together, the two families successfully invested in Panorama, a department store chain in Colombia and Panamá, by that time safe havens for the Venezuelan business community. However, managerial control was in the Muller's hands, leaving the Sánchez family with a 30 percent share and little say about the future of the company.

As for Video Magic, it was registering a 33 percent decrease in income, and the number of stores had reduced from 65 in 2006 to 42 in 2008. This signaled a major change in the home entertainment industry into more interactive internet-based and individual choice-driven activities.

The family was facing major dilemmas. Business rationality pointed to reinforcing internationalization even if this seemed to be at odds with their attachment to Venezuela. On the other hand, new business models had to be explored beyond Sánchez & Co.'s traditional imports and retail know-how, in a trade-off between family control and renewed competitive advantages.

While entering the meeting room, in which his father, siblings and trusted directors were sitting, Juan Miguel hoped he was not going to be the first Sánchez to give in to dire circumstances.

DISCUSSION QUESTIONS

1. What has been, over time, the main competitive advantage of Sanchez & Co.?
2. When facing a hostile environment in Venezuela, how did Sanchez & Co. overcome their difficulties?
3. What advantages and risks does the current situation pose for Sanchez & Co.?
4. What course of action should Juan Miguel and his family take to reap the endowment effects of their accumulated social capital?

INTRODUCTION

How do firms like Sánchez & Co. remain resilient in a hostile environment? Several scholars have selected hostility as the most frequently used dimension to characterize external adversity for organizations (Miller and Friesen, 1983; Zahra, 1996). There appear to be strong reasons to believe that at least some family controlled businesses (FCBs) are resilient (Chrisman et al., 2011), which means that they have the ability to avoid, absorb, respond to and recover from situations that could threaten their existence (Lengnick-Hall and Beck, 2005).

According to Gedajlovic and Carney (2010) the value of 'generic non-tradable assets (GNTs)' such as reputation and networks of a firm enable long-lived firms to build their resilience capacity. Internal social capital and social exchange have been pointed out as some of the characteristics that increase resilience in family firms (Long, 2011; Chrisman et al., 2011). Some evidence has also been found of FCBs being able to achieve stronger resilience both during and after an economic crisis (that is, a form of hostile environment), compared with non-family businesses, because of their long-term orientation, their familiness and their social capital (Amann and Jaussaud, 2012).

The role of internal social capital as an enhancer of the resilience capability of FCBs has been supported by Long (2011) and Chrisman et al. (2011). However, little research has been carried out as to the role of *external social capital* in increasing the family firms' resilience when facing hostile environments. Based on Sharma (2008), the essence of our research is based upon the idea that if the internal capital stocks are insufficient, the firm needs to reinforce them with external capital investments. Thus, through the bridging of the social capital, the FCBs may then have access to other resources and can then mobilize them for their benefit.

In this chapter we explore how bridging social capital influences a family firm's resilience in hostile environments. This is accomplished through careful case analyses of six family controlled businesses from different countries. Our results point towards the finer nuances of the bridging social capital and the effects of such nuances on the resilience pathways adopted by long-standing firms.

The chapter is structured as follows. The first section briefly illustrates the theoretical background that will serve as the framework of our study. We introduce the literature on the definition, content and stocks and flows of social capital. Furthermore, we introduce the construct of resilience, considered as a capability that shapes the actions of family firms in a hostile environment. The second section provides the method employed in this study. This is followed by a section on the findings and derivation of theoretical propositions. The chapter concludes with a recapitulation of key findings and a discussion of implications for research and practice.

THEORETICAL BACKGROUND

Describing adverse environments has not been an easy task, although several scholars have selected hostility as the most frequently used dimension to characterize adversity external to organizations (Miller and Friesen, 1982, 1984; Zahra, 1996). Specifically, Zahra and Neubaum (1998) propose four levels of characterizing hostility: (1) macro environmental hostility, which refers to the existence of unfavorable conditions in the general context of the firm. This level is related to political, regulatory and economic conditions that may reduce the company's degree of liberty to create and follow strategies (Miller and Friesen, 1984). (2) Market hostility, which refers to the existence of unfavorable conditions within the industry that limit the firm's operations. This includes the historical evolution and the characteristics of the industry as well as the conditions of supply and demand that may affect the company's performance and growth (Porter, 1980). (3) Competitive hostility, which refers on the one hand to the intensity of competition in a given industry and to the power of different rivals, and on the other hand to the actions taken to gain opportunities (Grant, 1998; Slater and Narver, 1994). (4) Technological hostility, which refers to radical changes in technological resources and capabilities available within the industry (Zahra et al., 1995).

Facing Hostile Environments: Resilience Capability in FCBs

In this chapter, we use the lens of resilience capacity to explore the pathways family firms adopt when faced with a hostile environment. Resilience capability is defined 'as the organizational ability and confidence to act decisively and effectively in response to conditions that are uncertain, surprising, and sufficiently disruptive that they have the potential to jeopardize long-term survival' (Lengnick-Hall and Beck, 2009: 41).

In general, the resilience capacity influences an organization's response to environmental change and it can help organizations redefine their business models and strategies as the environment changes. Likewise, according to Lengnick-Hall and Beck (2009: 43), this capability 'prepares organizations to effectively manage disruptive, unexpected and potentially debilitating changes by ensuring the means needed for recovery and renewal are available; absorbing shocks and complexity; broadly accessing resources; crafting creative alternatives; and executing transformational change' (McCann, 2004).

An organization's resilience capacity is achieved from interactions among specific cognitive, behavioral and contextual factors (Lengnick-Hall and Beck, 2005). Specifically, cognitive resilience deals with the generation and selection of alternative actions and with a firm's decisiveness in initiating activities (Lengnick-Hall and Beck, 2009). Behavioral resilience is related to a firm's innate reaction when disruptive conditions appear. These actions include the development of particular routines, resource configurations and interaction patterns that implement the firm's response (Lengnick-Hall and Beck, 2009). While contextual resilience refers to the set of interpersonal relationships that provides a basis for quick response to environmental conditions, in the same manner, this kind of resilience also includes a network of potential resource donors which allows the organizations to expand the options and resource combinations available to face the disruptive conditions (Lengnick-Hall and Beck, 2009).

Social Capital: Increasing Resilience in FCBs

Social exchange theory suggests that social regularities, such as family social capital or the associated concept familiness (for example, Habbershon and Williams, 1999; Habbershon et al., 2003; Pearson et al., 2008), are the result of either rational choice or symbolic ritual. Social exchange has been indicated to be one of the characteristics that increases resilience in family firms (Long, 2011; Chrisman et al., 2011). According to DeCarolis et al. (2009) social exchange implies 'the existence of resources that can be easily mobilized at the time of impact', and therefore it 'greatly facilitates the capacity to confront the events'. In the case of FCBs this can be matched by the firm's ability to build on the family's heritage, and more broadly on the family's social capital.

Nahapiet and Ghoshal (1998: 243) define social capital as 'the sum of the actual and potential resources embedded within, available through, and derived from the network of relationships possessed by an individual or social unit'. The social capital theory focuses on how the quality, content and structure of social relationships affect other resource flows and further facilitate the sustainability of an organization (Wright et al., 2001; Salvato and Melin, 2008), providing information, access to technological knowledge and markets, as well as to complementary resources (Hitt et al., 2001, 2002).

Attempts to conceptualize social capital more thoroughly have resulted in different taxonomies and characterizations, where the distinction between internal and external ones is the most common. *Internal social capital* or 'bonding' is the network of relations among actors within a collectivity, such as a business organization or a family, and focuses on the internal characteristics that reinforce cohesiveness therein (Adler and Kwon, 2002; Yli-Renko et al., 2002; Kontinen and Ojala, 2010). On the other hand, *external social capital* or 'bridging' can be explained as a process of creation and mobilization of network connections tying a focal actor to others, through direct or indirect links, and allowing them the opportunity of acquiring recognition, favorable negotiations and access to resources among a set of benefits (Adler and Kwon, 2002).

Most of the family business related research on social capital has focused on 'bonding', although Salvato and Melin (2008) have considered both internal and external ties as facilitating factors in strategic adaptation to the dynamic environment and the transgenerational value of creation, and this, as a result of restructuring and recombining relations both within and outside the family. However, little research has been carried out as to the role of external social capital in increasing family firms' resilience when facing hostile environments. This study focuses on external relations (that is, 'bridging'), which have been recognized by Sharma (2008) as a way for FCBs to meet their resources needs and thus establish beneficial norms of reciprocity between the actors involved (Miller and Le-Breton Miller, 2005). Following this line of research, we aim to explore the influence of bridging social capital on the resilience capability of FCBs in different hostile environments.

METHODS

Research Design and Setting

We used an inductive, multiple-case research design (Eisenhardt, 1989) and followed the STEP (Successful Transgenerational Entrepreneurship Practices) research method's guidelines (Nordqvist and Zellweger, 2010) involving six FCBs. Multiple cases permit a replication logic in which cases are treated as experiments, with each serving to confirm or disconfirm inferences drawn from the others (Yin, 2009). This process typically yields more robust, generalized theories than those found in single cases (Eisenhardt and Graebner, 2007).

The research setting was of FCBs facing hostile environments at any time of their life cycle. The current study focuses on understanding how social capital is used for FCBs when facing hostile environments. In this sense, this setting is an appropriate one for two reasons: (1) A methodological reason that explores in-depth the moments when the environment has become dangerous for these companies and allowed researchers to identify and analyze the role of social capital at a specific moment (hazard time), and to compare it with a basal state (stable time); (2) A reason of practical significance that facilitated an understanding of how FCBs face hostile environments to prevail over time.

Sample

Our selection of cases was based on theoretical considerations because the random selection of cases is neither necessary nor preferable, and extreme examples are most appropriate when seeking to extend a theory (Eisenhardt, 1989). The first consideration when selecting our cases was the evidence of dimensions of adverse environment on the firm's family context (that is, macro environmental hostility, market hostility, competitive hostility and technological hostility). The second was replication logic. After the pilot case (Dencker & Co. case) was analyzed, we chose more cases for replication that might explain how bridging social capital is used when family firms act under adverse environmental conditions. We used six cases from a list of 84 from the STEP project database (see Nordqvist and Zellweger, 2010), two of them refer to Venezuelan FCBs and were written by the same research team.

The rest of the cases did not meet the research setting due to the fact that some of them did not have episodes of hostile environments, and others lacked information as to the mechanisms used to face uncertainty. Table 8.1 summarizes various characteristics of the firms in the sample. Fictitious names were used in order to maintain the low profile of the owners and the corporate image of the respective firms.

Data Analysis

As is typical in inductive research, we analyzed the data by first building individual case studies synthesizing the information provided by the master (analytical) cases, archival data and webpages (Eisenhardt, 1989). A central aspect of case writing was the triangulation between master cases and archival sources to create richer, more reliable accounts (Jick, 1979). As an assessment on the emerging case stories, a second and third researcher read the original master cases and formed an independent view, which was then incorporated into each case to provide a more complete view of each firm. The case histories were used for two analyses: within-case and cross-case. The internal-case analysis focused on developing relationships to describe how the content and flow of bridging social capital

Table 8.1 Description and summary of the findings

Firm*	Descriptive information		Summary of findings			
	Industry and no. of employees	Year founded and family generation	Contacts used in a hostile environment	Exchanged capital stocks	Kind of link	Proposition
Azucarera El Abuelo (Costa Rica)	Sugar mills (manufacturer) 300–650* depending on the harvest period	1958 Gen: 2nd and 3rd	Local competitors	–Marketing –Branding –Opportunity for new business –Sales	Geo and sector concentrated	1,2
Pastas Sorrento (Venezuela)	Food production; pasta industry; pasta production 400 employees	1955 Gen: 2nd and 3rd	Local competitors	–Knowledge –Information	Geo and sector concentrated	1,2
Dencker & Co. (Germany)	Logistics and freight 110 employees	1900 Gen: 3rd	Clients: not just one name Suppliers: not just one name	–Transaction, sales –Service –Pride and commitment	Sector diversified	3,5

Table 8.1 (continued)

Firm*	Descriptive information		Summary of findings			
	Industry and no. of employees	Year founded and family generation	Contacts used in a hostile environment	Exchanged capital stocks	Kind of link	Proposition
Sverige Machines (Sweden)	Manufacture of machines for soil and planting 550 employees	1962 Gen: 2nd	Local farmers International farmers	–Knowledge –Information to develop products –Sounding board –Information to enter in new markets	Sector diversified	3,5
Grupo Navidad (El Salvador)	Manufacture and distribution of pharmaceutical products 1000 employees	1950 Gen: 2nd	International suppliers: Wella and Dewitt	–Privileged conditions –Grant sales –Grant products –Strong brand	Geo diversified Sector concentrated	2,4,5
Foto Rápida (Venezuela)	Trade and services in the images sector 200 employees	1862 (last 80 years in the photographic and imaging trade) Gen: 4th and 5th	International supplier: Fuji Film	–Payment flexibility –Access to products	Geo diversified Sector concentrated	2,4,5

Notes: *Fictitious names were used in order to maintain confidentiality.

enhance resilience in the cases studied. A core aspect of this inductive process is that we allowed the emergence of constructs from the data compiled during this process, rather than being guided by specific hypotheses (Eisenhardt, 1989). Though we noted similarities and differences among the cases, we left a margin for further analysis once we had completed all the case write-ups in order to maintain the independence of the replication logic. Cross-referencing case analysis began after all cases were finished. Using standard cross-case analysis techniques (Eisenhardt, 1989) we looked for similar constructs and relationships across the multiple cases.

FINDINGS

Hostile Environment and Bridging Social Capital in Our Cases

In this section we present a summary of each case, which highlights the situation of hostility faced by the FCBs, as well as some evidence of the use of their social capital.

Dencker & Co.: a German freight forwarding and logistics company
Since 2006 the German logistics and freight forwarding market has faced intense competition. New players eventually compete with established firms on price levels that are difficult to sustain. Consequently, lots of companies go out of business every year, causing high turnovers and considerable low margins.

> Especially the few desperate business men that simply buy a truck and start moving stuff are a threat to us. Without any background in organization aspects, they drive the prices down (. . .) Still, the stream of new players has never been as large. (Second-generation leader)

Throughout the years, the Dencker family has always been involved in the freight forwarding business, developing long-lasting relations with customers and suppliers which span generations and deal with aspects that go well beyond pure business connections. One of the outcomes is a superb relationship between Dencker and these business partners when compared to other industry players. This relationship is highly valued when contracts are concluded. Additionally, their long-time partnerships with some clients and suppliers lower the risk profile. For Dencker, the close and personal connection becomes an asset in a competitive context in which a lot of non-family businesses have a hard time replicating and coordinating for themselves.

Grupo Navidad: a Salvadoran pharmaceutical lab and retailer

In the last ten years the pharmaceutical sector in El Salvador has been highly competitive, with a large number of international and local laboratories providing a wide range of products and services. The fierce competition helps regulate the prices.

Carlos's (a second-generation member) networks in El Salvador were multiple, practically encompassing all major actors in politics, the government, and so on. In both domestic and international arenas, he has received various distinctions strengthening his and the company's image, keeping it in a privileged position vis-à-vis local competitors. All these features of his personal track record and his business group history have built him a wide network of relationships in both the private sector and the government of El Salvador. However, when the company faces hostile environments its network of international suppliers takes on added importance. From the early years of the company, Carlos has understood the importance of building ties with international players as he considered them central to the company's growth. For example, Wella Laboratories of the UK granted him their first representation to distribute their products in El Salvador. More recently, Carlos entered an agreement with Dewitt, an English laboratory, to manufacture its products at the Grupo Navidad and then distribute them in the region. Such relationships with international suppliers have acted as barriers to entry against local and regional competitors, not only assuring Grupo Navidad's survival in turbulent times, but also the development of new options.

Sverige Machines: a Swedish manufacturer of machines for soil and planting

In the mid 1980s, Sverige Machines of Sweden attempted to expand its production into seeding drills. However, the seeding methods in farming were changing considerably, and very soon a Swedish agricultural policy changed traditional farming, which included the use of seeding drills. The over-production, low profitability and agricultural policy in two of Sverige Machines' most important markets, Sweden and Finland, led to an increasingly difficult situation for the company in the early 1990s. As a result, in 1991 sales plummeted to almost half of those in 1989, resulting in diminished profits and lay-offs.

In 1990, intensive product development started to focus on two new agricultural systems: a seeding drill called 'Speed' and a harrow called 'Sonic'. The product development work for these products was done by a small group of co-workers in conjunction with a number of farmers used as a sounding board. Eventually, after a long and costly product development process, the firm launched the 'Speed' seeding drill. It soon became a major success and, as had several other of Sverige Machines' previous products, it revolutionized the market. In 1993, sales increased at the same time as Sweden's entrance into the European Union gave hope to the Swedish farmers, since they would be included within the European Agricultural Policy. The new product development by the company, working closely with the farmers, helped spark what had been an economically low period into the launch of a new era. As noted by the company's 40th anniversary book:

> The difficult years became the take-off for a fantastic boom, which in turn would generate an impressive growth over many coming years.

Although formal networking had never been an explicit source of capital, circumstances of market change and opportunities of collaboration brought out the power of informal ties.

Azucarera El Abuelo: a Costa Rican sugar mills manufacturer

The sugar industry in Costa Rica was mainly affected by environmental factors such as climate, labor force regulations, governmental decisions, trade agreements (for example, the Central American Free Trade Agreement, CAFTA) and social trends.

El Abuelo produced three different types of sugar which were sold entirely to the Liga Agricola Industrial de la Caña de Azúcar (The Industrial Agricultural League for Sugar Cane (LAICA)) – an important organization for all of the sugar producers in Costa Rica, in charge of coordinating the production, industrialization and marketing of sugar-derived products. LAICA bought the sugar produced by all the farmers and distributed it both locally in Costa Rica and to foreign markets such as the United States and Europe. Every time environmental factors affected the sugar industry, LAICA generated strategies to defend and protect its affiliates. For instance, when social trends such as sugar-free diets affected the industry, LAICA started working on healthier options such as creating a 'light' sugar to satisfy market needs. Alberto, the founder of El Abuelo, was a former president of LAICA, and his son is, at the time of writing, its current president. Presiding LAICA has given them the opportunity to build important industry networks both locally and globally.

Foto Rápida: a Venezuelan photographic retail company

In 2003, the Venezuelan government introduced foreign exchange controls, thereby limiting access to foreign currency transactions. Importing companies were severely affected by this measure as they were no longer able to purchase their products overseas at reasonable prices. These controls placed Foto Rápida at a competitive disadvantage compared to multinational competitors. The head of the international business division of Foto Rápida remarked:

> Our competitors, specifically Kodak, enjoyed greater freedom to deploy price strategies; it was easier for them given their condition of subsidiaries. The multinational condition grants them better credit terms when shipping goods and allows them to gain a competitive advantage in prices. For our provider, we are really a customer; accordingly, exchange controls put us at a disadvantage.

When the government introduced foreign exchange controls, thereby restricting access to transactions in foreign currencies, Foto Rápida took advantage of its ties with the international suppliers to maintain access to products. This problem was understood by its main supplier, which, based on trust built over the years, granted them benefits in negotiations and allowed flexibility in payments to Foto Rápida, while stabilizing the exchange control contingence.

Pastas Sorrento: a Venezuelan pasta producer

From 2000–07, the Venezuelan national government implemented restrictions on foreign currency transactions and regulated the prices of certain foodstuffs and other essentials. As a result, the government-regulated sale prices did not cover the actual cost of producing pasta with flour blends. Production costs surpassed sales prices by over 300 percent.

The networks this family had developed within the national and international pasta-making industry, as well as the business knowledge amassed over half a century, helped the business survive in times of turmoil. As a non-family board member said:

> Though it requires much time and dedication to build relationships and contacts, in the end the effort was worthwhile (. . .) Not only did it open up opportunities, but it also drew on knowledge and information.

While the family did not, as such, use its contacts and relations to further develop the company, the current president of the company had always invested time and effort in cultivating relationships between members of the pasta industry. This bridge-building helped to enhance the company's reputation and recognition. In 1978, he led the movement to create Avepastas – the Venezuelan Association of Manufacturers of Pasta Products – an association that he has chaired since its founding. Relations and networking with the members of the Venezuelan pasta industry gave Pastas Sorrento access to privileged and new information, which helped the company to anticipate the national government's intentions and react promptly by introducing innovative products and adaptive strategies.

Cross-Case Analysis

A critical cross-case analysis highlights the influence of external social capital on the resilience capability of family enterprises. However, as elaborated below, the temporality and stability of the effect on resilience capability of the focal entity varies based on the positioning of the bridge partners geographically as well as within the same industry or beyond.

Bridges between actors in the same environment: improving resilience steadily

When Pastas Sorrento was affected by the regulatory threats imposed by the national government, leading the sales price of pasta products to plummet even below the production costs, all members of the pasta industry manufacturers association (Avepastas) experienced reduced profits, questioning their survival. Thus, the forces of the hostile environment promoted an exchange of knowledge and information between Pastas Sorrento and other members of this association. As Pastas Sorrento's founder was also the creator of Avepastas, the company was well-positioned to proactively develop new products and escape price regulations. A similar behavior was observed in the case of Azucarera El Abuelo. When the environment affected the sugar industry, the network of producers (LAICA) generated strategies for the defense and protection of its members. The free flow of information, ideas, knowledge and relationships with other industry players in LAICA helped with the marketing and branding strategies, thereby opening up new opportunities for all manufacturers.

Both Pastas Sorrento and Azucarera El Abuelo could take advantage of their bridging capital due to the high levels of respect, friendship and prestige they built with their ties. Because many of the FCBs build their networks according to their resources and the possibility to give back, some concentrate their main ties in the same or unique economic sector (see Table 8.1). In this way a hostile environment that could affect the existence of one member of the net could also affect the other member's existence (see Figure 8.1), leading to both parties having the same needs or threats, enabling participation in a reciprocal exchange of resources. In formal terms:

Proposition 1: When FCBs and their ties belong to the same economic sector, the forces of the hostile environment affect them in a similar manner, leading to exchanging capital flows in both directions of the network (from FCBs to their network and vice versa).

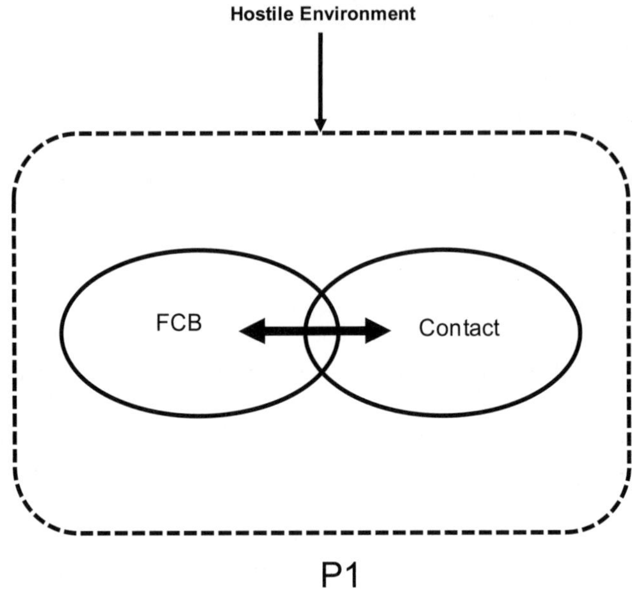

Notes:
Bold arrows indicate flows of capital
Fine arrows indicate environmental forces.

Figure 8.1 Social capital flows within a hostile environment

When capital flows are bi-directional between FCBs and other enterprises operating in the same hostile environment, the FCBs could get sustained access to resources such as knowledge, information, financial capital and advice. At the time of impact, such mobilization of resources can facilitate the FCBs' capacities to absorb environmental shocks. Through its bridging ties, Pastas Sorrento and Azucarera El Abuelo have the means to survive steadily through their crises. Azucarera El Abuelo got marketing facilities, branding and opportunities to develop new businesses from its external ties, enabling it to resist the shock produced by the shrinking market. In same way, Pastas Sorrento had access to privileged knowledge and information that allowed the company to cope with the threat imposed by the price regulation. In both cases, their strong external ties, based on trust, allowed these FCBs to enhance their resilience by scoring high in their absorption capability. In formal terms:

Proposition 2: When capital flows are from FCBs to external ties and vice versa (bi-directional flow), the FCBs' resilience improves steadily through its absorption capability.

Bridges between actors from different environments: improving resilience temporarily

When the actors of the network belong to different economic sectors, the behavior of the capital flows in hostile environments is different. For example, when the government did not support the kind of farming in which the seeding drill was designed to perform, the sales of Sverige Machines decreased rapidly in the early 1990s, shrinking the company's profitability and causing lay-offs. Given this situation, Sverige Machines co-opted with another key stakeholder within its environment – the farmers. A small group of co-workers brainstormed with farmers to develop new products that eventually helped the firm to launch new seeding drills. Soon these drills became a major success. As with several other of Sverige Machines products before, the seeding drills revolutionized the market. Although the farmers benefited from the technology developed by Sverige Machines, they were not directly affected by the regulations. If the government prohibits any kind of farming with the seeding drills, the farmers can use another type of machinery, thereby not affecting their activities directly. In this instance, the social capital that was found to be beneficial was between two different types of stakeholders – one directly affected by the hostile environment and the other not so.

A similar pattern was observed in the case of Dencker & Co. When the environment affected the German logistics and freight forwarding market, their main networking activities were not directly affected. Some of those relationships between their clients and suppliers have grown far beyond pure business connections. One of the outcomes is a superb relationship between Dencker and its business partners in comparison with other industry players. Although the market is becoming more hostile to the freight and logistics companies, Dencker's suppliers and customers do not feel the same rivalry, thus ensuring the flow of capital such as loans and flexible payment terms. These patterns allow us to suggest that when an FCB has its main contacts in different economic sectors (diversified industry), the forces of hostile environments affect only one side of the network (see Figure 8.2). In formal terms:

Proposition 3: When FCBs and their ties belong to different economic sectors, the forces of the hostile environment affect them in different magnitudes, leading to the giving of capital flows from the ties to the FCBs (in one direction of the network).

The pattern of capital flows not only seems to depend on a concentrated or diversified industry, but some of the cases studied showed that although

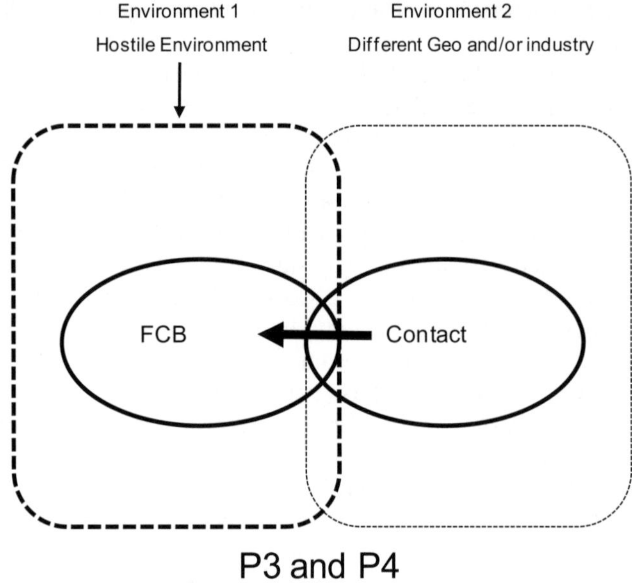

Notes:
Bold arrows indicate flows of capital
Fine arrows indicate environmental forces.

Figure 8.2 Social capital flows across diversified links

FCBs and their network(s) belong to the same industry sector, the capital flows were only in one direction while the environmental forces were present. That is the case for Grupo Navidad, in which its main links (Wella and Dewitt Laboratories) belong to the same pharmaceutical sector, providing support while the Salvadoran and Central American markets were adverse. Good commercial conditions, granted products and marketing advantages flowed from Wella and Dewitt to Grupo Navidad, in spite of the forces of the competitive pharmaceutical market. Foto Rápida's capital flows showed a similar pattern. When the Venezuelan government introduced foreign exchange controls, limiting access to transactions in foreign currencies, the FCBs were severely affected by the threat of no longer being able to purchase their products overseas at reasonable prices. Foto Rápida took advantage of its international links to maintain access to its products. This problem was understood by its main supplier, which, based on trust built up over the years, granted benefits in their negotiations and allowed a certain flexibility in payments while exchange control contingency became stabilized. Apparently, even in the same economic sector, the forces of a hostile environment can affect just one contact within a network when the actors in that network are located in different regions or countries (Geo diversified, see Table 8.1 and Figure 8.2). In formal terms:

Proposition 4: When an FCB and its ties belong to different regions or countries, the forces of the hostile environment affect them in different magnitudes, leading to the unidirectional transfer of capital flows from actors in the non hostile environment to those affected by the hostile environment.

When capital flows move in one direction under disruptive conditions, the FCBs could get intermittent access to resources such as knowledge, information, financial capital and advice. This mobilization of resources, at the time of impact, could provide the FCBs with an immediate capacity to face or absorb the events. Through their bridging ties, Dencker and Sverige Machines have the means to survive through several of their crises. In both cases, their strong external ties, based on trust, allow these FCBs to enhance their resilience by scoring high in their absorption capability. However, if the threat should prolong or repeat itself, and both FCBs do not pay back some capital stocks to their external ties, the relation could wear off or disintegrate the capital in the transmission system. In formal terms:

Proposition 5: When capital flows are from external links to the FCBs, the FCBs' resilience improves temporarily through its absorption capability.

DISCUSSION AND CONCLUSIONS

In this chapter we investigated how bridging social capital influences a family firm's resilience in hostile environments. After conducting a comparative analysis of six cases, we characterized two pathways that may shed light on how the flow of capital between FCBs and their ties could contribute to their resilience capability. Bridging social capital contributes to achieving an FCB's resilience capability by increasing its potential resources through donors (ties), which allows the FCB to expand the available options when facing disruptive conditions. However, the impact of this network of potential resources on an FCB's resilience capability could vary depending on the environment (location and economic sector) in which the ties are present (see Figure 8.3).

When FCBs and their ties belong to the same industry and location, the resources exchanged when the environment becomes hostile are exchanged in a committed way, thus steadily improving the absorption capability of the FCB. Both the FCB and its ties feel the threat with the same intensity and continue to interchange resources until both sides overcome the crisis.

If the FCBs and theirs ties belong to the same industry and location the probability of sustainably absorbing the brunt of the hostile environment will be greater (highly sustainable resilience). Azucarea el Abuelo and Pastas Sorrento are examples of this. Both companies have their ties in the same industry and the same place (location). This ensures the sharing of resources steadily in the event that the country's macro environment becomes hostile, or in case the industry becomes hostile.

When FCBs and their ties belong to different environments, when one of the environments turns hostile the resource moves are made from one side to another until the crisis is overcome. The systems characterized by the FCBs and their contacts belonging to different industries and different regions could represent a high-risk burden for one side of the system in the long term if the hostile environment becomes frequent and unrelenting (see Figure 8.3). Although short-term imbalances in capital flows are to be expected, the sustainability of both extremes of the systems (FCBs and contacts) over the long term, calls for a balance between the inflows and outflows, which must be achieved and maintained in the course of time (Sharma, 2008).

When FCBs and their ties belong at least to the same industry or at least to the same region (location), there will be some probability of facing the steadily disruptive conditions imposed by the environment. Grupo Navidad and Foto Rápida's ties are in the same industry, which assured them some ability to absorb, in a sustainable way, the events produced when the industry turned hostile. However, these FCBs have little capacity to absorb, in a sustainable way, the events imposed by the hostile environment of the region, as their main contacts are in other countries. On the other hand, Severige Machines and Dencker & Co. have their ties in the same region (see Figure 8.3), which assures a sustainable resilience when the macro environment turns hostile, but not when the industry does so.

In this study we did not find any evidence of social free-riding affecting the systems when FCBs face hostile environments. However, the conditions that motivate such negative consequences are likely to lead to promising insights in the future. We observed some nuances of bridging social capital as the directionality and temporality of resource flows varies between similar and different stakeholders within the hostile environment. Variations in such flows are also observed when the relationships are between an actor facing a hostile environment and another one that is not in such an environment.

Our findings can have both theoretical and practical implications. By

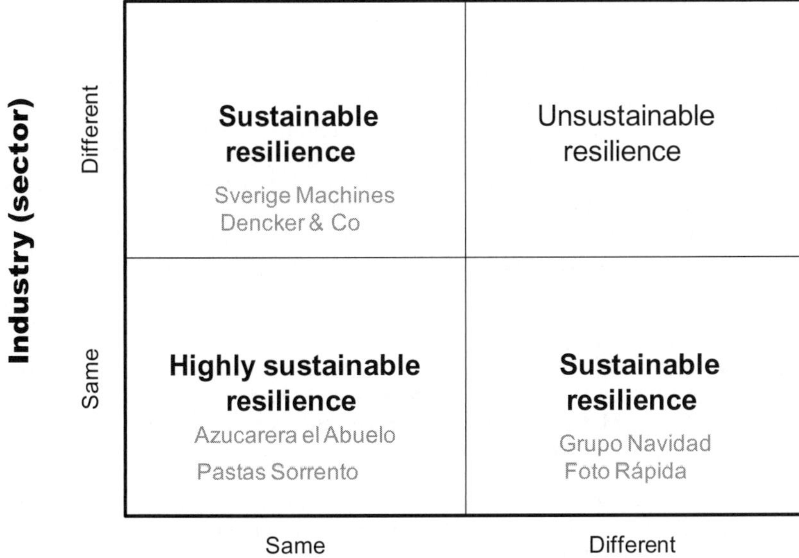

Figure 8.3 Resilience capability depending on FCB's network location (in hostile environments)

pointing out the influence of the location and economic sector in which the FCB's ties are present, this study aims to extend Salvato and Melin's (2008) considerations about the role of *external social capital* in a hostile environment, as well as the thoughts of Sharma (2008) about the *balanced flow of capital* between FCBs and their ties. As for the practical implications, our results reinforce the critical role of active participation in industry associations, supporting similar findings in other studies (for example, Parada et al., 2010). Our findings encourage FCBs to think of the multidimensionality of bridges with external actors both within their own industries and locales, but also beyond. The cost of building different types of bridges varies but so do the benefits. Investment in building social capital strategically can ensure resilience not just temporally, but also steadily.

REFERENCES

Adler, P.S. and S.W. Kwon (2002), 'Social capital: prospects for a new concept', *Academy of Management Review*, **27**, 17–40.

Amann, B. and J. Jaussaud (2012), 'Family and non-family business resilience in an economic downturn', *Asia Pacific Business Review*, **18** (2), 203–23.

Chrisman, J.J., J.H. Chua and L.P. Steier (2011), 'Resilience in family firms: an introduction', *Entrepreneurship Theory and Practice*, **35**, 1107–19.

DeCarolis, D.M., Y. Yang, D.L. Deeds and E. Nelling (2009), 'Weathering the storm: the benefit of resources to high-technology ventures navigating adverse events', *Strategic Entrepreneurship Journal*, **3** (2), 147–60.

Eisenhardt, K.M. (1989), 'Building theories from case study research', *Academy of Management Review*, **14** (4), 532–50.

Eisenhardt, K.M. and M.E. Graebner (2007), 'Theory building from cases: opportunities and challenges', *Academy of Management Journal*, **50** (1), 25–32.

Gedajlovic, E. and M. Carney (2010), 'Markets, hierarchies and families: toward a transactions cost theory of the family firm', *Entrepreneurship Theory & Practice*, **34**, 1145–72.

Grant, R.M. (ed.) (1998), *Contemporary Strategy Analysis: Concepts, Techniques, Applications*, 3th ed., Cambridge, MA: Basil Blackwell Inc.

Habbershon, T. and M. Williams (1999), 'A resource-based framework for assessing the strategic advantages of family firms', *Family Business Review*, **13** (1), 1–25.

Habbershon, T., M. Williams and I. MacMillan (2003), 'A unified systems perspective of family firm performance', *Journal of Business Venturing*, **18** (4), 451–65.

Hitt, M.A., R.D. Ireland, S.M. Camp and D.L. Sexton (2001), 'Strategic entrepreneurship: entrepreneurial strategies for wealth creation', *Strategic Management Journal*, **22**, 479–91.

Hitt, M.A., R.D. Ireland, S.M. Camp and D.L. Sexton (2002), 'Strategic entrepreneurship: integrating entrepreneurial and strategic management perspectives', in M.A. Hitt, R.D. Ireland, S.M. Camp and D.L. Sexton (eds), *Strategic Entrepreneurship: Creating a New Integrated Mindset*, Oxford: Blackwell Publishers, pp. 1–16.

Jick, T.D. (1979), 'Mixing qualitative and quantitative methods: triangulation in action', *Administrative Science Quarterly*, **24**, 602–11.

Kontinen, T. and A. Ojala (2010), 'Bridging social capital in the foreign market entry and entry mode change of family SMEs', *Electronic Journal of Family Business Studies*, **4** (1), 24–38.

Lengnick-Hall, C.A. and T.E. Beck (2005), 'Adaptive fit versus robust transformation: how organizations respond to environmental change', *Journal of Management*, **31** (5), 738–57.

Lengnick-Hall, C.A. and T.E. Beck (2009), 'Resilience capacity and strategic agility: prerequisites for thriving in a dynamic environment', in C. Nemeth, E. Hollnagel and S. Dekker (eds), *Resilience Engineering Perspectives, Vol. 2*, Aldershot, UK: Ashgate Publishing, pp. 39–69.

Long, R.G. (2011), 'Social exchange in building, modeling, and managing family social capital', *Entrepreneurship Theory and Practice*, **35** (6), 1229–36.

McCann, J. (2004), 'Organizational effectiveness: changing concepts for changing environments', *Human Resource Planning*, **27** (1), 42–50.

Miller, D. and P. Friesen (1982), 'Innovation in conservative and entrepreneurial firms: two models of strategic management', *Strategic Management Journal*, **3**, 1–25.

Miller, D. and P. Friesen (1983), 'Strategy making and environment: the third link', *Strategy Management Journal*, **4**, 221–35.

Miller, D. and P. Friesen (1984), *Organizations: A Quantum View*, Englewood Cliffs, NJ: Prentice-Hall, Inc.

Miller, D. and I. Le Breton-Miller (2005), 'Management insights from great and struggling family businesses', *Long Range Planning*, **38**, 517–30.

Nahapiet, J. and S. Ghoshal (1998), 'Social capital, intellectual capital, and theorganizational advantage', *Academy of Management Review*, **23**, 242–66.

Nordqvist, M. and T. Zellweger (2010), 'A qualitative research approach on studying transgenerational entrepreneurship', in M. Nordqvist and T. Zellweger (eds), *Transgenerational Entrepreneurship: Exploring Growth and Performance in Family Firms across Generations*, Cheltenham, UK and Northampton, MA, USA: Edward Elgar, pp. 39–57.

Parada, M.J., M. Nordqvist and A. Gimeno (2010), 'Institutionalizing the family business: the role of professional associations in fostering a change of values', *Family Business Review*, **23** (4), 355–72.

Pearson, A., J. Carr and J. Shaw (2008), 'Toward a theory of social capital: a social capital perspective', *Entrepreneurship Theory and Practice*, **32** (6), 949–69.

Porter, M. (1980), *Competitive Strategy*, New York: Free Press.

Salvato, C. and L. Melin (2008), 'Creating value across generations in family-controlled businesses: the role of family social capital', *Family Business Review*, **21** (3), 259–76.

Shanker, M.C. and H. Astrachan (1996), 'Myths and realities: family businesses' contribution to the US economy – a framework for assessing family business statistics', *Family Business Review*, **9** (2), 107–23.

Sharma, P. (2008), 'Commentary: familiness: capital stocks and flows between family and business', *Entrepreneurship Theory and Practice*, **32**, 971–7.

Slater, S.F. and J.C. Narver (1994), 'Does competitive environment moderate the market orientation performance relationship?', *Journal of Marketing*, **38**, 45–55.

Wright, J.P., F.T. Cullen and J.T. Miller (2001), 'Family social capital and delinquent involvement', *Journal of Criminal Justice*, **29**, 1–9.

Yin, R. (2009), *Case Study Research: Design and Methods*, Thousand Oaks, CA: Sage.

Yli-Renko, H., E. Autio and V. Tontti (2002), 'Social capital, knowledge, and the international growth of technology-based new firms', *International Business Review*, **11** (3), 279–304.

Zahra, S.A. (1996), 'Governance, ownership, and corporate entrepreneurship: the moderating impact of industry technological opportunities', *Academy of Management Journal*, **39** (6), 1713–35.

Zahra, S., S. Nash and D. Bickford (1995), 'Transforming technological pioneering into competitive advantage', *Academy of Management Executive*, **9** (11), 17–31.

Zahra, S. and D. Neubaum (1998), 'Environmental adversity and the entrepreneurial activities of new ventures', *Journal of Developmental Entrepreneurship*, **3** (2), 123–40.

9. Reputation for what? Different types of reputation and their effect on portfolio entrepreneurship activities

Eric Clinton, Robert S. Nason and Philipp Sieger

MLS – THE ROLE OF REPUTATION IN SOLVING A STRATEGIC DILEMMA

In 1932, Ryan Smith Senior began his working life at the age of 16 in partnership with his brother delivering coal, sand and gravel in Dublin city, Ireland. From these humble beginnings emerged Tarastone Limited, which quarried and supplied stones to the construction industry. By 1961, Tarastone had expanded overseas and its success continued through its merger with Infrastructure Development Limited in 1970 to form Infrastructure Development Holdings (IDH) plc. Frustrated by the restrictions of a large public company, Ryan resigned his position as chief executive officer (CEO) of IDH in 1974.

In 1978, Ryan Smith Senior started MLS. The first infrastructure project of this company was the construction of the South Link Bridge across the River Liffey, linking north and south Dublin. This project was developed and built in conjunction with the Irish government as a public–private partnership (PPP). Ryan first established political contacts through his role as CEO of IDH and his membership of the Irish political party Fianna Fáil, where he met influential Irish politicians and entrepreneurs. Following the award of the contract, a fixed price of €7.4m was negotiated. In return for the construction of the South Link Bridge, MLS secured the contractual right to collect a toll on the route for 30 years. Construction started in April 1983 for a contract period of 80 weeks. The contract was completed at the start of week 81, at a cost of €7.7m. By February 1985, one million vehicles had used the bridge, and the predicted usage of 11,000 vehicles per day had been reached. The construction of the South Link

Bridge and the subsequent tolling contract reflected the mutual trust and understanding between the Irish state and MLS.

In 1987, a further PPP was established to build a 3.3 km stretch of motorway and the North Link Bridge in the north of Dublin city. The deal was one of the most profitable ever signed between a private company and the state. Ryan Smith Senior and MLS's initial investment, €140 million, generated profits of more than €900 million. The North Link is one of the most important cogs in the Irish infrastructure network. It traverses the Liffey Valley and connects the orbital motorway (the M50) with the airport and the M1 motorway to Belfast. Almost 100,000 vehicles per day pass through this toll bridge. In the following years, the strong working relationship between the Irish state and MLS continued with the development of further capital-intensive infrastructure projects throughout Ireland.

Commenting on such long-term relationships, Ryan Smith Junior, son of Ryan Smith Senior and the current chairman of MLS, states: 'infrastructure by its nature involves interaction with the public authorities, being regulated by the state in the waste business or partnering with the state in the roads business'. Over the years, the Smith family and MLS have built a favorable reputation in the infrastructure industry in Ireland as noted by Ryan Sr's grandson, Sean Smith:

> the Smith family has been well respected in the infrastructure industry in Ireland. This Smith family reputation adds credibility to business transactions and propositions . . . when most people think of MLS, they associate it with the Smith family.

In 1999, Ryan Smith Senior passed away. His death marked the loss of one of Ireland's foremost entrepreneurs. The Irish media described him as 'one of the outstanding businessmen of his generation' (Millennium Edition *Irish Times*, 2000). He was continually pursuing new projects or looking at ways to make existing products more efficient. Some undeveloped ideas include a gas project in Dublin Bay, a car park under St Stephens Green and a tunnel for Dublin Port. Indeed, the week before he died he was in government offices showing members of the Department of Transport radical plans to reposition existing railway bridges in Dublin city. From 1999 on, however, Ryan Smith Junior led MLS into the twenty-first century, perpetuating the entrepreneurial passion of his father. Sean Smith notes that his father 'loves new businesses, he loves getting stuck in there, working at a corporate level'.

However, despite all these favorable preconditions, MLS was at a critical strategic turning point at the beginning of the 2000s, as its exclusive tolling rights were to expire in a few years, drying up a major source of income. Ryan Smith Junior wondered about the future. Three generations of his family had been involved in the construction industry for nearly 80 years. Should they remain in the route-way development and construction business? Should they try to source new opportunities in that context, such as new PPPs? Or should they diversify their product and service offering to pursue emerging attractive opportunities? They were considering internationalizing into the US market but had to consider whether their strong networks and good name would be as useful overseas.

For Ryan Smith Junior, three factors were especially important in setting the future strategic direction of the company. First, his own entrepreneurial thirst that needed to be satisfied. He was particularly attracted to renewable energy and waste management. Ryan's vision for such a portfolio strategy was driven by the global macro factors of climate change, security of energy supply and resource depletion. These factors underpinned the belief that significant growth opportunities would continue to emerge in the markets for renewable energy, bio energy, recycling and waste management.

Second, he realized that MLS in general and the Smith family in particular had developed into a 'magnet' for business opportunities. He once mentioned that 'the reputation of MLS as a family firm is a huge selling point when conducting ventures with other family firms'. His son Sean supports this view: 'the ability to use the Smith name and its link with MLS instantly gets you a foot in the door'. Frank Miller, the CEO of MLS notes, 'there is an endless stream of people trying to sell ideas and investment opportunities to the Smith family. It is like a full time job trying to review the business proposals we receive.' A concrete example of a promising opportunity was Atlantic Energy, a wind energy business founded by Dr Michael Murphy, the former CEO of Bord na Móna (state energy supplier). He needed significant capital investment (€120 million) to locate large wind turbines across the wind-swept Irish coastlines.

Third, at this strategic turning point, the Smith family was in a very favorable financial position. They had sold part of their investment in a hotel chain for close to €508 million, so they had the slack financial resources to invest in new opportunities. But how would their intangible resources be best put to use?

With these thoughts as a starting point, Ryan Smith Junior noted down the main questions that needed to be answered to solve that strategic dilemma.

REVIEW QUESTIONS

1. What resources have led to the success of the Smith family and MLS?
2. If one thinks of reputation as a resource, what type of reputation does the Smith family and/or MLS have?
3. Could the different types of family reputation be an advantage or disadvantage to firm development?
4. What resource-related factors should the Smith family consider when making a decision to continue with the infrastructure business or diversify into other entrepreneurial activities?
5. What are the reputational risks involved in your chosen strategy? The reputation of MLS and the Smith family has been built up over more than 80 years. Could that reputation erode? How? Should the family really put their main asset at risk?

INTRODUCTION

It is widely acknowledged that different types of resources constitute the building blocks of firms' long-term competitive advantage. The resource-based view (RBV) postulates that firms develop a competitive advantage based on their ability to exploit the value potential of these resources (Barney, 1991), where reputation is seen as one of the key asset bases (Grant, 1991; Wernerfelt, 1984). Due to its intangible nature, a firm's reputation is difficult for competitors to replicate and can create a significant barrier to entry (Landon and Smith, 1997; Roberts and Dowling, 2002). Reputation has been linked to financial performance (Fombrun and Shanley, 1990), increased trust (Deephouse, 2000) and value creation (Rindova et al., 2010). Recently, reputation resources have been linked to portfolio entrepreneurship activity (Sieger et al., 2011).

The RBV in general and reputation in particular are of special relevance in the family firm context. First, the systemic interaction between the family and the business sphere creates unique resources and capabilities (Habbershon et al., 2003). Second, reputation is an especially valuable resource due to identity overlaps between the family and the business, its advantages to family firms in general and its particular relevance for corporate strategy in such firms (Craig et al., 2008; Miller and Le Breton-Miller, 2007). Third, reputation in the family firm is particularly valuable since it can be leveraged across a variety of domains due to its generic non-tradable asset (GNT) nature (Gedajlovic and Carney, 2010).

However, there remain significant gaps in knowledge regarding the role of reputation in family firms. We attempt to fill these gaps using a single in-depth STEP (Successful Transgenerational Entrepreneurship Practices) case across family and firm levels of analysis (Nordqvist and Zellweger, 2010). First, previous research has largely treated reputation as a homogenous construct with a presumed positive impact. The implicit assumption is that firms aspire to develop and protect a positive reputation (Dyer and Whetten, 2006), where a 'bigger is better' approach is adopted, since having greater stocks of valuable and rare resources will be beneficial. Little research though has paid attention to the possibility that reputation may be a multidimensional construct or consist of different types. We argue that there is a need to move beyond a stock approach to a nuanced perspective of types of reputation. Firms, as individuals, do not only develop a positive or negative reputation, but rather develop a reputation for various types of behaviors, attitudes or orientations. We identify long-term orientation, trusted business partnership and entrepreneurial spirit as distinct types of reputation. These detailed reputation components allow for the reputation of firms to be analyzed in less dichotomous (high/low or positive/negative) terms and opens up the possibility to link to more specific firm outcomes.

Second, there is relatively little empirical research on family firm reputation development, and its impact on firm outcomes (Zellweger and Kellermanns, 2008). One of the few areas where reputation has been examined is in the development of family business portfolios. In this context, industry and meta-industry reputation has been linked to family portfolio activity (Sieger et al., 2011). We explore this link further by drawing out the distinct types of reputation and demonstrate how they contribute to the development of family business portfolios.

The chapter is organized as follows. First, we review the existing research on reputation and the unique context of family portfolio entrepreneurship. Second, we use an in-depth case study to identify distinct types of reputation and develop empirically testable propositions. We close with suggestions for future research.

THEORETICAL FOUNDATIONS

Reputation

Reputation is predominantly viewed as a broad construct which can provide many positive benefits to a firm (Roberts and Dowling, 2002; Rumelt, 1987; Shamsie, 2003). Fombrun (1996: 72) defines corporate reputation as a 'a perceptual representation of a company's past actions and future prospects that describes the firm's overall appeal to all of its key constituents when compared to other leading rivals'. Essentially, reputation is concerned with stakeholders' perceived evaluation of the firm in terms of 'affect, esteem and knowledge' (Deephouse, 2000: 1093).

In general, firms that have a positive public image are rewarded with better financial performance and firms that are performing well become the 'first choice' with investors, employees and customers (Schultz et al., 2000). Reputation also has the propensity to create value for the firm by signaling to existing or potential stakeholders (suppliers, customers, employees and investors) the reliability and credibility of the product or service being offered (Fombrun and Shanley, 1990).

In the family firm context, reputation has been perceived as a double-edged sword. Reflective of the dark sides of family firms, Litz and Turner (2012) suggest that unethical or immoral business-related behavior can create a negative reputation in one generation that is often difficult to change for subsequent generations. However, reputation can also be positive, as a non-economic goal and perk to being a family member (Tagiuri and Davis, 1996; Sharma, 2008; Sorenson, 1999). The social recognition of belonging to the family of a prominent family firm often stems from their community involvement. Family businesses pride themselves on the employment of a community based workforce, sourcing resources locally, supporting community charities or engaging in social entrepreneurship endeavors (Craig et al., 2008). The identity overlap between family and business instils a need for reputation preservation to maintain the firm's positive public image (Miller and Le Breton-Miller, 2007; Zellweger et al., 2013). The development of reputation capital warrants a long-term perspective since intensive short-term advertising cannot equate to a proven reputation for superior performance over many years. As family firms are typified by their stability, continuity in ownership provides an embryonic environment for the creation of reputation capital (Zellweger, 2007).

While reputation is regarded as an important resource in general (Grant, 1991), it can be classified as a GNT (generic non-tradable asset) as defined by Gedajlovic and Carney (2010). A GNT is a firm-specific asset that is generic in its application. Reputation is one of the primary GNTs because it is generic in the sense that it is an intangible asset which can benefit a firm in a variety of different ways, but non-tradable because it is inextricably bound with the history and idiosyncrasies of the business family.

More recent scholarship has clarified the construct of reputation around two primary dimensions: perceived quality and prominence (Rindova et al., 2005, 2010). Perceived quality emerges from the economic perspective. It is based on how stakeholders evaluate a company based on a particular attribute (quality of products for instance) and is more concerned with the perceptions of customers. Prominence emerges from an institutional perspective, is based on the public awareness and recognition of a company, and is more concerned with the perceptions of stakeholder groups and institutions within a particular organizational field (Rindova et al., 2005). We build on the work of Rindova et al. (2010) and follow in the perceived quality dimension of reputation. We focus on this dimension because of its natural link to the RBV and the important influence of stakeholder groups on family firms regardless of their specific organizational field (Zellweger and Nason, 2008). Family firms often operate in multiple institutional contexts (Sieger et al., 2011) and stakeholders of any field may evaluate a firm based on a multitude of attributes. We specifically identify three particularly salient attributes, which may be considered types of reputation, and link them to portfolio entrepreneurship activity.

Portfolio Entrepreneurship

Increasingly, entrepreneurship scholars, practitioners and policy makers are using portfolio entrepreneurship to investigate firm growth and performance (Carter and Ram, 2003; Westhead et al., 2005). Portfolio entrepreneurship describes an individual's interest in multiple firms (Kolvereid and Bullvag, 1992; Rosa and Scott, 1999; Ucbasaran et al., 2001). Portfolio entrepreneurs are seen as an important subgroup in the entrepreneurial pool who make a significant contribution to wealth creation (Scott and Rosa, 1996). Such portfolio entrepreneurs offer greater growth prospects than novice or serial entrepreneurs (Westhead et al., 2005). Thus, an understanding of portfolio entrepreneurship activity plays a seminal role in explaining local, national and international entrepreneurial development (Carter and Ram, 2003).

Research on portfolio entrepreneurship has explored the motivations for entrepreneurs to engage in portfolio development activity. Motivations or triggers cited for portfolio development include an individual's desire for autonomy, independence, achievement, risk diversification and growth opportunities (Donckels et al., 1987; Westhead and Wright, 1998). A related realm of research investigates the desirable qualities for establishing a portfolio business, including prior experience, an established network, a strong reputation and a proven track record (Wiklund and Shepherd, 2008). Portfolio entrepreneurship activity is particularly relevant to family firms in light of their long-term investment horizons (Zellweger, 2007), desire for family employment (Carter and Ram, 2003), risk diversification and increased wealth creation opportunities (Sieger et al., 2011: 329). Carter and Ram (2003: 372) suggest 'family dynamics have a significant effect on both the decision to engage in portfolio strategies and also the processes which are used in the portfolio approach'.

Building on prior research in portfolio entrepreneurship in family firms, Sieger et al. (2011) investigate the portfolio development process. They find that both industry-specific and meta-industry reputations influence the development of a business portfolio over time. However, while these authors focus on the contextual nature of reputation as a resource, they do not specifically evaluate the exact type of reputation, meaning the reputation for what exactly? We address this gap by focusing on reputation attributes which have evolved over a long period of time and through diversification stages that represent a specific type of reputation. As will be shown, the types of reputation we identify are primarily situated on the meta-industry level.

METHODOLOGY AND CASE CHARACTERISTICS

In this chapter, we rely on the STEP case about the Smith family in Ireland. This unique case allows in-depth insights into the role of different types of reputation in the context of portfolio entrepreneurship. In general, the same methodological approach as for all other STEP case studies was applied.[1] Referring to the different sub-dimensions of reputation that we intended to identify, dictionary codes were intuitively derived by two of the authors. Two of the three authors independently coded the interview transcripts with primary concern for different dimensions of family reputation. In that process, three dimensions of reputation emerged, namely long-term orientation, trusted business partners and entrepreneurial spirit. All coding was imported to a centralized database.

Table 9.1 Interviewee profile

Informant	Number of interviews	Family or non-family	Position in the firm
Ryan Smith	3	Family	Chairman, MLS Group
Sean Smith	3	Family	Business Development Manager, MLS Group
Denzel Chipfield	1	Family	Board of Directors, MLS Group; CEO Pharma Vet plc
Jamie Fisher	2	Non-family	Financial Advisor, MLS Group
Frank Miller	2	Non-family	CEO, MLS Group
Markus Hill	1	Non-family	Financial Advisor, MLS Group

Table 9.2 Critical events in the development of MLS

Dates	Key issues and events	Countries
1978–97	Initial public–private partnership (PPP) with the Irish state for the construction of an infrastructure route-way	Ireland
1998	Investment in water treatment (Irish Anglian Water). A venture started by a relation of the Smith family	Ireland
1999	Following strategic review and deregulation initiatives in both the renewable energy and waste management industries MLS enters both respective sectors nationally and pan-European	Ireland, UK, Europe
2001	Further expansion through its investment in wind energy (Atlantic Energy)	Ireland, UK, Continental Europe and USA
2001	Investment in telecommunications (Irish internet)	Ireland
2003	Following the success of the first PPP negotiated by Ryan Smith (Senior), Ryan Smith (Junior) successfully negotiates a second PPP with the state for the construction of a second route linking north and south Dublin ('North Link')	Ireland
2006	Further expansion of the firm's portfolio through the firm's involvement in bio-energy (Woodford). Alignment with Virgin Fuels to expand operations in North America	Germany, UK & USA
2008	Investment in solar power energy (East Energy Systems)	USA
2008	In line with the corporate strategy on renewable energy MLS expands its portfolio by investing in wind energy (The Energy Group)	USA
2008	Expansion of its renewable energy business through investment in the ethanol business (Renewable Energy Inc.)	USA

The coding in the database was then compared by the third author. Two scenarios were presented from this analysis: both authors agreed on the marked text, or only one author marked the text. In the case of disagreement, the third author acted as a judge. Initial agreement was reached in excess of 80 percent of the cases coded.

Table 9.1 offers a profile of interviewees of the Smith case. Table 9.2 identifies the critical events in the development of the MLS group.

FINDINGS FROM THE SMITH FAMILY

In the following we discuss the three forms of reputation that we identified, including a reputation for: long-term orientation, trusted business partners and entrepreneurial spirit. We relate each of them to family portfolio entrepreneurial activities.

Long-Term Orientation

MLS, a business controlled by the Smith family for three generations, has largely focused on building infrastructure in Ireland. The impetus for the establishment of the business was the strong political capital of Ryan Smith Senior through his involvement in the Fianna Fáil political party. Such political contacts were to prove instrumental in securing long-term contractual commitments with the Irish government in the form of PPPs. PPPs offered a solution to the demand for much-needed investment in infrastructural projects, aligned with a need for fiscal conservatism. PPPs are collaborations between public bodies (local authorities, central government) and private companies for the delivery of a product or service. The PPP model is built on the premise of mutual benefit to both the public and private sector, such as access to private sector revenues to fund public services, the allocation of risk between public and private sector bodies, and a reduction in project costs resulting from synergistic qualities (Connolly and Wall, 2009). In return for the development of large infrastructure projects that would later be key to the country's transport network, MLS was awarded the tolling rights for 30 years. Through the development of the South Link Bridge, MLS demonstrated to government, suppliers, developers and employees its status as a long-term business partner. This appetite for long-term projects and significant capital investment saw the firm secure subsequent PPPs with the Irish state for the development of the North Link Bridge and other route-ways nationwide.

The turn of the twenty-first century saw MLS and the Smith family face a significant strategic dilemma based primarily on two factors. First, the expiration of the tolling rights to the South Link and North Link toll bridges in the coming years. Second, with the sale of a shareholding in a chain of hotels the family netted a significant financial windfall of €508 million. The family shareholders must decide if they should continue in the infrastructure development business or gravitate towards emerging opportunities like that of green energy or waste management. The family were particularly attracted by emerging opportunities in renewable energy. In particular, one individual – Dr Michael Murphy – was seeking investment in his wind energy business and saw the Smith family with their entrepreneurial foresight and disposable capital as the ideal partner. For the Smith family, the long-term investment nature was aligned with their patient financial approach. Furthermore, as the former CEO of the Irish gas company (BordGas), Dr Murphy was aware of the willingness of the Smith family to invest in large capital projects. After much discussion, the family felt that Dr Murphy shared their values and acquired 51 percent of the emerging business. The family investment was primarily used to erect wind turbines and construct renewable energy power stations on Ireland's Atlantic Ocean-facing west coast.

Following the initial venture into renewable energy (wind), the family decided to make further sizeable capital investments. Indeed, over the past decade, the asset base of the firm has moved from a national to an international focus, with 80 percent of the asset base sourced outside of Ireland. The 'tentacles of MLS' have truly spread worldwide, noted Frank Miller, the non-family CEO of the company. In his words, the 'family's long-term focus and willingness for capital investment has been key . . . it is a huge advantage to us to have the family shareholding aligned with our future strategic direction; they see the potential within the industry and recognize the significant investment needed to generate opportunities'.

By the turn of the twenty-first century MLS had repositioned itself as a utilities company with a thirst for expansion. This expansion was primarily achieved through merger and acquisition activity. Examples of acquisitions include UK and Irish family firms Waste Services (UK) Ltd, Verdant Group plc, Waste Exchange Services, Bailey Waste Recycling, Rainbow Refuse Ltd and North American firms including Tensington Waste Management, a fourth-generation firm, family-owned since 1910, Materson and Finon Falls, family-owned since 1924, and Leicester Paper Processors, a fourth-generation family firm.

The acquisition process was greatly aided by the values and reputation the Smith family had developed both nationally and internationally in the infrastructure business. Acquisition targets, many of which are family firms, were attracted to the long-term commitment of MLS; all firms talk of the intrinsic Smith family values and culture and the alignment with the family-orientated package that the MLS group was offering. CEO Frank Miller notes: 'many of the firms we do business with have a significant family presence . . . issues of long-term orientation and commitment to the industry, community and organisational stakeholders often take precedence over short-term financial return . . . therefore, the 80 years of Smith family commitment to the infrastructure industry is invaluable for our international growth'.

MLS's management are big proponents of the family's long-term vision as 'the family shareholding possess the key ingredients for our growth objectives, primarily their long-term orientation, which is conducive to capital intensive research and development projects we are undertaking' (Markus Hill, Financial Advisor, MLS). Such sentiments are supported by the family Chairman: 'if we were short-term in our vision we would not be as entrepreneurial in the existing companies' (Ryan Smith, Chairman, MLS).

These findings illustrate that the family can influence firm reputation in a way that engenders a perception amongst stakeholders of a long-term orientation. As a result, long-term orientation represents a unique type of reputation in family firms and is distinct from having a generally positive reputation. Further, a reputation for long-term orientation can be conducive to long-term entrepreneurial investments, developing projects, attracting and generating opportunities, as well as diversification and internationalization efforts. Put differently, this makes us believe that a reputation for long-term orientation is an important antecedent to portfolio entrepreneurial activity in family firms, as it is very helpful in attracting, identifying and exploiting entrepreneurial opportunities. More formally stated:

Proposition 1: A business family's reputation for long-term orientation is positively related to portfolio entrepreneurship activity.

Trusted Business Partners

As noted earlier, the family firm has a significant interest in mergers and acquisitions activity. The types of firms they are acquiring are often small, rural family-run firms in industries such as quarrying, waste management and farming. The belief of family management is that 'while many of the acquiring firms may receive greater financial returns from private equity firms they decide to merge with MLS as they are inspired by the well-established and respected family legacy attributed to the firm. Many firms believe they will get a fairer deal from a family controlled company than a non-family controlled company and in many respects I think they do' (Markus Hill, MLS). Further expanding on this, Frank Miller, the CEO of MLS, contends: 'people (acquiring firms) are attracted to what the Smith's, especially Ryan, stands for, the values he possesses, his work ethic, his drive for creativity and innovation . . . while firms appreciate what we do they also like what we stand for'. The long-standing values and culture instilled through family involvement is greatly respected and an attractable commodity to other firms. Frank Miller adds: 'we do not have the touch and feel of a big corporate'. This is supported by Ryan Smith Junior, who says that 'although the MLS group is a PLC, when acquiring firms hear that the primary shareholder is a family called the Smith family, and they hear about our legacy, they like the values we possess and what we stand for'. He continues, 'we are dealing with people who possibly share our own family values, they do not like dealing with a faceless company that they cannot relate to, and particularly in the US as most of the big companies we partner with, started out as family companies'. Frank Miller also illustrates further that the personal accountability and legacy in the infrastructure industry has been extremely effective in securing deals with prospective partners, 'Ryan has been invaluable in developing relationships with business owners, many of whom are family businesses, in North America'.

The PPPs formed with the Irish government showcase the family's status as a trusted business partner. The success of the PPP model has been well-documented both nationally and internationally, earning the firm rich credibility as a good business partner.

As a whole, the MLS case demonstrates how a family can influence firm reputation to become known as a trusted business partner. This distinct type of reputation helps in attracting opportunities, be it in the form of firms potentially to be acquired, partnerships, joint ventures or government deals. Hence, we pose the following proposition:

Proposition 2: A business family's reputation as a trusted business partner is positively related to portfolio entrepreneurship activity.

Entrepreneurial Spirit

A passion for entrepreneurial activity has always been 'part of the DNA' of the Smith family. A look at the three generations of family involvement in the firm clearly displays this entrepreneurial gene. Starting with the founder of MLS, Ryan Smith Senior was passionate about new business and spreading the tentacles of the business far and wide, as his son Ryan Junior states 'entrepreneurship was his passion, he was continually seeking out new opportunities and ways to improve the status quo'. Hence, he was classified by many 'as the foremost entrepreneur of his time', as Frank Miller, the MLS CEO, emphasizes.

The second generation of Smith family involvement brought structure and professionalism to the firm. Having completed his formal education, a master of business administration at the Wharton School (University of Pennsylvania), Ryan Smith Junior returned to MLS to offer formal guidance to his father. However, Ryan and his family as major shareholders were faced with a major strategic decision in light of a financial windfall from the sale of a family share in a hotel chain and the pending expiration of exclusive tolling rights with the Irish state. Should they simply invest the financial windfall in a secure bank account or pursue emerging entrepreneurial opportunities?

Reflective of the desire for new business and growth they decided to reinvest the earnings back into the business and pursue the emerging industries of renewable energy and waste management. This decision saw the firm grow to a multiple of five in terms of profits, employee numbers and asset base.

Third-generation members also exude the entrepreneurial spirit and need for innovative independence. The family strives for entrepreneurial opportunities and recognizes that innovation, risk-taking and autonomy are necessary for future aspirations. They appreciate the need for entrepreneurial performance to ensure their transgenerational survival. Commenting on this passion for entrepreneurship, Ryan Smith Junior states: 'opportunistic would describe us in a business sense rather than in a family sense . . . we (the family) are not main stream in our thinking, we would want to break the mould . . . we want to grow the business, we want to exploit opportunities'. This inherent entrepreneurial spirit has been successfully nurtured and the mindset passed onto future generations, evident through the magnitude of successful ventures established by the successive generations. Commenting on the current generation, Ryan Smith Junior notes that 'Sean has the entrepreneurial spirit and drive that his grandfather possessed previously'.

Recognition of the entrepreneurial spirit of the Smith family has resulted in a rich interest from prospective partners in tapping into the capital stocks of the family. Parties are eager to offer ideas, prototypes and emerging opportunities to the family in the aspiration of tapping their entrepreneurial capabilities. Such opportunity attraction is coming to the Smith's from multiple industries and from various levels in the production process. Markus Hill contends 'there is an endless stream of people trying to sell them (Smith family) ideas and investment opportunities, it is nearly a full-time job dealing with propositions'. Sean Smith, member of the third generation, contends 'there is continual flow of ideas from both start-ups and existing business trying to channel the resources we possess, this is especially evident following our decision to diversify the strategic direction of the group'. He continues: '. . . we possess the established networks, we have access to capital (banks), suppliers, retailers . . . we have means for both horizontal and vertical integration which we have created over our 80-year involvement in the industry and this is particularly appealing to emerging opportunity'.

The entrepreneurial spirit and desire for entrepreneurial opportunity has been a core ingredient in the family's reputation. 'Firms align them-

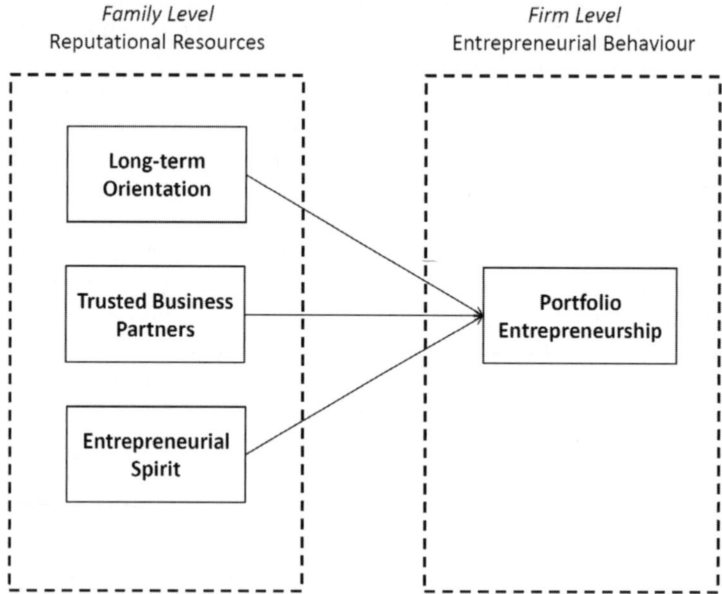

Figure 9.1 Research model

selves with the entrepreneurial mindset of the Smith family, they identify with the need to embrace change and create opportunity . . . the Smith family have a proven reputation for successful venturing within the respective industries', says Frank Miller, CEO of MLS.

Building on these insights, we suggest that families can infuse their firms with an entrepreneurial spirit which becomes known by stakeholders. This creates a distinct type of reputation for an entrepreneurial spirit which is not prevalent in all firms, even those with a positive reputation. A family firm with a reputation for entrepreneurial spirit will be more likely to attract new opportunities, thus resulting in enhanced portfolio entrepreneurial activity. More formally stated:

Proposition 3: A business family's reputation for entrepreneurial spirit is positively related to portfolio entrepreneurial activity.

DISCUSSION

This study set out to shed a more nuanced light on reputation as a family-influenced resource and its role for portfolio entrepreneurial activity at both family and firm levels. Using the MLS STEP case from Ireland, we identify three different types of reputation, namely reputation for long-term orientation, for being a trusted business partner and for entrepreneurial spirit, and identify positive linkages to portfolio entrepreneurial activity. Figure 9.1 provides a summary of our research model. By this we contribute to the literature in three main ways.

First, we extend resource-based research on reputation by introducing three different sub-dimensions of the construct that are positively related to portfolio entrepreneurial activity. More specifically, we challenge the traditional 'the more the better' approach prevalent in RBV research and strongly support the notion that various types of reputation need to be considered separately (cf. Dyer and Whetten, 2006; Sieger et al., 2011; Zellweger and Kellermanns, 2008). This more fined-grained approach to reputation is useful in distinguishing reputation differences and their corresponding effects on performance between family and non-family firms (Deephouse and Jaskiewicz, 2013).

Second, we contribute to research on portfolio entrepreneurship by providing further depth in the types of resources that are critical in this process. In particular, we link portfolio entrepreneurship with emerging research on transgenerational entrepreneurship (Zellweger et al., 2013). We offer a more fine-grained understanding of how family-influenced resources can contribute to entrepreneurial activity, and ultimately the long-term success of the business family. Third, we speak to family business scholars who call for a more in-depth investigation of the distinctive family-influenced resources (Chrisman et al., 2005; Habbershon and Williams, 1999; Pearson et al., 2008). We demonstrate the explanative power of in-depth case studies by showing that unique insights about specific family-influenced resources, such as reputation, can be generated.

Viewing family firm reputation as a multidimensional construct enables new theorizing on the topic. For instance, so far unaddressed is the way in which the reputational dimensions of long-term orientation, entrepreneurial spirit and trusted business partners are related to each other. While some dimensions may be mutually reinforcing, others may be conflicting. For instance, the elements of risk and proactivity inherent in an entrepreneurial spirit (Lumpkin and Dess, 1996) may be in conflict with the stability and 'safe' choice of a trusted business partner. For this reason, family firms may develop unique constellations of reputation with varying levels of each reputation type. Still little is known about how individual stakeholder perceptions of reputation are aggregated, but the view of reputation as a constellation of dimensions may offer insight into this process. In addition, while reputation is externally oriented, future research on reputation constellations may draw from efforts examining the internally oriented research identity. Research on identity has demonstrated that individuals and firms have multiple identity concerns with varying levels of salience (Zellweger et al., 2013). Further research may also identify archetypes within reputation constellations (Miller and Friesen, 1978) and link them to firm outcomes besides portfolio entrepreneurship.

In addition, our study is based on a single case study and our findings may thus not be generalizable to all family businesses. However, while we believe that our findings offer some basic insights that might be transferable across institutional and cultural contexts, we call for further research to replicate and validate our findings on a larger sample of firms from different regions in the world. More specifically, future studies need to address the implications of the cultural context on family reputation to strengthen the external validity of our findings. This research should incorporate different geographical locations and sociopolitical contexts. In addition, future research could also address the question of how to ensure the transgenerational transfer of this resource. To date little empirical research has been completed on the cross-pollination of resources across family generations and we argue that this is a fruitful area for exploration. Finally, our propositions could be tested empirically, with appropriate measurement instruments in a regression or structural equation model.

CONCLUSION

This study has filled an important gap in the literature through an intensive exploration of a single family-influenced resource, reputation. We offer a more nuanced perspective of different types of reputation by identifying reputations for (i) long-term orientation (ii) an entrepreneurial spirit and (iii) trusted business partners. As each of those dimensions is positively related to portfolio entrepreneurship activities, we contribute to numerous streams of literature and open up avenues for promising future research.

NOTE

1. For detailed information on methodological aspects such as research design, procedures, data collection and analyses please refer to the corresponding chapters of this book, as well as to published academic articles built on STEP cases (for example, Nordqvist et al., 2008; Sieger et al., 2011; Zellweger and Sieger, 2012).

REFERENCES

Barney, J.B. (1991), 'Firm resources and sustained competitive advantage', *Journal of Management*, **17** (1), 99–120.

Carter, S. and M. Ram (2003), 'Reassessing portfolio entrepreneurship', *Small Business Economics*, **21** (4), 371–80.

Chrisman, J.J., J.H. Chua and L. Steier (2005), 'Sources and consequences of distinctive familiness: an introduction', *Entrepreneurship Theory and Practice*, **29**, 237–47.

Connolly, C. and T. Wall (eds) (2009), *Public Private Partnerships in Ireland: Benefits, Problems and Critical Success Factors*, Dublin, Ireland: Gill & MacMillan.

Craig, J., C. Dibrell and P. Davis (2008), 'Leveraging family-based brand identity to enhance firm competitiveness and performance in family business', *Journal of Small Business Management*, **46** (3), 351–71.

Deephouse, D.L. (2000), 'Media reputation as a strategic resource: an integration of mass communications and resource based theories', *Journal of Management*, **26** (6), 1091–112.

Deephouse, D.L. and P. Jaskiewicz (2013), 'Do family firms have better reputations than non-family firms? An integration of socioemotional wealth and social identity theories', *Journal of Management Studies*, **50** (3), 337–60.

Donckels, R., B. Dupont and P. Michel (1987), 'Multiple business starters. Who? Why? What?', *Journal of Small Business and Entrepreneurship*, **5** (1), 48–63.

Dyer, G. and D.A. Whetten (2006), 'Family firms and social responsibility: preliminary evidence from the SP 500', *Entrepreneurship Theory and Practice*, **30** (6), 785–802.

Fombrun, C. (1996), *Reputation: Realizing the Value From the Corporate Image*, Boston, MA: Harvard Business School.

Fombrun, C. and M. Shanley (1990), 'What's in a name? Reputation building and corporate strategy', *Academy of Management Journal*, **33** (2), 233–58.

Gedajlovic, E.R. and M. Carney (2010), 'Markets, hierarchies and families: toward a transaction costs theory of the family firm', *Entrepreneurship Theory and Practice*, **34** (6), 1145–72.

Grant, R.M. (1991), 'The resource-based theory of competitive advantage: implications for strategy formulation', *California Management Review*, **33** (3), 114–35.

Habbershon, T.G. and M. Williams (1999), 'A resource-based framework for assessing the strategic advantage of family firms', *Family Business Review*, **12** (1), 1–25.

Habbershon, T.G., M. Williams and I.C. MacMillan (2003), 'A unified systems perspective of family firm performance', *Journal of Business Venturing*, **18** (4), 451–65.

Kolvereid, L. and E. Bullvag (1992), 'Novices versus experienced business founders: an exploratory investigation', in S. Birley, I. MacMillan and S. Subramony (eds), *Entrepreneurship Research: Global Perspectives*, London: North-Holland, pp. 275–85.

Landon, S. and C.E. Smith (1997), 'The use of quality and reputation indicators by consumers: the case of Bordeaux wine', *Journal of Consumer Policy*, **20** (3), 289–323.

Litz, R. and N. Turner (2012), 'Sins of the father's firm: exploring responses to inherited ethical dilemmas in family business', *Journal of Business Ethics*, **113** (2), 297–315.

Lumpkin, G.T. and G.G. Dess (1996), 'Clarifying the entrepreneurial orientation construct and linking it to performance', *Academy of Management Review*, **21** (1), 135–72.

Millennium Edition *The Irish Times* (2000), 'Performance and growth', *The Irish Times*, accessed at www.irishtimes.com.

Miller, D. and P.H. Friesen (1978), 'Archetypes of strategy formulation', *Management Science*, **24** (9), 921–33.

Miller, D. and I. Le Breton-Miller (2007), 'Kicking the habit: broadening our horizons by studying family businesses', *Journal of Management Inquiry*, **16** (1), 27–30.

Nordqvist, M., T.G. Habbershon and L. Melin (2008), 'Transgenerational entrepreneurship: exploring EO in family firms', in H. Landström, H. Crijns and E. Laveren (eds), *Entrepreneurship, Sustainable Growth and Performance: Frontiers in European Entrepreneurship Research*, Cheltenham, UK and Northampton, MA, USA: Edward Elgar, pp. 93–116.

Nordqvist, M. and T. Zellweger (eds) (2010), *Transgenerational Entrepreneurship: Exploring Growth and Performance in Family Firms across Generations*, Cheltenham, UK and Northampton, MA, USA: Edward Elgar.

Pearson, A.W., J.C. Carr and J.C. Shaw (2008), 'Toward a theory of familiness: a social capital perspective', *Entrepreneurship Theory & Practice*, **32** (6), 949–69.

Rindova, V.P., I.O. Williamson and A.P. Petkova (2010), 'Reputation as an intangible asset: reflections on theory and methods in two empirical studies of business school reputations', *Journal of Management*, **36** (3), 610–19.

Rindova, V.P., I.O. Williamson, A.P. Petkova and J.M. Sever (2005), 'Being good or being known: an empirical examination of the dimensions, antecedents, and consequences of organizational reputation', *Academy of Management Journal*, **48** (6), 1033–49.

Roberts, P.W. and G.R. Dowling (2002), 'Corporate reputation and sustained superior financial performance', *Strategic Management Journal*, **23** (12), 1077–93.

Rosa, P. and M. Scott (1999), 'The prevalence of multiple owners and directors in the SME sector: implications for our understanding of start-up and growth', *Entrepreneurship & Regional Development*, **11** (1), 21–37.

Rumelt, R.P. (1987), 'Theory, strategy and entrepreneurship', in D. Teece (ed.), *The Competitive Challenge: Strategies for Industrial Innovation and Renewal*, Cambridge, MA: Ballinger, pp. 137–57.

Schultz, M., M.J. Hatch and M.H. Larsen (eds) (2000), *The Expressive Organization: Linking Identity, Reputation, and the Corporate Brand*, Oxford: Oxford University Press.

Scott, M. and P. Rosa (1996), 'Opinion: has firm level analysis reached its limits? Time for rethink', *International Small Business Journal*, **14** (4), 81–9.

Shamsie, J. (2003), 'The context of dominance: an industry-driven framework for exploiting reputation', *Strategic Management Journal*, **24** (3), 199–215.

Sharma, P. (2008), 'Commentary: familiness: capital stocks and flows between family and business', *Entrepreneurship Theory & Practice*, **32** (6), 971–7.

Sieger, P., T. Zellweger, R. Nason and E. Clinton (2011), 'Portfolio entrepreneur-

ship in family firms: a resource-based perspective', *Strategic Entrepreneurship Journal*, **5**, 327–51.
Sorenson, R.L. (1999), 'Conflict management strategies used by successful family businesses', *Family Business Review*, **12** (2), 133–46.
Tagiuri, R. and J. Davis (1996), 'Bivalent attributes of the family firm', *Family Business Review*, **9** (2), 199–208.
Ucbasaran, D., P. Westhead and M. Wright (2001), 'The focus of entrepreneurial research: context, process and issues', *Entrepreneurship Theory and Practice*, **25** (4), 57–80.
Wernerfelt, B. (1984), 'A resource-based view of the firm', *Strategic Management Journal*, **5** (2), 171–80.
Westhead, P. and M. Wright (1998), 'Novice, serial and portfolio founders: are they different?', *Journal of Business Venturing*, **13** (3), 173–204.
Westhead, P., D. Ucbasaran, M. Wright and M. Binks (2005), 'Decisions, actions, and performance: do novice, serial, and portfolio entrepreneurs differ?', *Journal of Small Business Management*, **43** (4), 393–417.
Wiklund J. and D.A. Shepherd (2008), 'Portfolio entrepreneurship: habitual and novice founders, new entry, and mode of organizing', *Entrepreneurship Theory and Practice*, **32** (4), 701–25.
Zellweger, T. (2007), 'Time horizon, costs of equity capital and generic investment strategies of firms', *Family Business Review*, **20** (1), 1–15.
Zellweger, T. and F.W. Kellermanns (2008), 'Family firm reputation: an investigation of antecedents and performance outcomes', paper presented at the annual meeting of the Academy of Management, Anaheim, CA.
Zellweger, T. and R. Nason (2008), 'A stakeholder perspective to family firm performance', *Family Business Review*, **21** (3), 203–16.
Zellweger, T.M., R.S. Nason, M. Nordqvist and C.G. Brush (2013), 'Why do family firms strive for nonfinancial goals? An organizational identity perspective', *Entrepreneurship Theory and Practice*, **37** (2), 229–48.
Zellweger, T. and P. Sieger (2012), 'Entrepreneurial orientation in long-lived family firms', *Small Business Economics*, **38** (1), 67–84.

10. Conclusion: exploring transgenerational entrepreneurship: implications and conclusions

Philipp Sieger, Kavil Ramachandran and Pramodita Sharma

INTRODUCTION

Transgenerational entrepreneurship, defined by Habbershon et al. (2010: 1) as the 'processes through which a family uses and develops entrepreneurial mindsets and family influenced capabilities to create new streams of entrepreneurial, financial and social value across generations' has previously been explored in the context of Europe (Nordqvist and Zellweger, 2010), Latin America (Nordqvist et al., 2011) and the Asia Pacific (Au et al., 2011). Building on this foundational work, this book set out to explore one specific aspect within the transgenerational entrepreneurship framework: the role of intangible resources in family enterprises around the world. These strategic firm resources enable the creation of sustainable value across generations of leaders, products or services, and economic and social life cycles. Scholars contend these resources are valuable, rare, inimitable and non-substitutable, thereby significant for sustained organizational competitive advantages (for example, Barney, 1991).

Each chapter in this book examines how enterprising families utilize their unique family-influenced intangible resources to create economic and non-economic value across generations. Drawing on the resources available within the Successful Transgenerational Entrepreneurship Project (STEP), the chapters investigate 26 business families from 12 countries to shed a nuanced light on the creation of different types of intangible resources and their impact on family based entrepreneurship and long-term value generation. Viewing the chapters as a whole, the book differentiates between internal and external intangible resources and links them to distinct outcomes.

As becomes evident in the next section, each chapter of this book is a thought-provoking read that makes a valuable contribution to research and practice. After highlighting the theoretical and practical implications of each chapter below, we attempt to consolidate the findings to determine how best to consider the development and deployment of intangible resources for sustained growth of family enterprises. Given the embryonic level of understanding on this topic and the unique insights presented from different parts of the world, this chapter closes with reflections for future work.

RESEARCH AND PRACTICAL IMPLICATIONS

Each of the eight chapters in this book provides unique insights. As you will notice in our elaboration below, the first five chapters largely focus on processes for development and deployment of intangibles that pertain to individuals within a family enterprise. Examples include values, virtues, tacit knowledge, learning and bonding social capital. The last two chapters are externally focused on the bridging social capital and reputation of a family enterprise as they pertain to relations with or perspectives of individuals beyond the boundaries of a family enterprise. The connecting chapter by Balunywa, Rosa, Ntamu, and Nagujja (Chapter 7) underscores the challenges of maintaining the delicate balance between internally and externally focused intangible resources as the family leaders attempt to satisfy the competing demands of stakeholders within and beyond the boundaries of their enterprise. Let us begin a reflective journey of the chapters in this book.

Internally Oriented Intangible Resources in Family Enterprises

'Family firms and entrepreneurial families as breeding grounds for virtues' by Orozco and González

Scholars agree that values play a very important role in family firms (for example, Yu et al., 2012). However, the exploration of a theoretical link between family values and firm outcomes is only just beginning (Tàpies and Ward, 2008). This is the starting point of the Colombian chapter. Building on insights garnered from 66 interviews with family and non-family members in eight family business cases, the authors use the existing understanding of the distinction between resources and capabilities and differentiate between values and virtues. The combinative power of the virtues of courage and temperance that guide enterprising families when operating in a hostile environment littered with kidnappings, terrorist threats, weak regulatory institutions and unstable political structures is revealed. This chapter makes three key contributions: (i) the processes used by a family to seed and breed values – the deep-rooted beliefs of a family – in an enterprise are revealed; (ii) values are then distinguished from virtues that trigger actionable and visible behaviors; and (iii) insights are shared on how the virtues impact firm-level outcomes such as the wisdom of knowing when, how and how much to grow a family enterprise. These interesting findings have several implications for research, teaching and practice.

Researchers will find value in this chapter as it contributes to the literature on familiness by its explicit focus on intangible resources of values and virtues and their relationships with different firm-related outcomes. The study provides empirical support from a Latin American context to reinforce that family firms are a fertile ground for developing values and virtues. This demonstrates how a family firm's values and virtues can be a source of sustained competitive advantage in family firms compared to their non-family counterparts. The chapter also points to the important issue of dynamism, as values and virtues may change over time. It extends the existing research on values in family firms in general as it provides nuanced insights into the development of different values over time, how these values become actionable, and explicitly links them to relevant outcomes.

The above insights are likely of interest to family business owners, managers and advisors, as well as teachers and students in family business courses. These readers will enjoy reflecting on this chapter as it reveals how successful Colombian families are dealing with the important issue of how to reinforce familial values in actionable forms in family enterprises. A major challenge very often faced by business families is the articulation and explanation of the process of living their values. The dilemmas of deciding whether or not to grow in potentially lucrative directions that may compete with the core values of the family are revealed. Since virtues represent the practice of values, families may develop ideas about how to align the performance metrics of their enterprises with the core family values. This chapter provides pragmatic ideas on how the capability to nurture and develop unique values and virtues may constitute a competitive advantage for family firms in the long-term.

Beyond the illustrative benefits of values across generations and from the family to the business system, this chapter suggests how feedback and reinforcement mechanisms can keep family values alive even when its members are separated by physical distance. Furthermore, the Colombian insights may assist business families in critically reflecting on the type, strength and life cycle of their own values and virtues, and how they could be used to generate desirable outcomes. Perhaps a family coefficient of their values and virtues could be developed to calibrate the development and changes over time.

'Professionalization of the family business: decision-making domains' by Gimeno and Parada

Building on previous works on decision-making processes in family firms from a leadership and succession perspective (see review by Long and Chrisman, 2013), the Spanish STEP team takes a novel approach and investigates decision-making processes from a professionalization perspective. Based on two Spanish case studies of an older and a younger family firm established in 1838 and in the 1960s, respectively, this chapter brings to life the unfolding of the process of professionalization in family firms over time. By splitting the domains of decision-making into administrative, operational and strategic, the authors illustrate how professionalization practices emerge and change in different domains over the life cycle of a firm. Leaders of family enterprises must find ways to build firm capabilities for making decisions along each domain. And, the capabilities and decisions needed for continued growth of an enterprise change over time. Founders and experienced managers tend to rely more on intuition when making decisions, while less experienced managers are more comfortable with analyses-based decisions. For effective functioning of family enterprises over time, the three domains of decision-making require a different mix of intuition and analysis. The gradual transformation of systems and structures, combined with the development of skills and competencies, enables professionalization of the family enterprise.

This chapter views professionalization as a process of organizational transformation characterized by the codification of knowledge, clarification in role definition and the creation of different decision-making domains. In doing so, it makes at least five contributions for its scholarly and practitioner readers. First, by taking this perspective, it moves the attention of its readers to think of professionalization as an organizational level process, rather than individual level, which dominates previous writings. Second, by asking the question '*what* is being professionalized?', it directs the attention of its reader towards the need for clear articulation of the foci of professionalization rather than the inherent assumption in the literature that every part of a system is simultaneously professionalized. Third, in attempting to understand the process of professionalization, the authors shed light on the different mindsets and capabilities needed for the three decision-making domains of an enterprise – administrative, operational and strategic. Fourth, in comparing a younger and older family firm in the same context, the dynamic and nuanced nature of the process of professionalization is revealed. And, fifth, by illustrating the process by which each domain of decision-making gets professionalized, the chapter contributes to our understanding of factors that enable transgenerational entrepreneurship and success.

Given the limited understanding of the process of professionalization of a family enterprise over time, the above insights are valuable for students, teachers, practitioners and researchers alike. Recognition and development of its critical decision-making skills is fundamental to the professionalization and success of any organization. However, for leaders of family enterprises, seeing their firm as distinct from themselves can be challenging given the alignment of identities (for example, Sharma, 2004). Beyond the logical acceptance of the separation of business from the family or individuals in it, this research reinforces the importance of emotional intelligence of family entrepreneurs in order to professionalize their ventures (cf. Goleman, 1995). For enterprising families desirous of longevity beyond the founding or current generation of leadership, this chapter is particularly relevant as it provides ideas for reducing the dependence on the current leaders by using a milestone approach to train the next generation of family or non-family successors. The responsibilities can gradually move from administrative to operational to strategically oriented decisions as the organization makes progress on its pathway to professionalization.

'Transgenerational entrepreneurship and entrepreneurial learning: a case study of Associated Engineers Ltd in Hong Kong' by Cheng, Ho and Au

This chapter illustrates the pathway used by an enterprising family in Hong Kong to enable the entrepreneurial learning of the founder's descendants. Developing and sustaining entrepreneurial capabilities within the family is crucial for transgenerational entrepreneurship. Yet, the process of evolution and retention of entrepreneurial spirit in founders' descendants has yet to be understood. By analyzing how entrepreneurial learning takes place in the case of Associated Engineers Ltd (AEL), this chapter makes a contribution to the understanding of this critical yet poorly understood learning process. AEL uses several age-appropriate learning methods and activities to build the entrepreneurial skills and confidence of next-generation family members. This case signals the moderating effect of entrepreneurial learning on the relationship between entrepreneurial orientation and firm performance; and also, on the relationship between family-influenced resource pools and firm performance. Empirical testing of these propositions in other companies and contexts will be useful in future research.

By illustrating how a systematic proactive approach to entrepreneurial learning can take place across the firm's and family's life cycle, this study shatters the myth that entrepreneurial learning 'just happens' unconsciously without much reflection or effort. Instead, it highlights the role that education and experiential activities play in this learning. This insight that meaningful and strategic entrepreneurial learning can be a powerful tool to achieve transgenerational success opens up avenues for novel consulting and advisory efforts. Family members and students can reflect on their past experiences to understand the role played by each in determining their current levels of entrepreneurial skills and confidence. Furthermore, educational and experiential milestones can be planned to ensure continuous development of entrepreneurial and leadership skills and a strong future of their family enterprises.

'Successful family business ownership transitions: leveraging tacit knowledge' by DeWitt and González

While tacit knowledge has been examined by many scholars before, both in family and non-family contexts (for example, Chirico and Salvato, 2008; Polayni, 1966), what is novel about this chapter is how this knowledge residing within a family business can be leveraged to achieve long-term success despite ownership transitions outside of the founding family. The case of Curtis Packaging in the US leads to intriguing insights into the flow of tacit knowledge from one controlling family to another by an insightful new entrepreneurial leader of the enterprise. An experienced professional, this new leader used an astute combination of learning from and with the experienced non-family employees who had worked at Curtis with the founding family. Together, this new leader and seasoned 'insiders' developed systems and structures to leverage the tacit knowledge sourced within the enterprise and position it for growth and longevity.

The Curtis case has several implications for research and practice. On the longevity of an enterprise, it illustrates how the strengths of a firm can continue over time, despite the exit of the founding family from its ownership and leadership. The importance of retaining the name of the firm to signal continuity both to insiders and outsiders must be noted. In terms of tacit knowledge, this case demonstrates that while a new controlling owner may have significant experience outside the firm, the first step towards regeneration and growth of the continuing firm is to learn from and with the non-family 'insiders' who are rich reservoirs of tacit knowledge.

Regarding succession, it is interesting to see how the involvement of non-family members serving as a form of 'bridge generation' helped secure the longevity of this firm even though for some transitioning years it could no longer be characterized as a 'family firm'. Later in its history, it was converted back to the status of being a family firm, albeit under a different controlling family from the founders. This company's experience over time in moving in and out of being a family firm, and with control moving from the founding family to another unrelated controlling family, suggests the importance of thinking beyond the two-dimensional view of succession to consider hybrid or different succession forms. It may not be only family-internal or family-external, but may also include intermediate forms such as with non-family insiders who efficiently contribute to an effective influx of tacit knowledge. While ownership and leadership transitions naturally constitute challenges to the firm, they can also represent an opportunity to ensure continuity, longevity and growth of an enterprise. Obviously, how ownership and leadership transitions between family members and non-family members and the related tacit capital can be efficiently managed is an interesting field for service providers. For students, in addition, this case illustrates the role of tacit knowledge in the succession context, whereas succession may not be limited to family members. As the authors correctly indicate, long-term success may be rooted in exploiting the best of both the family world and the business world.

'The role of social capital in succession from controlling owners to sibling teams' by Cisneros, Chirita and Deschamps

Succession from one generation to the next is one of the most frequently studied topics in the family business literature (for example, Yu et al., 2012). However, it is a bit curious that while there has been an understanding that transitioning from one controlling owner to another is only one form of leadership transition in family firms (for example, Lansberg, 1999), most of the available literature focuses on this transition (for example, Sharma, 2004). The process involved in successfully transitioning a family firm from a controlling owner to a sibling team has not received much scholarly attention. Therefore, this chapter, based on six cases of French-Canadian family firms that have transitioned from controlling owners to sibling partners, is both refreshing and thought-provoking. The authors adopt the family business succession model of Handler (1994) and find that the selective transfer of tacit knowledge from the controlling owner to the next generation members based on the skills, competencies and interests of these members is a precursor to such collective successions. Moreover, the reputation and networks of the controlling leader and the firm have trigger effects on sibling team succession in later stages.

The chapter adds to the embryonic research on sibling team succession (for example, Cater and Justis, 2009). It integrates research on social capital and tacit knowledge transfer to better understand transition from a controlling owner to a sibling team, illustrating how the explanatory power can be enhanced by combining insights from family business literature and other streams of research outside the context of these firms. Practitioners and students alike will enjoy reading this chapter for inspiration on how an enterprise might be successfully transferred from one controlling owner to a team of siblings. The importance of shared vision, strategy and values of the new leaders, combined with their complementary styles of functioning and interests is revealed. The study sheds a nuanced light on the transfer of social capital as a critical success factor in such transitions.

When considering inter-generational transition, this chapter provides hope and inspiration for family firms desirous of moving from a controlling owner to sibling partnership stage when several children may want to take over the firm. It shows that no competition or 'winner takes all' may be necessary. Instead, by pooling their intangible and tangible resources, multiple next generation members can contribute to the entrepreneurial growth and longevity of a family firm. Advisors can help families going through this form of leadership transition to develop strong governance mechanisms that are likely to become more critical in such situations than recycling the controlling owner form across generations (cf., Lansberg, 1999).

The Balancing Act between Internal and External Intangible Family Resources

'Opportunities and dilemmas of social capital: insights from Uganda' by Balunywa, Rosa, Ntamu and Nagujja

While the five chapters discussed above focus largely on intangible resources that reside within the boundaries of family enterprises, and the next two focus on externally residing intangibles, this chapter is unique in several aspects. It analyzes a family business case in the under-researched African context. Although the African continent is formed of 54 countries recognized by the African Union, there is currently not much research on family enterprises in this region. This chapter starts with an interesting account of family and business life in three significantly different regions of Africa. After this, the focus moves to Uganda and its turbulent history, where the focal case is set. This contextual part of the chapter is stimulating reading as it sheds light on the different forms of family and social life prevalent in our world. The inherent strength of family bonds is revealed as this internally focused intangible resource helps this enterprising family to absorb environmental hostility and reap the advantages of opportunities that emerge as a result of such turbulence.

More surprising insights await the reader as the chapter moves to its topical focus of social capital. The tussle and dilemmas of family enterprise leaders are revealed as they try to balance their energy on development and deployment of externally focused bridging social capital and the needs of their family enterprise. For the first time in the literature, the detrimental effects of high reservoirs of the externally focused bridging social capital are brought to life.

This chapter offers various contributions to the existing literature. On a general level, the study extends the existing body of research on transgenerational entrepreneurship to the African continent and thus adds an interesting cultural and contextual perspective. Specifically, unique insights into how families and family businesses are affected by social, cultural and political factors are gained. Referring to existing research on social capital (for example, Arregle et al., 2007; Nahapiet and Ghoshal, 1998) and familiness (Habbershon et al., 2003), this chapter opens up a new perspective by illustrating how family-influenced bonding and bridging social capital can have both positive and negative effects on transgenerational value creation. So far, existing research seems to have taken a 'the more the better' perspective on social capital with regard to entrepreneurial outcomes while underestimating the potential negative effects. This, of course, may not be solely applicable in the African context, but also in other regions and continents, which calls for additional research efforts to understand the dark and bright sides of social capital. Such research is likely to provide a more fine-grained understanding of social capital's relationship with performance outcomes.

For business family members, the implications are obvious: while there are well-touted benefits of social networks and capital, this intangible resource also has its dark side. This awareness hopefully leads to a critical reflection of the social capital that a family has, and how negative effects could be prevented. In essence, families have to be clear about their purpose for and the costs of maintaining rich social networks. They should also see how family human resources are allocated between direct business activities and others. There is always the threat of drift, thanks to social pressures, that families should be conscious of. Hence, business families may derive additional guidelines on how to cope with intra-family dynamics and relationships. This, as a whole, might increase the likelihood of transgenerational success. For service providers and students of family business studies, this chapter is a reminder to consider the positive and negative aspects of social capital, keeping in mind that nurturance of an intangible, albeit important, resource, requires the time and energy of the controlling leaders – a scarce resource by itself that should be expended prudently.

Externally Oriented Intangible Resources in Family Enterprises

'Bridging for resilience: the role of family business social capital in coping with hostile environments' by Rodriguez, Auletta and Monteferrante

Transgenerational entrepreneurship strategies used by family firms operating in hostile environments have been previously studied by the STEP scholars largely from Latin America (for example, Nordqvist et al., 2011). Building on this work, this chapter investigates how generic non-tradable (GNT) intangible resources such as reputation and social networks enhance the resilience capacity of family enterprises (cf. Gedajlovic and Carney, 2010). Based on their comparative analysis of six family firms from Costa Rica, El Salvador, Germany, Sweden and Venezuela, these authors find there are two pathways used by family firms to build their resilience capacity. These pathways are contextual as they vary by location and economic sector. When the host company and its ties are in the same industry and location, resources and social networks are exchanged steadily until both overcome the external crisis. On the other hand, if one company is facing a hostile environment but the other is not, the resources move from the one in a steady environment to the other, until the disruptive conditions pass. Over time, the flow of resources is balanced, however, and no evidence of social free-riding was found.

Readers of this chapter are reminded of the critical role of the external environment in the survival and growth of enterprises (for example, Sharma et al., 2012). As hostile environments may exist in various forms and in different contexts, resilience capacity is a crucial determinant of the transgenerational success of family firms. Scholars may build their future research to gain insights into how family firms design capital exchanges with external ties to cope with hostile environments. Family business owners and advisors may find inspiration for the different pathways used by successful firms to continue their entrepreneurial growth despite the harsh external environment. Proactive adaptation and management of social linkages with near or distant external ties is found useful. Applying principles of portfolio allocation and management of resources, families may prudently hedge risks and uncertainties existing in different markets. In turn, such strategies may increase the probability of transgenerational success. Lastly, students should realize the significant importance of incorporating the realities of the external environment when considering strategies to build resilience or transgenerational success of family enterprises.

'Reputation for what? Different types of reputation and their effects on portfolio entrepreneurship activities' by Clinton, Nason and Sieger

Based on the Irish case of the Smith family's MLS company established in 1978, this chapter questions the assumed homogeneity of 'reputation' in the literature which inadvertently neglects its different facets and forms (for example, Dyer and Whetten, 2006). Three distinct dimensions of reputation are observed in the MLS case – (i) long-term orientation, (ii) trusted business partners, and (iii) the entrepreneurial spirit of the Smith family. Each of these facets has a positive impact on the availability of growth opportunities presented to the company by prospective partners. This, in turn, positively influences its portfolio entrepreneurship activities. It is interesting to see how the entrepreneurial spirit of the family takes a slightly different shape in each of the three generations studied in this research. While the founding generation started with passion, seeking new opportunities far and wide, the second generation brought structure and professionalism to the firm. Innovative independence defines the third generation that currently leads this enterprise.

In directing scholarly conversations to the possible dimensions of reputation, this research signals the need to develop a nuanced view of reputation, challenging the inherent assumption of the uni-dimensionality of this construct (for example, Deephouse and Jaskiewicz, 2013; Fombrun, 1996). Various dimensions of reputation are introduced as critical drivers of portfolio entrepreneurship activity (Rosa, 1998; Sieger et al., 2011).

For practitioners and students of family business studies, this chapter encourages reflection on the core question in the title – 'reputation for what?' Careful self-assessment of this question may lead to an understanding of how this intangible resource could be nurtured and deployed to orchestrate portfolio entrepreneurial activities of a firm to ensure generation-spanning success? Family business advisors and consultants might tailor their service offerings to include an objective assessment of a firm's reputation to help identify dimensions that are strong or weak. And, what aspects of reputation could be harnessed for longevity and transgenerational entrepreneurship.

A SYNTHESIZED VIEW OF INTANGIBLE RESOURCES AND CAPABILITIES

Family entrepreneurship is a fairly young branch of study. While the development and orchestration of resources and capabilities have captured the attention of many scholars (for example, Habbershon and Williams, 1999; Penrose, 1959; Sirmon and Hitt, 2003), the critical role of intangible resources and capabilities has only recently begun to be explored (Molloy et al., 2011). Chapters in this book join the exploration by deepening our insights into the processes that help build and transfer intangible resources and capabilities to ensure transgenerational entrepreneurship in family enterprises in contexts not previously studied.

A brief glimpse of the interesting findings and implications from each chapter in this book was shared in the previous section. Taking an inside-out approach, we find that the core values of the controlling family have a

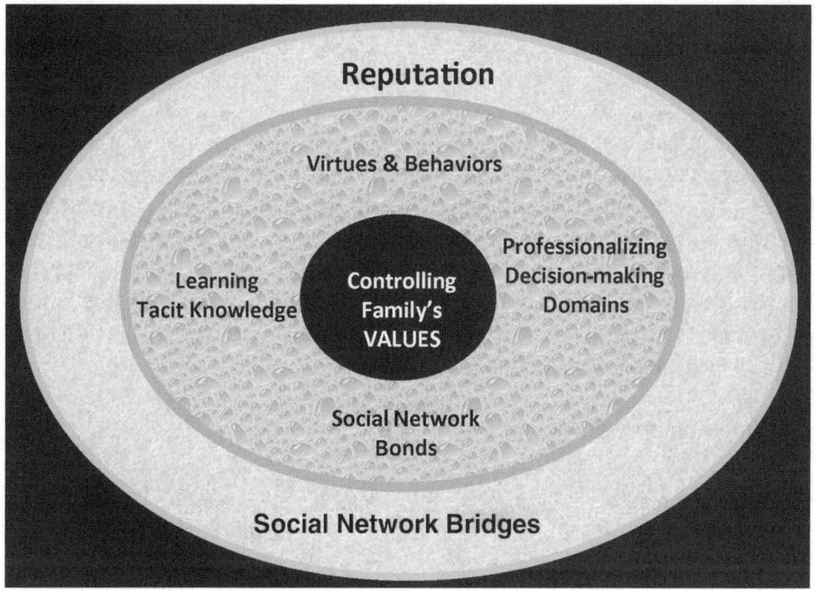

Figure 10.1 Ripples of intangible resources and capabilities

ripple effect on the behaviors and transmittal of knowledge, learning, professionalization and the bonds between family and non-family members in an enterprise. The processes and pathways through which intangibles like tacit knowledge, learning and networks make their way from one generation of leadership to the next are uncovered. The patient in-depth longitudinal research extending into multiple contexts helps to give shape to the nebulous processes that lead to professionalization in the different domains of decision-making in family enterprises. When researchers cast their critical analytical light on the frequently used construct of 'reputation', its multidimensionality, depth and relationship with the core values become visible. And, viewing social capital closely, its light and dark sides are brought to the fore. The ripple of intangibles from the deepest core of family values into the enterprise and their halo effect on the firm's social networks and reputation in the external environment can be illustrated using concentric circles as shown in Figure 10.1.

In this section, we share a few overarching observations that span across chapters and aid our understanding of intangible resources and capabilities for entrepreneurship to flourish across generations. These thoughts may trigger ideas for research investigations as well as for reflective practitioners and students of family business studies.

(1) Intangible Resources and Capabilities, Though Nebulous, Are Critical for Enterprising Firms

Unlike tangible resources, the metrics of their stocks are harder to define, and their movement and flows from one level to the next more difficult to visualize. Yet, a picture seems to appear based on in-depth longitudinal investigations in different contexts. Values emerging from the deepest core of the controlling family (Chapter 2) signal what behaviors are acceptable, learning that is important so that tacit knowledge can be carried from one generation to the next (Chapters 3 and 4). When looking at the family enterprise from outside its boundaries, the glow of its reputation and bridges becomes visible (Chapters 7, 8, 9).

(2) Dimensionality of Intangibles

In looking at the variables in Figure 10.1 and reading prior related literature, some of these concepts may appear uni-dimensional. However, the in-depth patient investigations begin to reveal the multidimensionality of several of them. For example, the Irish chapter (Chapter 9) asks the question 'reputation for what?', signaling the incomplete nature of statements like 'company X has a good reputation'. And, the Spanish chapter (Chapter 3) peels off the layers of 'professionalization', asking 'professionalize what?' and illustrating the ease and complexity of professionalizing different aspects of an enterprise. Even for variables such as 'social capital', whose dimensionality has been discussed in previous literature both in family and non-family contexts (for example, Adler and Kwon, 2002; Pearson et al., 2008), the difficulties of maintaining the delicate balance between the externally focused bridges and internal bonds is revealed by the Ugandan study in Chapter 7.

(3) Pathways to Imbue the Entrepreneurial Spirit in the Next Generation

Pathways are found to vary from an organic 'watch me do it' style (for example, Chapters 2 and 3) to a more structured style, found in Chapters 4, 5 and 6, where the senior generation proactively thinks of the interests and talents of the next generation of family members and the opportunities they need to build their entrepreneurial skills and confidence. The challenges of delegating and sitting back to let the new leaders take on the reins and cast their own impressions and shadows on the enterprise become evident, testing the courage and temperance of the senior generations (for example, Chapter 2).

(4) Variance of Internal Context and Family Structures

This variance plays a significant role in whether 'transgenerational' means that leadership is moved from one controlling owner to the next, as in Chapter 9, or whether control moves from a controlling owner to sibling teams, as in Chapter 6, in the context of nuclear or extended families, as in Chapters 4 and 9 respectively (cf., Lansberg, 1999). While the latter is more challenging than the former, partially because of the lack of knowledge of such transitions, perhaps the least understood are instances of the continuity of an enterprise and its core values without the continuity of the founding family in ownership or management of the firm, as illustrated in Chapter 5.

(5) External Environment

The external environment significantly varies in the studies presented in this book. While some, like those in Chapters 5 and 6, are set in the relatively stable environments of the USA or Canada at the time of investigation, other chapters illustrate how enterprising families cope with and find opportunities in the uncertainties of the political environment. Examples include the handover of Hong Kong from Britain to China and the continuity of innovative pathways by AEL (Chapter 4) and the hostility of the Ugandan environment and opportunities it presented for the Sentongo family (Chapter 7).

The book is the collaborative effort of 23 scholars from the Asia Pacific (3), Africa (3), Europe (6), Latin America (6) and North America (5). This reflects the capabilities of shared values and virtues, professionalism, entrepreneurial thinking and strong global networking of the authors through a global applied project like STEP. Research presented in this book is focused on enterprising families in the 12 countries of Canada, Colombia, Costa Rica, El Salvador, Germany, Hong Kong, Ireland, Spain, Sweden, Uganda, the USA and Venezuela. It is noteworthy, however, that, with the exception of Chapter 8, which compares cases in five different countries, most chapters in this book present research set in one external environment. In most instances, however, the longitudinal and in-depth nature of investigations extends over several decades and generations, providing a view of how the process unfolds over time. Together these studies paint a rich mosaic of knowledge that we hope will lead to future investigations comparing multiple contexts. Incidentally, the book conveys the power of the intangibles in creating sustenance in society. We have only seen the tip of the intangibles iceberg.

REFERENCES

Adler, P.S. and S.-W. Kwon (2002), 'Social capital: prospects for a new concept', *Academy of Management Review*, **27** (1), 17–40.

Arregle, J.L., M.A. Hitt, D.G. Sirmon and P. Very (2007), 'The development of organizational social capital: attributes of family firms', *Journal of Management Studies*, **44** (1), 73–95.

Au, K., J. Craig and K. Ramachandran (2011), *Family Entrepreneurship in Asia Pacific: Exploring Transgenerational Entrepreneurship in Family Firms*, Cheltenham, UK and Northampton, MA, USA: Edward Elgar Publishing.

Barney, J.B. (1991), 'Firm resources and sustained competitive advantage', *Journal of Management*, **17** (1), 99–120.

Cater, J.J. and R.T. Justis (2009), 'The development of successors from followers to leaders in small family firms an exploratory study', *Family Business Review*, **22** (2), 109–24.

Chirico, F. and C. Salvato (2008), 'Knowledge integration and dynamic organizational adaptation in family firms', *Family Business Review*, **21** (2), 169–81.

Deephouse, D.L. and P. Jaskiewicz (2013), 'Do family firms have better reputations than non-family firms? An integration of socioemotional wealth and social identity theories', *Journal of Management Studies*, **50** (3), 337–60.

Dyer, W. and D. Whetten (2006), 'Family firms and social responsibility: preliminary evidence from the S&P 500', *Entrepreneurship Theory & Practice*, **30** (6), 785–802.

Fombrun, C.J. (1996), *Reputation: Realizing Value From the Corporate Image*, Cambridge, MA: Harvard Business School Press.

Gedajlovic, E. and M. Carney (2010), 'Markets, hierarchies, and families: toward a transaction cost theory of the family firm', *Entrepreneurship Theory and Practice*, **34** (6), 1145–72.

Goleman, D. (1995), *Emotional Intelligence: Why It Can Matter More Than IQ*, New York: Bantam Books.

Habbershon, T., M. Nordqvist and T. Zellweger (2010), 'Transgenerational Entrepreneurship', in M. Nordqvist and T. Zellweger (eds), *Transgenerational Entrepreneurship: Exploring Growth and Performance of Family Firms across Generations*, Cheltenham, UK and Northampton, MA, USA: Edward Elgar, pp. 1–38.

Habbershon, T.G. and M.L. Williams (1999), 'A resource-based framework for assessing the strategic advantages of family firms', *Family Business Review*, **12** (1), 1–25.

Habbershon, T.G., M. Williams and I.C. MacMillan (2003), 'A unified systems perspective of family firm performance', *Journal of Business Venturing*, **18** (4), 451–65.

Handler, W.C. (1994), 'Succession in family business: a review of the research', *Family Business Review*, **7** (2), 133–57.

Lansberg, I.S. (1999), *Succeeding Generations: Realizing the Dream of Families in Business*, Boston, MA: Harvard Business School Press.

Long, R.G. and J.J. Chrisman (2013), 'Management succession in family business', in L. Melin, M. Nordqvist and P. Sharma (eds), *SAGE Handbook of Family Business*, London: Sage Publications.

Molloy, J.C., C. Chadwick, R.E. Ployhart and S.J. Golden (2011), 'Making intangibles "tangible" in tests of resource-based theory: a multidisciplinary construct validation approach', *Journal of Management*, **37** (5), 1496–518.

Nahapiet, J. and S. Ghoshal (1998), 'Social capital, intellectual capital, and the organizational advantage', *Academy of Management Review*, **23**, 242–66.

Nordqvist, M., G. Marzano, E.R. Brenes, G. Jimenez and M. Fonseca-Paredes (2011), *Understanding Entrepreneurial Family Business in Uncertain Environments: Opportunities and Resources in Latin America*, Cheltenham, UK and Northampton, MA, USA: Edward Elgar Publishing.

Nordqvist, M. and T. Zellweger (eds) (2010), *Transgenerational Entrepreneurship: Exploring Growth and Performance in Family Firms across Generations*, Cheltenham, UK and Northampton, MA, USA: Edward Elgar.

Pearson, A.W., J.C. Carr and J.C. Shaw (2008), 'Toward a theory of familiness: a social capital perspective', *Entrepreneurship Theory & Practice*, **32** (6), 949–69.

Penrose, E.T. (1959), *The Theory of the Growth of the Firm*, Oxford: Basil Blackwell.

Polayni, M. (1966), *The Tacit Dimension*, Gloucester: Peter Smith.

Rosa, P. (1998), 'Entrepreneurial processes of business cluster formation and growth by "habitual" entrepreneurs', *Entrepreneurship Theory & Practice*, **22** (4), 43–61.

Sharma, P. (2004), 'An overview of the field of family business studies: current status and directions for the future', *Family Business Review*, **17** (1), 1–36.

Sharma, P., J.J. Chrisman and K.E. Gersick (2012), '25 years of family business review: reflections on the past and perspectives for the future', *Family Business Review*, **25** (1), 5–15.

Sieger, P., T. Zellweger, R.S. Nason and E. Clinton (2011), 'Portfolio entrepreneurship in family firms: a resource-based perspective', *Strategic Entrepreneurship Journal*, **5** (4), 327–51.

Sirmon, D.G. and M.A. Hitt (2003), 'Managing resources: linking unique resources, management, and wealth creation in family firms', *Entrepreneurship Theory & Practice*, **27** (4), 339–58.

Tàpies, J. and J.L. Ward (2008), *Family Values and Value Creation: The Fostering of Enduring Values within Family-Owned Businesses*, New York: Palgrave Macmillan.

Yu, A., G.T. Lumpkin, R.L. Sorenson and K.H. Brigham (2012), 'The landscape of family business outcomes: a summary and numerical taxonomy of dependent variables', *Family Business Review*, **25** (1), 33–57.

Index